D0021834

AUG 2 0 2020

NO LONGER PROPERTY OF
SEATTLE PUBLIC LIBRARY

A WOMAN LIKE HER

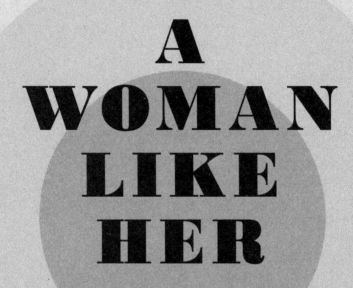

A WOMAN LIKE HER

The Story Behind the Honor Killing of a Social Media Star

SANAM MAHER

MELVILLE HOUSE
Brooklyn | London

A Woman Like Her

First published in 2018 in India as *The Sensational Life and Death of Qandeel Baloch* by Aleph Book Company
Copyright © Sanam Maher 2018
All rights reserved
First Melville House Printing: February 2020

Melville House Publishing
46 John Street
Brooklyn, NY 11201
and
Melville House UK
Suite 2000
16/18 Woodford Road
London E7 0HA

mhpbooks.com
@melvillehouse

ISBN: 978-1-61219-840-8
ISBN: 978-1-61219-814-5 (eBook)

Library of Congress Control Number: 2019949143

Designed by Marina Drukman

Printed in the United States of America
10 9 8 7 6 5 4 3 2 1

A catalog record for this book is available
from the Library of Congress

For my father, Mumtaz, and my mother, Rehana

"You're going to miss me when I'm gone. You're so terrible, with your double standards. You like to watch me, and then you like to say, 'Why don't you just die?' Will you be happy when I die? When I die, there will never be another Qandeel Baloch. For a hundred years, you will not get another Qandeel. You're going to miss me."

—QANDEEL BALOCH

CONTENTS

Author's Note   xi
Prologue   xvii

THE BALOCH FAMILY   1
"PEOPLE SAY THIS IS NO JOB FOR A WOMAN"   16
THE MODELS OF ISLAMABAD   26
"HOW I'M LOOKING?"   46
THE BLUE-EYED CHAIWALA   55
"GUYS, WHO WANT TO WATCH MY NEXT NASTY CLIP?"   69
THE HELPLINE   90
"I'M GOING TO DO SOMETHING THAT GETS EVERYONE WORRIED"   127
THE MUFTI   140
"I'M TELLING YOU THAT MY LIFE IS IN DANGER"   162
THE MEDIA AND THE MURDER   177

Epilogue   214
Acknowledgments   224
Notes   226
Index   231
About the Author   235

AUTHOR'S NOTE

In February 2016, Issam Ahmed, a journalist from the international news agency Agence France-Presse, interviewed a twenty-five-year-old Pakistani woman for a story on how the country's youth interacted with social media. Qandeel Baloch, the country's first social media celebrity, had more than 700,000 followers on Facebook, 40,000 followers on Twitter, and a popular YouTube channel. "Young people can communicate online in relative freedom," Ahmed reported. He described Baloch as a "Kim Kardashian-type figure."

Ahmed was curious about whether Qandeel's social media posts had any greater intent beyond gaining likes and followers. He thought her photographs and videos were funny, refreshing and cool, yet every time she posted something, she would receive a flood of abusive comments. So why did she keep going? It was gutsy, he thought. What did she want people to take away from what she was doing? When he first spoke with Qandeel, she was suspicious of these questions. It was the first time she had been interviewed for the foreign press, but more importantly, it was the first time that she was hearing that her social media activity had meaning.

Qandeel had caught Ahmed's attention after a video she posted on Facebook mocking a presidential "warning" not to celebrate Valentine's Day—deemed a "Western" holiday—was viewed more than 800,000 times in less than two weeks. In the video, made on a cellphone as she lies in bed, Baloch wears a low-cut red dress, and her full lips are painted scarlet. The sheets match her outfit, and her dress rides up her legs to reveal her thighs. "They can stop to people go out," she says in broken English, "but they can't stop to people love." She says the same thing once more, this time in Urdu, with an exaggerated American accent, as though she is not used to speaking the language. "No matter what they do, they can't stop people from loving." She whispers the message again: "*logon ko pyaar karnay se nahin rok saktay.*" These politicians are "*ghatiya*" (shameless) and "idiots," she says with disgust. "At least Imran Khan doesn't do this. That's why I always support Imran Khan," she notes. She adds a personal message for the former cricketer turned prime minister: "Imran, happy Valentine's Day. I know you're alone and you don't have a Valentine. I don't either. I'm also alone. And I don't want you to be my Valentine. I just want you to be mine . . . Forever."

The video shows us everything that Pakistanis loved—and loved to hate—about Qandeel: she played the coquette, dished out biting critiques of some of Pakistan's most holy cows, and gave her heart away to politicians, actors, singers, and cricketers. We snickered at her accent and the way she spoke, and marveled at her gumption. She was the stuff of a hundred memes and the butt of our jokes.

Qandeel's daily posts on Facebook, Twitter and YouTube were a mixed bag—she had a headache, she was bored, she had a song stuck in her head, she would try on a new dress—and seen by thousands. Her posts went up at night, when Qandeel said she couldn't sleep, and they were forgotten by her viewers by the time morning came.

Until they became more risqué—by Pakistan's standards, at least.

In March 2016, Qandeel uploaded a video that couldn't be swept aside so easily. She promised a striptease for her viewers if Pakistan's cricket team won an upcoming match against India. For many of her fans, Qandeel had gone too far. "Before you post these sort of videos think about your religion and your family . . . this is too much," one viewer commented. Others were not so polite. "Please shoot her wherever you find her," wrote one user. "You slut, if you love getting naked why don't you go sit in a brothel?" asked a female Facebook user. "Have some shame. I don't know what kind of family you come from, are they so dishonourable?"

Four months later, she was dead. Her brother Waseem confessed to strangling her in their family home, in what would be described as an "honour killing"—a murder to restore the respect and honour he believed Qandeel's behaviour online robbed him of. "You know what she was doing on Facebook," Waseem said when he was arrested and asked why he murdered her. She was twenty-six years old.

In the days after her death, many Pakistanis expressed happiness that Qandeel had been "punished" for behaving the way that she did. When he was asked about Qandeel's murder, the leader of one of the largest religio-political groups in Pakistan, Maulana Fazlur Rehman, stated, "We are Muslims and Pakistan has been made in the name of Islam . . . shamelessness and exhibitionism are a scourge in our society, spread through women like her." I saw acquaintances in my own social media feeds having arguments about whether what had happened was right or wrong, whether Qandeel "deserved" what had been done to her. On social media, many women who condemned the murder or confessed that they had been fans of Qandeel faced a torrent of abuse—some temporarily shut down their Facebook or Twitter accounts after receiving threats. Offline, many of the men and women I knew condemned Qandeel's death but then, in the next breath, followed their statements with " . . . but if you think about it . . . "

In the year before Qandeel was murdered, 933 women and men were killed for "honour" in Pakistan, according to the country's Federal Ministry of Law. Those are only the number of cases that were reported by friends and families—many honour crimes are not reported or covered up as a family can collude to protect one of their own. The victims are often believed to have broken a code that their community or family lives by, and their "crimes" can include anything from chatting with a member of the opposite sex on a cell phone or marrying someone of their own free will rather than having a marriage arranged by their parents.

The average Pakistani would find it challenging to recognize the faces or remember the names of any of these men and women. Their stories and our dismay at yet another killing fade with the newsprint from our fingers as we read about them.

But Qandeel was different. Her murder was splashed across the front page of every newspaper. She had appeared in our social media feeds every day, her videos nestled among photographs, status updates, or tweets by our friends and family. Whether we loved, loathed, or ignored her, it was difficult to turn away from the image of her shrouded remains, her hands and feet covered in henna by her mother—a ritual from Shah Sadar Din, the village she was born and then buried in, that declares that this woman left the world with honour. Her family did not close ranks around their son and brother, the murderer. Even in death, Qandeel was exceptional, it seemed.

When I began working on this book in July 2016, I asked myself how one woman could crystalize such disparate views on how a Pakistani woman can and should behave and what happens when she breaks the rules. I felt that in Qandeel's story—her journey from a village in Punjab to the metropolitan city of Karachi and nationwide fame—lay the answer. A media frenzy had followed her death, locally and internationally. While she had been alive, Qandeel had largely been ignored by the foreign press. In death, she captivated it. She was written about by every major media outlet, including the *New York Times* and *Vogue*. Her obituaries praised her as a woman who "gave voice to a generation of Pakistani women," and "an incredibly fearless Pakistani women's rights campaigner who had zero fucks left to give." It was the opportune moment to discuss Pakistani society, culture, and an apathetic government that didn't seem to care about the violence committed against women. The men and women in Qandeel's life were quickly given roles to fit the news cycle's narrative: a Pakistani woman who had tried to live life on her own terms and was brutally murdered by her own brother; a father who wept on camera as he praised her as better than his sons; a mother who talked fondly about her whispered confidences with her daughter, the way they would share every detail of their lives with each other. A short documentary introduced us to the benevolent friend of the family who was acting as their lawyer and representative. After months of reading and watching everything put out about Qandeel, I thought I knew what my book was going to be about. I thought I knew the whole story.

But after my first week of interviews with her family and friends, I was bewildered. By the time I met them in November 2016, Qandeel's parents were weary of the media attention, and their resolve to punish their son was weakening. The lawyer was not so benevolent. After months of interviews and camera crews and photographers and sound bites, most of the people who had known Qandeel were telling me what they thought I wanted to hear about her. Their memories of her were coloured by grief, or by their desire to appear a certain way. In Shah Sadar Din, the village that Qandeel was from, many people were irritated by the media attention. It was "bringing them a bad name." As interest in Qandeel's story grew outside Pakistan, it became more common to encounter people who claimed to have been very close to Qandeel and would swear that they had extensive proof of their friendship with her, although phones were always damaged, stolen, or lost, and the messages they contained from Qandeel irretrievably, conveniently gone. I had conflicting accounts of her life and personality, and I now also had my own perceptions, as a consumer of her photos, videos, tweets, songs, and interviews. I felt frustrated by my inability to verify what I was told about Qandeel, but at the same time was fixated by the idea of truly knowing her, of finding some thread that would lead me to unravel her story.

It took me some time to realise that even if Qandeel had been sitting right in front of me, it would not have made a great difference to my understanding of her. Many of the articles and documentaries about her that have been published and aired since her death have promised to tell us the "real story" of Qandeel Baloch, and I have been asked many times in the course of researching this book about the inside story of her life and death.

Today, Qandeel cannot speak for herself, and even when she could, she said very little about her life. I realised that it isn't my job to provide the reader with every dirty little detail of Qandeel's life, but to ask why they would want them at all. I began to ask other questions. What kind of place created a woman like Qandeel? Why did her story receive such great attention? Why are we still so fascinated by her, and when we watched her videos or saw her latest photograph, what was her image reflecting back to us?

Qandeel's every appearance, video, interview, tweet, or Facebook post was in character. She created a story about herself—part truth, and part lies and exaggerations. The story allowed her to be whoever we wanted her to be, and the small fibs are as much a part of the real story of Qandeel—if not more important—as the filtered memories of her friends and family. Qandeel's words, translated by me but otherwise unchanged, appear as italicized sentences throughout the book. I feel it is necessary to allow her to have a voice as we tell the story of her life and death.

I knew that this book wouldn't only be about Qandeel, but also about the kind of place that enabled her to become who she did—a place that ultimately found that it could not tolerate her. The book uses parts of Qandeel's life in order to open up into a story about Pakistan and young Pakistanis at this particular moment, when, with the touch of a button, we are connected to the world like never before. While we might tread in a global space of ideas and possibilities online, we're still very much grounded in a society and culture that may not allow for those possibilities. In Qandeel's story and some of the others in the book, I have sought to reveal what happens when those two worlds collide.

This text is adapted from a previous edition and includes editorial changes for the American edition. Some names have been changed to protect privacy.

Sanam Maher
Karachi, August 2019

PROLOGUE

She is eight or nine years old when it happens.

She is inside a room with baked-mud walls, a mud floor. There is little of beauty in this room. Everything is functional, everything is shared, the overwhelming colour is of the beige walls. But there is a television, and she moves and writhes her body like a woman on this television. She doesn't have the woman's curves, but she sways her girlish hips in time with her anyway.

She longs to be outside. But she has been punished and must stay indoors. "What is wrong with you?" her mother had asked as she plucked her from the scrum of boys she had tried to play with. It is hot in the room. She wishes she could be swimming in the canal outside her home, and thinks of the cool slip of water against her skin, how each stroke of her arms and the furious pumping of her feet stirs a rush of mud. She could barely ever see in that brown gloom. The grit stung her eyes and coated her hair and left her skin with a wash of fine silt. Above, the sky would be cloudless, the sun a gold coin. It is a different world under the water. Just imagine, she thinks, if I could glide to the furthest reaches of the canal, past the fields, swoosh into the greater surge of the river and swim right out of this village. For now, however, the whole world comes to her, streaming into her home through a big bowl-shaped satellite dish in the courtyard.

She puckers her unpainted mouth. She doesn't know what the woman on the television yearns for, but she wants whatever it is. She knows the words to all these songs and she loves to sing, mouthing each word, her face twisted with the longing, the pleading. Ten years from now, the songs she will love, the ones she'll sing into her phone and then play back and share with the whole world (or whoever is out there, listening to her sing at night when she is alone in her home and can't sleep) will sound the same.

There's someone in the doorway. Her older brother is leaning against the frame of the door, watching her dance. She wants him to be proud. To marvel at the way she imitates the woman on the screen. He'll tell her parents and they'll stroke her hair and tell her she's more beautiful than any of the women on television. They'll plead with her to do a little dance for them. No, not just them, but for anyone who comes to the house. They'll turn on the music and give visitors a glimpse of just how she sashays and sways and knows all the words to every song. Just one, they'll cajole, just sing one verse for us. Our little nightingale. Let us hear that sweet voice. Do you know how far you'll go with a voice like that?

She puts everything she's got into that dance for her brother. He's the one who named her when she was born. She loves to watch him as he stands in the courtyard of their home, scowling, scissoring the air with his swift karate kicks. She tries to do it just like him. When he's not there, she sneaks into his room and tries on his shirts and pants and looks at herself in the mirror, the cuffed hems of the trousers falling fatly around her ankles. He strides towards her and she beams. She looks up at him in anticipation, thinks of how he'll retell this moment to their parents . . . and that's when he knocks the breath right out of her.

Her cheek smarts, she stumbles to the side, bright motes before her eyes. He raises his warm open palm once more, but she sees it coming this time, feels the gasp of air as his hand rushes towards her and she scrambles away. He is shouting and their mother runs into the room. Will she think of this moment, years later, when she dances in—no, not in, but for—a huddle of men at a wedding, when her fingers brush the rupee notes that these men shower on her? The papers will caress her feet. She will tread on them. The bridegroom, drunk with happiness or actually drunk, will sway. Someone will fire an AK-47 in the air, and the rat-a-tat will startle her just a little. She will be sweating in her tight black jeans and T-shirt. A scarf, fringed with small shiny discs, will feel too snug tied around her waist. Or is that someone's arm? (Later, she would swear that she hated that sort of thing. She would never do that. She didn't even know those kinds of dances.)

Is that what her brother had pictured, what he had feared, when he saw her dancing in that room?

Will her mother remember that day when she walks back into the same room more than a decade later with small knots of journalists, their cameras slung around their necks, dark blooms of sweat on their shirts in the July heat? The journalists will hear about the time the girl's brother slapped her when he saw her dancing.

By then, hundreds of thousands of people will have seen her dance. They will have seen her pull the white bathrobe she stole from a five-star hotel down over her shoulders. It'll slip to her hips, a single knot holding it together at her waist. In that lime-green slip of a bikini, she'll caress her breasts and trace the curve of her stomach. "This was just the trailer," she will tell these people. "Do you want to see more?"

THE BALOCH FAMILY

I t takes a little over two hours to drive from Multan, a city in southern Punjab, to the village of Shah Sadar Din. After many checkpoints, where officers shake down the young men on motorbikes, some riding two or three at a time, their thin arms curled around each other's waists, you'll see a silty brown river snaking past men lounging on charpoys by its banks. On the way, if you admire the fields of sugarcane, each stalk taller than a man, your driver, a local who has played under the green sway of these plants as a child, will scoff. The *ganna* is short this year because there has been little water. He has seen these plants soar to fifteen feet. On the side of the road men and women stand by smoking steel vats, stirring a muddy treacle, folding crushed almonds and dried fruit into the soupy folds of the molasses. They sell packets of this liquid sugar along the highway.

You'll drive past a thicket of short, squat mango trees, sufaidas (eucalyptus) that are chopped for firewood, and date trees that in five or six months will yield bundles of silky-skinned fruit the size of a baby. The grass here is the brightest malachite. It is impossible to know where the sky ends and the azure, cloud-filled pools of water in the fields begin.

A thermal power station with lazy puffs of smoke curling from its cooling towers powers the entire region. Great swoops of cable arc from one pylon to the next, each tower a child's line drawing of a robot stand-ing astride our puny world. Within an hour of leaving Multan, you will reach the Recep Tayyip Erdoğan Housing Complex and its accompany-ing hospital, donated to the people here by the Turkish government after their homes were washed away during the floods of 2010. In the dis-tance smoke plumes from brick kilns, where men, women, and children spend their entire lives on their knees under the sun, cooling, patting, stacking, and packing red bricks that are sent across the country. They will never leave this burning land, always thousands of rupees short of freeing themselves from their debts to the kilns' owners.

Beyond the kilns, white canopies hover inches above the ground, protecting a swathe of GM crops. You'll pass warehouses, built better than most homes here, filled with the government's wheat reserves. And then you'll see the blaze of the mustard fields. If you have spent your life in a city, you will struggle to remember seeing a yellow so bright, a yellow like the neon gleam of a McDonald's sign in the night, like a New York taxi washed clean by the rain. After this, you arrive in the city of Dera Ghazi Khan and it will feel as though that mustard field is the last thing of beauty you will see for some time.

You will abruptly realise that no women feature in any of the adver-tisements on the billboards. It is the first time you have seen only men in ads for washing powder. You'll see women on the streets, but never their faces. Many of them wear what looks like a black ski mask with slits for their eyes under their hijab. The others wear a burqa that makes you feel naked under your *dupatta*. The burqa's fabric falls from a skullcap fitted to the woman's head. A thin funnel rises from this cap. The burqa has no slits for the eyes. The funnel allows air into the burqa so the women do not suffocate. If you have ever been caught in a dust storm, you'll un-derstand how these women see the world. When you stare at them, your contact in Dera Ghazi Khan, a journalist, tells you about a place not too far from here where the tribal belt of Balochistan province starts, where he says the women are not given any shoes. When you don't understand, he explains impatiently, "If you're not wearing shoes and you walk outside, where will your eyes remain? You'll never look up—never look at any man—if you're scared of where your naked foot might fall when you leave your home."

Less than an hour away from Dera Ghazi Khan, you speed past fish farms and a smashed tractor—five people dead, and no ambulance for miles—then pass a board that welcomes you to the village of Shah Sadar Din. Qandeel Baloch was born here.

In July 2016, the villagers watched as reporters from all over—not just from Pakistan, but from abroad, from the BBC, the *Guardian*, the *New York Times*—turned up in Shah Sadar Din to cover the story of Qandeel Baloch. It was a great time to be a local reporter. If you weren't covering the story, you were working as a fixer, an interpreter, a driver . . . the possibilities were endless. The local journalists took the visiting reporters to Shah Sadar Din over and over again. Everyone wanted to see where Qandeel came from. The villagers couldn't understand it. "My friend, you have come here for nothing," a man said to one of the reporters. "Strange people, coming here just like that." What did he mean? the reporter asked. "We have a tradition here that every second or fourth day some girl is killed and thrown in the river. You media guys are creating hype for nothing." A girl could be stuffed into a gunny sack or the kind of bag used to carry wheat or sugarcane and the bag could be filled with stones. The bag would sink to the bottom of the river. The girl would stay there, buried under the stones.

When I meet Qandeel's parents, three months have passed since the day she died. Any meeting with them must now be organized through a man named Safdar Shah, who introduces himself over the phone as their lawyer. A few days earlier, Qandeel's parents had told a reporter they have been forced to beg for food in Shah Sadar Din, where they returned after they were evicted from their house in Multan.[1] While their daughter was alive, they divided their time between Shah Sadar Din and Multan, and Qandeel paid the 10,000 rupees' rent for this house every month. Without her, they could not afford the rent. But Shah says the meeting will take place at the house in Multan, where Qandeel was murdered, and not in Shah Sadar Din. "It's no problem at all," he says airily. "Just don't come to the village. People here aren't happy about all the reporters who have been coming to meet the parents."

It takes around twenty-five minutes to travel from Multan's city center to Qandeel's home. We pass through the cantonment area and drive past the army club with its fat white onion domes and buildings whose walls bear neat lines of portraits of young men. The photographs change from grainy black and white—soldiers who died long enough ago to have roads named after them and paragraphs devoted to them in textbooks— to rosy-cheeked technicolour. These are pictures of *shaheeds* (martyrs)— men who have died in the line of duty for their country. Everything is perfectly ordered, from the manicured grass outside the city's only Mc-Donald's to the separate line for donkeys and cyclists at the checkpoints to get in and out of the cantonment. Just past the last checkpoint, we pass the sprawling skeleton of a building under construction, the new garrison library, which boasts enough space for 200,000 books, and then banks and a line of schools with names like Blossom Valley and Bloomfield.

Further on, as the road narrows and deteriorates, there are fewer women. Men crowd the vegetable carts and fruit stands and linger at shops selling household supplies, shoes and clothes. There are signs indicating a textile mill. Dung cakes slapped on the low red-brick walls of houses grow warm in the November sunlight. As we near the Karachi Hotel neighbourhood, the buildings thin out. The area is home to many who have come to the city from villages across Punjab seeking work. Small houses, narrow, one or two storeys high, constructed by landowners who rent them out for five to ten thousand rupees a month, are squeezed together on patches of land.

Someone is building a house just a few steps from the one that Qandeel rented for her parents. The scrub has been cleared, and the foundations reveal a simple, cramped layout: a kitchen, two rooms and what will probably be a bathroom. It is quiet, with the houses at some distance from the road. There are no squalling cars, no shrieking children playing in the street, no shops around the corner, no gurgle of water in open gutters. It does not have the familiar smells: there is no scent of sewage, no waft of food simmering on a stove, no piles of chicken fat, vegetable skins or cores of fruit festering in heaps on the side of the street. It seems to be deserted.

Safdar Shah's white car stands at the end of the lane, just before the sharp right turn to Qandeel's house. Only one of the four houses here is occupied. A woman emerges from it and narrows her eyes at us. "Media?" she asks. I nod, yes. "Do you have a card? Any phone number?" She takes my business card, and it disappears down the front of her shirt, probably tucked away with loose change and bits of paper with prayers scribbled on them. "Never know when you guys might come handy, right?" she says as she walks off.

Shah waits at the door to Qandeel's house. He wears a starched black *shalwar kameez* that puffs around him and rustles when he moves. His shoes have been scrubbed to a dull glow down to their pointed tips. He probably slicked down his hair this morning, but it has buffeted into wispy clouds. His light skin is flushed pink in the heat and his moustache is a jet black straight from a bottle. He looks like the kind of man who, if you ask him his age, will coyly reply, "How old do *you* think I am?"

"I know more about her than they could ever tell you," he says right away, as though picking up the thread of our earlier conversation on the phone. "Did I tell you I am a Syed? [A Syed is a Muslim who claims to be descended from the Prophet Muhammad's family.] We don't lie, you see."

Inside, Qandeel's father, eighty-year-old Muhammad Azeem, perches on a black imitation-leather sofa, his legs, stick-thin within the loose folds of a dhoti, pulled close to his chest. He absently strokes the puckered nub of flesh where one leg abruptly ends. He lost his foot six months ago when a car ran over it. "The daughter came here to have his leg fixed," Shah explains. "She came to Multan on the second day of Eid and she planned to get his treatment done and then fly back to Karachi. She said she was going to leave for India after that."

Qandeel's mother, Anwar bibi, looks like she is in her fifties. She is small, the hard rise of her collarbones under her kameez hinting at a thin frame. She sits on the edge of one of the two charpoys in the room. Her feet dangle inches above the floor.

Shah drives Azeem and Anwar bibi here from Shah Sadar Din when he needs them to meet a reporter or appear on a talk show. He brushes off a query about Anwar bibi's claim that she and her husband have been forced out of this house. The landlord doesn't mind if they stay here for some time for free, he explains, and anyway they now have around 100,000–150,000 rupees in donations from human rights groups and sympathizers.

I try to gauge Shah's relationship with Qandeel's parents but it's not clear how he helps them or what he does as their lawyer since they are represented by the district prosecutor in their daughter's murder case. "I go everywhere with them," he explains as he sits on the charpoy next to Anwar bibi. "I mean, they refuse to go anywhere without me. They tell me, 'If you go, we'll go with you.' Even if it's for their son's bail hearing. You see, we have known each other's families for generations. We have been together for eight generations. Our fathers were friends and their women come and go from our house. We Syeds don't usually go to other people's houses [I assume he means people who aren't as well off as his family] but we went to theirs. The one time Azeem had to go somewhere without me, he started weeping in the car. I asked him, 'Uncle, why are you crying?' Do you know what he said?"

Azeem is quiet. He does not tell us what he said.

Shah continues, "He told me, 'Safdar, promise me you won't leave me!' So I swore, 'As long as I am alive, I'll never leave your side.'" He points to Azeem. "You see, they have cell phones; people can call them, but nobody ever understands what they say."

While Anwar bibi seems to understand and speak some Urdu, Azeem responds only in Siraiki. He tends to mumble, his words gummy and sloshing and often unintelligible when he cries, which is frequently and in small bursts.

Shah says he is the family's *pir* (spiritual leader). In rural areas across Pakistan, particularly in the provinces of Sindh and Punjab, pirs offer everything from religious intercession to dispute resolution among their followers, known as *mureed*. In southern Punjab, where Azeem's family lives, many political parties turn to pirs—usually landed, wealthier residents of small towns and villages—in order to secure the votes of their followers. "I help them because we are all from the same village. Our lands border each other, and they are my mureed," Shah says. "Azeem Khan is my mureed. His children are my mureed, and their children and so on."

Both Azeem and Anwar bibi only stare at the television as Shah makes these statements. They watched their daughter on that screen in a handful of television dramas and morning show appearances. She would call them to let them know what channel and what time she would be on. "In those moments, while we were waiting to see Qandeel, life would feel great," Azeem says. As a child, she had told them she wanted to be a star. And now that she was singing, dancing and acting, they were happy for her.

Shah sighs. "She didn't talk to them for years. Didn't talk to the father for three years."

"I supported her," Azeem pipes up. "I used to send her money."

Shah continues as if he hasn't heard him, "Didn't talk to the mother for six years."

"She would call us sometimes," Anwar bibi says quietly.

"Oh she just ended all relations with them," Shah says. "She thought they wouldn't like what she was doing. She said she would never look back."

Qandeel's six brothers knew about the television shows she was on, and they didn't like it. "Tell her we never want to see her again," one of them told Anwar bibi. Qandeel had two sisters, and when she returned to Shah Sadar Din for her younger sister Shehnaz's wedding around 2010 her parents tearfully welcomed her home but said she couldn't stay. "Leave, or your brothers will pick a fight with us," Anwar bibi told her daughter.

Qandeel's neighbour in Shah Sadar Din remembers a night, perhaps during that visit, when Qandeel appeared at his house out of breath. Her brother Arif had a pistol and was threatening to kill her. "I had no idea what had happened," he recalls. "Qandeel had come there with a driver and she took off. After she left the village, her parents had told us all she was working at some mill." She did not want to come back to Shah Sadar Din after that. She found this house in Multan and told her parents that she would meet them there once a year.

"Our sons, their wives and children didn't bother with us after that, and we didn't bother with them," Anwar bibi says. "Our daughter took care of us and no one else paid us any attention. We didn't know much about what she did, and we didn't really understand it. She travelled to Malaysia, Sharjah, Dubai, and South Africa, but we had no clue why. What she's doing, what she's not doing—we didn't bother asking. It was her life."

By June 2016 they were alarmed. Their daughter's face and voice seemed to be on TV almost every week. These were not appearances that she called to tell them about. "We saw these photos on the news," Anwar bibi says. "They said Qandeel did an interview with a cleric. There were photographs of her sitting on his lap. Wearing his cap. Every day those pictures were shown on every channel. Over and over again." While Anwar bibi and Azeem were in Multan for a visit, they found out that some people were taking photos of their home in Shah Sadar Din.

"These *kameenay* [bastard] mullahs," sputters Azeem.

"Those bearded men," Shah suggests.

"Those bloody bearded ones!" Azeem continues. "They asked people, 'Who is Qandeel? Where is she from? What do you know about her?'"

Qandeel was worried. "Don't think badly of me," she told her father. "I haven't done anything wrong. I'm just fighting with someone."

Anwar bibi scolded her daughter. She didn't want her to do any interviews or talk about the cleric. "These people are bigger than you," she remembers saying. "Don't meet these people who are above your stature," she cautioned. Remember where you come from. Whose daughter you are.

A few days later, in the last week of June 2016, everyone found out who she was, where she came from and her father's name. She had been married and had a son. Stills of her passport and national identity card, with her real name, "Fouzia," were shown on the news. When news broke that Qandeel Baloch was really Fouzia Azeem of Shah Sadar Din, Waseem refused to leave his home. People were coming to the mobile phone shop he owned in the village with their phones. "Can you download your sister's latest videos on this for me?" they'd ask, sniggering. When Waseem's friends came to his house to enquire about him, why he hadn't been out drinking with them, why he wasn't coming to the hookah pani (shisha) spot any more, he told his mother to say he wasn't in.

Up until this point Waseem had kept in contact with his sister. "Whatever he asked her for, she gave him," Shah claims. "If he said he wanted a mobile phone that cost 80,000 rupees, she bought it for him. If he asked for one lakh [100,000] rupees, she sent it to him. She did everything for him and her sisters. When Shehnaz got married, she sent a truck loaded with things for the new bride, including an air conditioner."

"How did she make enough money to buy all those things?" I ask.

"Allah provides," Azeem interjected.

When the media revealed her real name and pictures of her passport and identity card appeared on TV and online, Qandeel called from Karachi. "I want to come home," she told her mother. Then she vacillated, changed her mind. She would send them money for Eid. She didn't want to leave Karachi.

A week later, she said she would come. "She said, 'I am so tired, I am so worried,'" Shah prompts.

"I am tired, I am worried," Anwar bibi repeats.

"I am tired of this life. . ."

"I am tired of this life. I want some peace."

When she finally did come to the house in Multan, Qandeel was perpetually on the phone. Azeem heard her talking to someone one day. "What have I done for you to hound me like this?" she snapped. "Why are you after me? What have I ever done to Pakistan? Why do you keep calling me?"

"These media people hounded her," Anwar bibi says. "They just wouldn"t stop. Hounded her beyond all limits."

It didn't stop even after she died. Reporters and camera crews followed her parents to Shah Sadar Din for the funeral. Azeem didn't attend but insists that there were hundreds of thousands of people there on the day. However, photographs and video footage of the funeral show just a few people: relatives, villagers, curious bystanders. Qandeel's body was covered and laid on a charpoy. A cleric stood before her, raised his palms to his ears and led the congregation, four rows deep behind him, in prayer. Shah stood right behind the cleric. "I handled all the arrangements," says Shah. "Azeem wasn't even there for the funeral. I was. He told everyone, 'Shah *sahib* will be there. I don't have the strength to come.'"

After the prayers Shah approached one of the reporters who had come to the village for the funeral. "You should interview me," Shah told him. "I know just what is going on here." His interview ran as breaking news that day. And since then Shah has stayed in touch with that reporter and others, providing them with nuggets of information and updates as the case progresses. He glues news clippings of his interviews or stories featuring his quotes or photographs into a thick oblong notebook, the kind that schoolchildren use.

"The media got her killed," Shah says with a sigh. "She just wanted to be famous. She wanted to make a name for herself. She wanted people to know that Qandeel exists. I once asked her, and we used to speak practically every day you know, if she knew why people spoke badly of her. They are jealous of you, I told Qandeel. They are jealous of your fame."

Five days after the world found out that her name was Fouzia Azeem, Qandeel received a letter from Fayyaz Leghari, a lawyer in Gadai, a town twenty kilometres from Shah Sadar Din. He wanted her to stop claiming to be a Baloch. In southern Punjab the tribal and feudal system has strong roots. Men and women use the name of their clan as their family name and defer to their tribal chieftain or the head of their clan on all matters. Political power is often held over decades by the heads of clans, and a tribal chief may be responsible for everything from building a new school or hospital in his village to resolving disputes within his tribe. Shah Sadar Din is home to members of many tribes, including the Ma'arah, which has its roots in the neighbouring province of Balochistan. Qandeel's family belong to the Ma'arah tribe and believe they are Baloch. However, Leghari did not accept that. "You have no relation [sic] with any Baloch family or tribe," Leghari wrote in his letter. He claimed that Qandeel's behaviour was bringing shame to everyone who was Baloch and he threatened to sue her for up to fifty million rupees if she did not stop using the name.

Safdar Shah spoke with Qandeel shortly after this, and he recorded the call. Their conversation, a little over thirty minutes long, found its way onto YouTube, and Shah often cites it as proof that he knew Qandeel and would chat with her. When I ask why he would leak a private conversation, he insists that "a friend" put it on YouTube. He has a theory about why Qandeel was threatened with legal action for using "Baloch," and it's a theory he spoke to Qandeel about in that leaked phone call. He repeats it often. He notes that actresses and models who come from well-known or rich families in Pakistan have found success in the film or fashion industry. "But if Muhammad Azeem's daughter appears on television, then she's not Baloch. Why? Because he's a poor man? Because he's from a small village? If the daughter of the former governor of Punjab becomes a model, she gets offers to work in films. Her brother doesn't kill her. Her father doesn't kill her. But if Muhammad Azeem's daughter becomes a model . . . " He trails off.

I don't get to find out if Azeem and Anwar bibi really believe this. The most they will talk about for now is their memory of the morning that they found Qandeel's body. The last thing Azeem remembers from the night before was how sleepy he felt when he lay down on his charpoy on the roof of the house, where he and his wife slept during the summer. "I woke up in the morning and my head was spinning," he says. Their son would later confess that he had spiked their glasses of milk with a sedative the night before.

"I was the first to wake up," Anwar bibi says. "I felt like my body was numb. I couldn't see very clearly. I held my hand against the wall for support and tried to go downstairs. I remember sitting on the stairs every few steps because I could not stand. The sun was out by this time and it was quite hot. I was sweating a lot and I thought that I might be feeling unwell because I had been lying in the sun for too long. I washed my face. I didn't feel like I could cook breakfast, so when the servant who worked at our house arrived, I gave her some money and told her to buy some food from the market. I called out to Qandeel. I said her breakfast was ready. I called her three or four times, but there was no answer. I opened the door to her room and saw her lying there on the charpoy."

With Shah deftly steering the conversation, Anwar bibi and Azeem's explanation for why Waseem killed Qandeel comes out as a muddled version of the story that has been told, retold and then untold over the last few months. A month before we meet, Anwar bibi and Azeem were interviewed on a talk show about their daughter.[2] They said that Qandeel was scared of her brothers and feared their reaction to the kind of work that she was doing. Azeem told a reporter that his daughter had confided in him about this, saying, "Baba, sometimes I feel my younger brother wants to kill me."[3]

Azeem explains that his daughter tried to placate Waseem. She said she had arranged for him to marry the daughter of a woman who used to come to her parents' house to give her massages and to oil her hair. But Waseem wasn't interested in getting married; he wanted his sister to stop the work she was doing. Anwar bibi says her daughter asked for a year, just one year, to cash in on her sudden fame. Qandeel promised her brother she would then leave show business.

When Waseem came to his parents' home in Multan in July 2016 while Qandeel was visiting from Karachi, Anwar bibi tried to send him back to Shah Sadar Din because Qandeel pleaded with her to do so. She gave him 20,000 rupees. He left, but returned three days later. Azeem then told his son that he wanted him to represent the family at their neighbour's funeral because he could not walk without assistance. Waseem agreed, and it was decided that he would stay the night in Multan.

Azeem and Anwar bibi had no idea about Waseem's plan for that night—that he had arranged for his cousin Haq Nawaz to come to the house later to help him kill Qandeel. They claim that Waseem and Haq Nawaz stole 200,000 rupees and some jewellery from Qandeel after they killed her[4] and pocketed 40,000 rupees belonging to Azeem before leaving the house in Multan that night. Anwar bibi and Azeem say that the moment they saw their daughter's lifeless body, they knew without a doubt that Waseem had killed her, and when the time came to file an official report, that is exactly what Azeem told the police. Later, Azeem would tell a reporter from the BBC that he had felt unwell and out of sorts from the effects of the sedative Waseem had given him and could barely remember what he had told the police. He claimed the police called him back to the station several times to amend his initial statement. Sometimes they would suggest what he should write down.

Today, they speak proudly of their daughter to me. They insist on calling her "Qandeel," the name she chose for herself, and not "Fouzia," the name they gave her. She is a *shehnshah* (a queen), the one whose name will always be remembered, the one who became famous, a brave-hearted girl who was a tomboy and loved to swim, ride bikes, run six miles at a time, and do karate. She was intelligent, far more than their other children, bringing home prizes for her work in school and becoming class monitor. She danced at the slightest hint of a tune. She was not naughty but knew how to stand up for herself. She beat up a man who teased her sister but was not cut out for hard work like harvesting, milking cows, cleaning, and cooking like the other women in the village. When she came to Multan for ten days at a time, she liked to sleep for much of the day. She liked to be fashionable. She loved children and spoiled them. She cried for her son when she lost custody of him.

"And now that she is gone, you must think of that child," Shah interrupts.

"Don't say things like that," Anwar bibi replies.

"I don't want that child," Azeem says, scowling.

"You need to get that child somehow," Shah tells them. "He is her *nishaani* [memory]."

A few weeks after she died, Qandeel's landlord in Karachi sent her parents a notice to collect her things and pay a few months of outstanding rent. The letter had the address of her apartment, and her parents finally found out where she had been living in Karachi. Azeem and Anwar bibi travelled there with Safdar Shah. 'This sofa you're sitting on?' Shah says, pointing. "Qandeel's. That table. Qandeel's. Want to see the rest?" Her clothes, wispy silk shirts, jeans and soft chiffon tunics, fill a steel cupboard in one room. In another—the room where Anwar bibi says she walked in that morning in July to find her daughter unresponsive, a cloth thrown over her face—a bright red and yellow suitcase lies on the floor, more clothes bursting out of it. A worn-out cotton robe from a hotel, a pink lace top, a royal-blue shirt, a leather jacket, tights, a black and blue scarf threaded with silver. The floral-patterned stole that she wrapped around her bare shoulders in one of her last television interviews.

"We brought back forty-five pairs of shoes with us!" Shah crows. "There was a great big cupboard outside one of the three rooms in her flat," he says. "It was so big, we couldn't move it. It was filled with her things. We asked the landlord if we could just leave it there. He refused. He said he would throw it out. So we tied ropes around it and tried to lower it downstairs. The rope slipped from our hands. That cupboard of hers fell. It smashed into bits and pieces."

Anwar bibi comes into her daughter's room and sits on one of the sofas brought back from Karachi. Sometimes Qandeel would take selfies as she lay back on those sofas, bored and alone in her apartment. Anwar bibi watches Shah rifle through the suitcase. "We brought back a truck full of stuff," he says, tugging at the tangled clothes. "Sofas, a fridge.

Her bed." The same bed on which she made most of her videos. Where she writhed and sang love songs and feigned a headache and promised a striptease and wept as she asked, "Why do you guys hate me so much?" That bed is now in Shah Sadar Din.

Anwar bibi buries her face in her palms.

Shah looks at her. "She gets a little crazy sometimes," he says.

It is the first time in our conversation that Anwar bibi has cried. "I feel so strange in here," she says. "My heart feels so sad. I feel suffocated. I feel helpless. We are helpless. When I see her things, I feel this way. People say to me now that she was good. They praise her now. If they had praised her then, she would not have left this world. She would not have angered her brothers. But what crime did my daughter commit? She was innocent. They killed an innocent. I feel sad for her and I feel worried for my son."

This is the most that she will say during our conversation. Shah looks around the room. "Do you know what we can do with all these things?" he asks. "These clothes, these shoes—they're of no use to these people. Where we live, no one wears these kinds of things. Do you think people would buy this stuff?"

In a corner, the top of a small fridge is covered with a smattering of junk: Mr White Smokers Toothpaste, with the end cut off to squeeze every last bit of paste from the tube, a small bottle of mustard oil, a scrubbing brush for nails, Comfort Morning Fresh fabric softener, a yoghurt and cucumber face wash for oily skin, a card for a twenty-four-hour taxi service in Karachi, a toothbrush, and what looks like a bar of pure gold. Shah's eye falls on this and he picks it up to examine it. He shakes it. It is a powder compact, its red and black embossed YSL logo slightly chipped. It is almost empty, with just a ground-down shimmering square of flesh-coloured dust.

Shah grins. "Here you go," he says, thrusting the compact into my hand. "Something for you to remember her by. Take it. It'll be *Qandeel ki nishaani* (a memory of Qandeel)."

"PEOPLE SAY THIS IS NO JOB FOR A WOMAN"

She is seventeen and he is her mother's cousin. She writes him letters, confessing her love for him. The words turn the mottled brown of old blood—her blood—as the years go by. On their wedding day she is led into a room filled with family and friends and seated beside him. A woman fastens something to his wrist. He dips his head forward as a garland of pink and cream flowers is hung around his neck. He feels the heft of a gold watch, the cool metallic press of a ring slipped onto his finger. His arm presses against hers and someone arranges the gauzy puff of her dupatta around her. They never hold hands. She stares at a spot on the floor. Someone takes a photograph.

More than a decade later, when the reporters find him, he will show them this photograph and tell them about the letters. They will look at the picture of the happy couple and think that for a girl marrying a man she loved so much, she sure does look miserable. But then again, what kind of shameless woman grins on her wedding day? Would she have smiled if she had known that this photograph would later be seen by thousands of people?

There is no love marriage. My parents forcibly married me to him. That's it.

It isn't long after the wedding that she comes home weeping, and tells her parents about the cigarettes stubbed out on her skin, of the electric shocks that tremble in her body, the threats of throwing acid in her face. "He hates me because I am beautiful and he is not," she says. "I am young and he is not. He hates me." He would not let her visit them or meet her brothers. "Something is wrong with this man. He wants to kill me."

Every time, her mother takes her back to her husband's home. "We are Baloch," Anwar bibi scolds her daughter as they make their way back to Kot Addu, an hour away from Shah Sadar Din, "and Baloch do not believe in running away like this. His home is your home now." Anwar bibi knows what the people in the village would tell her child: "He can beat you. He can break your body with sticks. He can set you on fire. Whatever he does, you have to stay there. That's it."

Anwar bibi would finally see the burn marks when she bathed her daughter's body and wrapped her in a shroud on the day of her funeral. Even then she told the blonde woman who came to interview her the same thing she had told her dead child all those years ago.

Months pass. The girl feels no joy when the baby comes.

They think she will settle down now that she is a mother.

I was married against my will. Any child born in that marriage is not mine, it's his.

You have a son, her husband snaps at her. What more do you want? But even six months later, even after she has grown to love the little boy, the answers to her husband's question continue to beat within her.

I want to go back to school, she thinks when her husband strikes her. I want to leave this place, she repeats when she knows that she will go to the nearest city, Dera Ghazi Khan, and not back to her parents' home. I want to get a job, she reminds herself as she waits in the dark to hear her husband's snores the night she runs away. I want to stand on my own two feet, she pleads as she clutches her child and waits at the gates of the women's shelter in May 2009.

Main iss liye paida nahin hui thi ke kissi mard ki jooti bun ke rahoon. [I wasn't born to be worth less than some man's shoe.]

"Name?" asks the woman sitting behind a glass-topped desk inside the Darul Aman, the government shelter home for women.

She gives her real name. The name her brother had chosen for her when she was born: "Fouzia Azeem."

"And his?"

She looks down at the baby nestled against her. She will never forget the misery she felt the day she learned she was having that man's child. And then the love that held her so tightly within its grasp that she endured months with a man she called an animal, just for this little boy.

"Mishal." It means "the light."

A few days later, she is transferred to a shelter in the city of Multan. "My parents keep coming here for me," she had told the officials at the shelter in Dera Ghazi Khan. "They just want me to go back to my husband. I'm in danger here." From the car window, she sees men and women squatting on the footpath outside a mosque in front of the Multan shelter. Some of the women cradle children in their dupattas. They sit there for days, refusing to leave without the woman they have come to claim. "She will run off with someone else if she stays here," the men argue with the shelter's guards when they tell them to go away. "We do not accept this," the women chime in. While they wait, they watch the female guards saunter to a kiosk at the corner to buy crisps, candy, and fizzy drinks for the women behind the gates. There are rumours the guards keep a close eye on the women inside so they can sniff out the most desperate. "We have a pretty, new one with us this week," the guards then whisper to landlords and politicians in the city. The women are not allowed to leave the shelter, but on some nights, with a thick enough wad of notes in the right hands, the gates are unlocked. At least, that's what everyone says about this place.

Every day women pound at the gates, pleading to be let inside, and they are led to Fatima's office. She has been in charge of the shelter for only a year, but she learned one thing very early on: "The women who end up here are the rebellious ones." But this place has a way of weakening that spirit. Perhaps it is the din of wailing children—and sometimes their mothers—that makes women want to return to whatever it was they escaped. Maybe this place makes them realise they aren't all that special. Once your eyes get used to how dark it is inside—windows are a risk—you will see that there are two kinds of women here: those who want to marry someone of their own choice and those who want a divorce. And no one can stay here forever.

Some women crack in two days. Better the devil you know, they say. Some women believe their father's or brother's or husband's earnest promises. After they leave, Fatima gets updates on them. They have locked her in the house. They have cut off her legs. They have killed her.

The new girl does not seem to be in any hurry to leave. Her parents travel for hours from their village to see her. She doesn't want to talk to them. She has no interest in any of the classes—religious lectures, handicrafts, stitching and embroidery—intended to keep the women busy. She fusses over her child and trails through the corridors crooning to herself. Sometimes she takes requests, and then the sweet strains of a love song slip under the cracks of the door to Fatima's office, silencing for just a few seconds the whine of complaints from the women who crowd around her desk like siblings snitching on each other.

At any given time Fatima is responsible for up to forty women at the shelter, and she would have forgotten all about the new girl, were it not for the day she gives her baby away. Fouzia says the boy is sick. She is terrified he will die.

If anything happens to him, God forbid, they will do a case on me. I had no choice.

"What kind of mother are you?" Fatima asks with disgust when Fouzia returns to the shelter after meeting her family, her arms empty. The boy is no longer hers. She doesn't seem to register a word Fatima is saying.

"Just try and meet him [the child]," her husband had said. "See what I do to you if you even try."

What have I done? Will my boy ever know his mother's name?

Fouzia doesn't weep, she doesn't talk back or walk off as Fatima berates her.

I thought when my child is older, he'll understand, he'll see the environment there in the village and feel that his mother was right, that she did what was right.

Maybe she has some fantasy for herself, Fatima thinks. She imagines herself living in a beautiful house, a rich woman with the world at her fingertips. Maybe she is one of the educated ones. They think they are very modern. I am an educated girl, these girls say when Fatima asks them why they ran away from their homes. I don't belong there.

"Why did you do this?" she asks Fouzia.

Even years later, she has not forgotten the girl's reply.

"I need to make my own life," she says. "Whatever I want to do, I cannot do it with a child hanging onto me. I'll become helpless."

The child could live with his grandparents. Maybe his father will want him.

Fatima tries to argue with her. "But your parents could help you . . . "

Fouzia will have none of it. "No. They will not listen to me, and I will not listen to them. They should let me live my life."

They sit in silence for a moment.

"You don't know what I have planned," Fouzia says as she rises from her chair. "Just let me do whatever I need to."

A few days later she is gone. The next time Fatima sees her face is on the news, and by then Fouzia is calling herself by another name, the name the world has come to know her by.

You need a good memory to remember the faces of all the women who come in just one day to the Faisal Movers bus depot seeking work. Subhan isn't likely to remember a face. He scarcely ever looks up from his phone when he sits across from the hostess applicants or their fathers, brothers or husbands. So when reporters and officials turn up in his office in July 2016 to ask him about a woman named Fouzia, he gives them the same answer over and over: "These girls stay with us sometimes for two weeks and sometimes for two months. How can I be expected to keep tabs on each one?"

Every girl is the same. He repeats mechanically the requirements for the position as they strain to hear him above the crackle of the loudspeaker every time the announcer presses her lips too close to the mike—Is she kissing it or trying to eat it? Subhan grumbles—to rattle off a string of departure times. Lahore, Karachi, Islamabad, Sahiwal, Rawalpindi, Sargodha, Faisalabad, Hyderabad, Quetta, Bahawalpur, Rajanpur. With a belch of black smoke and a smack on the rump from the ticket inspector, the buses roll out of the depot and across the country every half-hour, all day and all night.

"Education?" Subhan asks the prospective hostesses. "Matric," they reply. Some lie. Others have Master's degrees. These ones weep when he says he has nothing administrative for them. It is hostessing or nothing. He knows they won't refuse. "It's better than having nothing," some of them say, sniffling.

"Age? You need to be above twenty."

Most of them lie again.

"Do you want to be paid daily or monthly?" The answer tells him how desperate the girl is. Those who opt for daily pay have promised themselves this is just a quick stopover until something better comes along. They need the money to tide them over.

Hostesses welcome passengers on board the bus, recite the *safr ki dua* (prayer for safe journeys) and serve water, cold drinks and cardboard containers of biryani or sandwiches halfway through the journey. They earn a few hundred rupees for each trip, and some women clock up several trips a day to earn a bit extra. In 2016 the company announced that if a hostess did thirty trips in a month, she would get a 2,000-rupee bonus. It doesn't sound like much, but every rupee counts for these women. If any of the rival companies offer them even 100 rupees extra, they will leave.

The hostesses travel across Pakistan—a measure of freedom they would not have had otherwise—but Subhan knows the job isn't ideal. The girls who come here have no other choice. They don't have fathers or they have brothers who do nothing.

If a woman gets the job, Subhan dispatches her to a nondescript two-storey building outside the depot. The only male allowed inside it is a young boy who delivers cups of tea, cigarettes and greasy fast food to the hostesses. They take quick naps between trips or stay the night there, sleeping on thin foam mattresses thrown on the floor, stripping down to tight white T-shirts that they wear tucked into the shalwars that the company issues them. A new girl is pointed in the direction of the hostess in charge. Naseem has been here since 2002. It has taken her more than a decade to work her way out of the buses, to the ticket counter and finally into this air-conditioned office with her own computer. She pairs new hostesses with older ones for the first three or four trips, until the girl is confident enough to do the announcements and manage passengers on her own.

Naseem believes she can weed out the ones who will cause her trouble and spot those who will learn to step nimbly away from the hands that cup their bottoms or the fingers that "accidentally" caress their breasts as they hand out the food boxes to passengers. "Men observe the women to see what they're like," Naseem warns new hostesses. "They will treat you accordingly."

She doesn't care what the women do in their own time. She just doesn't want to hear about it. "People say this is no job for a woman," she likes to say. "They say we become bad in this line of work. But the ones who are already spoiled are bad even in their homes."

If a new girl knows what is good for her, she will nod her head vigorously at this point.

He doesn't immediately recognize her when he first glimpses her. Could it be . . . ? he wonders, squinting to see the girl's face in the bright afternoon sunlight. Traffic snarls around the *chowk* (intersection) and his bus is nowhere in sight. He calls out her name. She turns, startled. Who knows her name here?

When he gets back to the shelter, he goes straight to Fatima's office.

"Guess who I met today?" he asks. "Fouzia. Remember, the girl with the baby? The one who used to sing for us?"

They had all wondered what had become of her.

"How was she?"

Aslam pauses before answering the question. "Ma'am, she . . . I think she . . . " He fumbles for an answer.

"What?" Fatima is impatient.

"Ma'am I think she's doing something wrong . . . " He trails off.

"Like what?"

"I think she's working on stage as an actress."

"Stage? Did she tell you that?"

"Ma'am, she didn't have to. You know how these women . . . how they dress. A bit bright and gaudy."

He turns to leave. "Ma'am, if I'm honest, it did not feel good to meet her. She was standing at Ghoora Chowk all alone. Dressed like that. I asked if I could help her with anything, if there was any help I could offer. She told me she was leaving Multan. She said, 'Now I'm going to go much further than this.'"

It is 2011. She lives in Islamabad now. She meets a man who goes by the name Mec—a snappy little nickname he coined for himself as media event coordinator—and everyone tells her she needs to work with him if she wants to make it in the industry, if she really does want to become the singer she's dreamed of becoming for years. They meet in her friend's office and she waits quietly, watching his face as her friend plays a *naat*, a religious hymn she has sung for him. The phone isn't the best, and she thinks the recording makes her voice sound tinny.

He doesn't look too impressed.

"Mec sir?" she interrupts the naat. "Sir, listen to my naat, please. Let me sing for you."

Years later, he loves to recount this moment. He imitates her. He remembers looking across the table in that office of the marketing company where she worked and thinking how this woman from Multan who wears a hijab wants to enter showbiz? Yes! He would insist to everyone who asked about her once she became famous. She was a scarfian! A *hijab waali* [woman who wears the hijab]! "She came to the city from the village," he would remind them. "She couldn't become bold all of a sudden."

She has a good face. There's a bit of "innocency," he notes. And the voice isn't bad. Maybe she could land a couple of morning shows during Ramzaan (Ramadan) with these naats.

"Will you do ramp walks?" he asks.

She pauses. "Whatever you say, Mec sir."

The girl wants it bad. He doesn't want to seem too eager. "OK," he says. He agrees to work with her. She beams. "Don't be so happy, my dear. You're a bit overweight," he remarks. That takes the smile right off her face. But it's OK, he reassures her; even the fatties can be worked on. "You just need to have an artist within you."

It is the first time anyone has ever acknowledged that, yes, she has an artist within her. No one, not her family, not the man she married and left had believed in her. She had then fallen in love with a man she had met here in Islamabad, but even he had not supported her decision to stand on her own two feet. "I don't want you to get into showbiz," he had pleaded with her. He thought she was doing it for the money. "Don't worry about money. What do you want? A house? I'll get you a house. A car? What more do you want?"

What she wanted was to be a star. She left him.

Now that she had Mec on her side, the only thing holding her back was "Fouzia." If she wanted to be a star, she needed a star's name. A new name for a new life.

"Candy?"

No, that didn't work.

"QB?"

There was a popular singer who went by that, and she didn't want to share a name.

My childhood crush once gave me a name. It's the name everyone knows me by.

Q – queen

A – appealing

N – naughty

D – dazzling

E – elegant

E – exquisite

L – lovely

Qandeel.

But Qandeel who?

Qandeel from Shah Sadar Din, a girl who belongs to the Baloch Ma'arah tribe.

Qandeel Baloch.

Yes.

That works. Qandeel. It's a beautiful name. What does it mean?

Qandeel ka matlab hai roshni. Qandeel means "the light."

THE MODELS OF ISLAMABAD

In November 2016, I travel to Islamabad to meet Mec, Qandeel's manager, to learn more about her years as a model. He invites me to a rehearsal for a fashion show at a banquet hall.

The fashion industry in Islamabad, Pakistan's capital, is tiny. When Qandeel started out as a model here, she hoped it would get her noticed so that she could have what her heart was set on: a career as a singer. But in Islamabad, there was only one show a month on average and she was competing with dozens of aspiring models, all scrambling to be picked for the catwalk. Most of these models, and photographers and fashion designers eventually headed to Lahore or Karachi, vying for the chance to be part of the multiple couture and bridal fashion weeks organized there throughout the year or a glossy spread in the weekend magazines devoted to the lifestyles and fashion choices of a new crop of starlets, socialites and influencers.

As I wait for Mec, I am introduced to the show's organiser, a twenty-nine-year-old woman named Khushi Khan. She stands out. While most of the models at the rehearsal are young and small, with almost prepubescent bodies, all bony shoulders and arms that you could probably encircle with the fingers of one hand, Khushi is older than the others, and tall, with broad shoulders and a full figure. While many of the other girls have faces that are heavily made up, with thick liner drawn around their lips to ensure a full-looking pout and broad strokes of baby-pink blusher layered over powdery foundation the colour of weak tea, Khushi's face is scrubbed clean, and she has creamy pale skin, small eyes and a mouth with a perfect peaked Cupid's bow. She is ordinary, almost plain, with a shawl draped around her shoulders like a cape, which billows behind her as she walks.

A year ago Khushi was one of these girls, crowded into a room outside this banqueting hall, waiting to get her hair and make-up done, drinking cups of tea to calm her hunger pangs. Now, she is trying to work her way up the ladder from the ramp. "I like modelling, but what I would love to do is to organize the shows," she confides to me in a low, rasping and deep voice. "I've never organised a show before and everyone has told me, 'You can't do this.'"

When she couldn't find investors to lend her the money for this event, Khushi used her own savings. "I need to prove that I can do this," she says. "I'm not getting any benefit from this thing. Not one rupee. But hopefully the next one will bring me some benefit." She pauses. "*If* there is a next one." She needs to make sure the show is perfect.

"Funky walk!" shouts Khushi from her spot at the end of the catwalk.

The model, Sunny, skips down the runway as the DJ turns up the volume on one of the songs from the playlist for the show. It is a number from the 1999 Bollywood film *Taal*. Sunny looks like she may have been four or five years old when it was released. She is very thin, all sharp angles and skin stretched taut over prominent cheekbones and strong jaw. She teeters on a pair of six-inch platform heels that make her legs look like toothpicks piercing wedges of cheese. Sunny flicks her long mane of caramel-streaked hair and winks at a carpenter squatting on the floor, then beams at two men tying red satin sashes into fat bows on the backs of the chairs that line either side of the ramp. The men are still, quiet. Their eyes follow her, the sashay of her bony hips in skinny jeans, the shimmying shoulders under a lacy T-shirt. One of them raises his phone to take a photo of her.

"When you do a funky walk, you wear Western clothes, pants and a shirt, and you do a little shimmy and swing your hips while you walk," Khushi explains. "OK, normal walk!"

Sunny halts mid-prance. Shoulders pulled back, hands on her waist, elbows jutting out, she clip-clops forward in an imitation of the models she has watched walking the runway in YouTube videos. There are no smiles for the labourers now, only a grim-faced stare at the end of the catwalk where Sunny imagines a pool of flashing cameras and photographers yelling her name.

"Bride walk!"

Sunny's elbows droop. She slows down. Her movements are languid, every step forward weighed down by layers of silk brocade. Her fingers pluck at the border of an invisible dupatta to draw it across her face. She looks demurely down at her feet. Then she hears something and pauses. She looks up.

"Khushi, the call to prayer is sounding," she calls out. "I can't walk during the *azaan*."

The music is turned off. The labourers trail out of the room for the midday prayers.

"What about walking without the music?" Khushi asks. "We just need to make sure the ramp is fine."

Sunny strolls forward and then stumbles. Her pencil-thin heel is stuck in a tiny gap between the planks that were hammered together to create the ramp this morning. This is exactly what Khushi was worried about— the last thing she needs is for a model to tumble on the runway in front of the four hundred guests who will attend the show tomorrow. She yells for a carpenter. Sunny wriggles her foot out of the trapped shoe and lopes off the runway.

The event has been put together for a TV channel to celebrate one of its dramas airing a hundred episodes. A representative from the channel tells Khushi that he's brought over the awards that will be handed out to the show's actors, producers and directors. She goes over the guest list with him. He insists that two army brigadiers be seated on a crystal-studded cream-coloured leather sofa placed at the runway's halfway point. Other guests include gym instructors and a property developer.

The event includes a fashion show, live music and a children's tableau before the prizes are given out. "May Allah reward your hard work," the man murmurs to Khushi as he looks around the hall, which is usually rented out for weddings. An electrician has finally hooked up the lights, and Khushi watches as the catwalk glows in flashes of red, blue and green. "Inshallah," she says fervently.

Her real name is not Khushi—"happiness" in Urdu. Like Qandeel, none of the girls here use the names their parents gave them. Just a few days after she was born, Khushi's father was promoted. He worked for the national flag carrier, Pakistan International Airlines (PIA), and he named his baby girl after a dear friend, an air hostess. When this friend heard about the promotion, she came over with a box of *mithai* (sweetmeats) and gave the infant her first taste of sweetness, letting her lick a dab of honey from her finger. "Look," she said to the new father. "Her arrival has brought happiness into your home."

On the morning of 8 October 2005 Khushi was sitting outside her family home in Dhirkot, Kashmir, a little over three hours away from Islamabad, with her cousin. The two girls chattered away as they dipped pots into the cool stream of water that ran by the house. At 8:50 a.m. the velvet green blanket of shisham trees on the hills around Khushi's home seemed to shimmer like the surface of the stream. The ground trembled. Khushi remembers screaming her sister's name, not knowing if she answered because she could not hear a thing over the ringing in her ears. "Thirty-two hours later we finally found her in her bed, covered in concrete," Khushi says. "When the earthquake came, she probably didn't understand what was happening."

Seventy-five thousand people died that day. It was one of the worst natural disasters Pakistan had experienced. It was the month of Ramzaan, and after the rains stopped, after Eid went uncelebrated, the aid workers finally arrived. Fourteen-year-old Khushi and her four sisters spoke English, Urdu and Kashmiri, and were snapped up to help interpret for the international rescue teams streaming into the valley. By the time Khushi was fifteen, she was earning 25,000 rupees a month working with a community-based development project. "My father no longer had his job with PIA and our home was a pile of rubble," Khushi says. "We desperately needed the money, but my father insisted that I continue to go to school. I'd just started ninth grade, and I would go to work after classes."

Three years later, even as billions of rupees changed hands for development programmes and reconstruction efforts, children were still studying under the open sky and going home to clusters of temporary settlements. One day Khushi travelled to a village near Dhirkot, where the residents pleaded with her to help them get a school rebuilt. Their children had to walk to another village to go to school and many had dropped out because they couldn't make the journey. Khushi knew there wasn't much she could do. It was her job to interview locals, listen to their problems, create an agenda and present it to her employers. Aid trickled down slowly.

"I went home and told my father that I needed 30,000 rupees to help out a friend who was getting married," Khushi says. "Then I walked straight back to the village with that money and my savings." The villagers learned that she was terrified of water, and every day while the school was under construction three or four people would escort her across the swaying bridge over the river that ran beside the village. Eleven years after the quake, the village still does not have a proper mosque, and Khushi hopes to return some day with enough money to get one built. "I want to help build the mosque with my own hands," she says. "That's my wish. Inshallah."

Khushi left Dhirkot for the ruins of Muzaffarabad, just twelve miles from the quake's epicentre, to work for a Turkish NGO rebuilding schools and hospitals, but after six months the work had wrapped up and she was without a job. A friend mentioned an opportunity at a furniture shop in Islamabad that sold expensive, intricately carved wooden pieces to the city's bubble of foreign aid workers, diplomats and journalists. "I travelled to the capital for an interview and I was told, 'Your education isn't good, your way of talking is not good, and we need an educated girl,'" she recalls. She then applied to a real-estate firm in Islamabad where she was hired as a receptionist. She moved in with her brother and his wife in January 2009.

"Everything was new for me, and everything was different," Khushi says. "I only knew the village." Her boss was kind to her, treating her as a daughter while she struggled to find her feet. "There were [foreigners] there and I was expected to serve them alcohol even during the day when they would come for meetings," she says. Soon her boss's son was offering her alcohol. "He would say, 'Come to parties with me, come sit with me, have a drink with me,'" she explains. "'I told my boss, 'If I wanted to do bad things, I could go anywhere in Islamabad. I don't need to work here.'"

When she left that job, she spent three months doing nothing. Her engagement to a man she had met in Islamabad had ended, and she had no work. By then she had become the primary breadwinner in her family. "My brothers are good boys, but when their wives are around, their colours change," she says bitterly. "They don't make that much, and whatever money they bring home, they hand over to my sisters-in-law. That's just the way it is." Back in Dhirkot, her parents had come to rely on the 15,000 rupees she had sent home every month. In Islamabad she paid half the rent, another 15,000, to stay in her brother's apartment. She needed to make some money and fast.

When her sister sent her the designs for some clothes she wanted made, Khushi got her tailor to make copies. The clothes sold, and she set up a small boutique named after her mother, Gulshan. "I even had one or two designers stock their clothes with me," Khushi says. "We would split the money fifty–fifty." Soon she was selling shoes, costume jewellery and purses. Two years later, however, the boutique was gutted in a blaze. Her stock of clothes was burned to ashes.

"I was very disheartened," Khushi says. She was back to being unemployed. "I just went back to my village and I cried for two weeks."

She lay in her bed, unable to move. What now? she remembers thinking. How could she start again from scratch? But when she looked around her home, still without doors as her parents struggled to put things back together slowly after the quake, she knew there was no other way. She had to go back to Islamabad.

When she returned to the city, she applied for every position she could find. At her first job interview a man at a marketing firm sneered at her. "I was wearing a shalwar kameez and had a dupatta on my head," she says. "I didn't wear make-up. This man said to me, 'Sorry, you don't meet our standards.' Yes. That's exactly what he said, can you believe it?" The next few interviews weren't too different. "Why are you wearing a hijab?" "Your clothes aren't so nice." "Don't you have branded clothes?" She rattles off the responses she got. "Sometimes I would laugh about it. But it made me cry. What country was I living in where I couldn't get a job because I wore a hijab?"

She finally found work with a retailer who paid her 8,000 rupees a month to visit markets and convince shopkeepers to stock his shampoos, soaps and perfumes. She had earned 40,000 a month with the real estate company and struggled to make ends meet. The daily excursions to the market frightened her. Some shopkeepers were polite and sent her away with *chai paani* (refreshments). Others leered at her, asking her more and more questions about the products so she would linger, stroking her fingers as she handed them a bottle of shampoo or body wash. She lasted six months.

Khushi's father had always wanted her to be an air hostess. "You've got the height," he would remind her. "Your sisters do not." One evening a friend pointed out the same thing. "You're a tall girl," he mused. "Ever thought about modelling? You could make a lot of money very fast." His girlfriend Aliya was a budding designer and she needed someone for a shoot, he told Khushi.

But when Aliya met her, her face fell.

"I could see that she didn't like the look of me," Khushi remembers.

"We'll need to do a lot of changing with you," Aliya sighed. Khushi had never been to a beauty parlour in her life. "We'll need cutting, we'll need a dye," Aliya complained.

"I just thought, Who would make all that effort for me?" Khushi recalls. "Who would spend that kind of money on me?"

But Aliya rejected her anyway, saying, "Your thighs are too big."

Khushi reached out to her former boss at the real-estate company for help. She had known him since she was eighteen, and despite his son's behaviour, she'd stayed in touch. "Lose some weight and I'll pay for a makeover," he promised her. He introduced her to a photographer, who offered to put her in touch with some models who could mentor her. She needed a portfolio, a Facebook account, and a diet, the photographer advised. Khushi spent the next few weeks looking up exercise videos on YouTube and lost ten kilos by the end of 2015. Once she'd had a few photographs taken, her brother created a Facebook page for her and uploaded the images. Soon there was a message blinking in her inbox: "I'm having a show tomorrow. Can you come audition?"

"Do not wear a shalwar kameez when you go to the show," advised Summi, a model who had befriended her. "Shalwar kameez don't work here, and the only ones that do are the branded ones. Get yourself some jeans."

Khushi had never worn a pair of jeans in her life. She called her photographer friend in a panic. "Don't worry," he reassured her. "My friend will take care of you." He dispatched her to a shop in one of the largest malls in Islamabad, where a girl helped her choose four pairs of jeans and some shirts. When the time came to pay, the bill was a whopping 35,000 rupees. "They were branded clothes, you see," she explains. "Mango." Her former boss was called in to help. "I tried to pay him 10,000 rupees for the clothes, but he refused to take it from me," Khushi says. "I kept thinking, I've never taken money from anyone in my life before. I felt so ashamed, but I took it quietly. I didn't have a choice."

Back home, she timidly stepped out of her room to show her brother and sister-in-law her new outfits. "You've taken to wearing jeans and shirts, now don't start wearing anything less," her brother said, joking. She draped a big shawl around herself and headed to the rehearsal.

"Walk," commanded the show's organizer. Khushi took a few steps forward and the other models sniggered. "If you want to wrap your big shawl around you and walk the runway, then sit at home with a chadar draped around you," she snapped. "Take off your shawl." Khushi pulled it off, but kept tugging at her shirt as she crept forward. Once she reached the end of the runway, she froze. "I didn't want to turn around and walk back," she recalls, laughing. "I didn't want anyone to look at my bum in those jeans."

The organizer needed to see her walk in heels. Khushi had never owned a pair. "I was five feet nine!" she exclaims. "Why would I wear heels?" She was sent to the nearest market to purchase a pair of four-inch heels and then went home and put them on, tottering around so she could learn how to walk without stumbling.

The next day she went to the Pearl Continental Hotel in Islamabad for the show. The organizer pulled her to one side. "Walk with confidence," she advised. "Don't look around you. Just look right at the camera. Just think—there's only the lights, the camera and the applause. Look haughty, just like the professional models."

Her walk wasn't great, but Khushi got through the show without falling over. As far as she was concerned, that was a win. Once the photographs from the show came in, she put them up on Facebook. A few days later a male model messaged her. "Stop working for these small-time coordinators in these shows," he told her. "If you want to make it in this industry, you need to meet Mec."

Mec is one of those men who you cannot imagine ever having been a little boy. It's as if he's never been without his distinctive handlebar moustache, his brightly patterned satin ties, jackets that are a touch too long and shoes with an extra wedge of heel. He doesn't try to convince you otherwise. How long has he been in this industry? "It's been so long, I can't even remember." But if he had to estimate? "You could say that 80 percent of the models here in Islamabad were brought into this industry by me." How did all these girls find him? "Is that even a question? Everyone here knows Mec." How long has he been working with Khushi? "From the very beginning. Ever since I've been in this line of work." "It's been a little more than a year," Khushi, who is sitting with us, interjects.

It's the day of Khushi's show, and when the girls arrive they throw their arms around Mec's neck and bend to hug him where he is perched on a black pleather sofa. His face rises like a flower and they air-kiss him twice, their lips hovering near each rounded cheek with a smacking Muah! Muah! Yesterday, a new girl came to Khushi's rehearsal. She had come to Islamabad from Peshawar and wanted to work with Mec. Her head was covered with a dupatta and she wore a shalwar kameez with long sleeves that trailed past her wrists. She was quiet, lingering outside the circle of girls flitting around Mec. She's back today, her head uncovered. Someone has had a chat with her about how Mec likes to be greeted. She sidles up to give him a kiss and a quick hug.

The girls arrive in packs of three or four, clamouring for Mec's attention from the moment they enter the room.

"Sir, look at my dress!"

"Sir, where is my dress? I need to see if I brought the right make-up."

"Sir, I've brought my own dress. It's a bridal dress, sir—it's *so* beautiful."

They are bright and lovely, with tumbles of caramel or blonde hair, eager as kittens. Each one wants to be the girl Mec likes today, the one with the best make-up and most beautiful outfit, the one who will be the last to walk the runway. The showstopper. Mec is known to play favourites. "Sometimes, if a model catches his eye, he will forget the others in the rush to promote her," Khushi says. "Selfies on Facebook, special shoots, nice clothes, videos for YouTube."

Mec turns to the girl who has brought her own outfit. "Put it on and show me," he instructs.

"Sir!" She pouts. "What do you mean, sir? Sir, [my dress] is outstanding, trust me."

She gets a laugh out of him. "Behave yourself," he chides.

She giggles. The others seem to wilt.

They pull handfuls of sparkly silk and satin from their bags and he leaves the room so they can change. He pauses at the door. "Girls! Girls, listen," he says. He claps his hands. "Girls, you need to take care of your things, OK? Put everything in your bags and take it all backstage. Everything goes there. Nothing stays in this room." They nod in unison like schoolgirls on a field trip.

Mec is nervous about this show. It's for a TV channel, so that means he couldn't promise promotion to any other media outlets. "Now if I can't do that, then why would any designers give us their clothes?" he complains. The channel has a small budget for this event. It's not the kind of show he is used to. There are only twelve girls walking the runway and they'll get their make-up done at a parlour. "They didn't even have a budget for a make-up artist! Just imagine!" There's only one designer who has agreed to participate, and he is currently on his way over from Peshawar with the clothes on the back seat of his car. "No showsha, no glamouring, you know?" Mec sighs. He pulls out his phone to find out when the designer will arrive.

"Where have you reached?"

The man cannot hear him. He repeats himself. There's no answer.

"Where are you?" Mec snaps.

The voice crackles on the other end.

"Lo. You told me you'd be here at eleven a.m."

There are some excuses about traffic.

"Just come. Quickly." He sulks. "I was going to remind you to get me some paneer. Now forget it."

The man says something that gets a wide smile from Mec. "OK, baba, OK. Thank you. Come. We're all waiting for you." Mec hangs up. He looks mollified. "You know, the cheese in Peshawar is excellent. And this designer is coming from there, as I told you. Bring me some, I told him. He's bought me a kilo. A kilo!" One of the girls walks in. She wears a heavily embroidered kameez that cinches under her breasts and flows out.

"Sir, isn't it beautiful? Didn't I tell you?" she asks. She sways from side to side. The sequins on the fabric are motes of light.

Mec agrees that it is beautiful.

"Can I wear my tights under this?"

He gives his permission.

The girl turns to leave and then pauses. "Sir, can you get the toilets cleaned? It's smelling so much."

Mec gives her a tight smile. "Sweetie, can't you see that I'm giving an interview here?" he says in a sing-song voice. "Is this the time to talk to me about toilets?" Any chance she had of being the showstopper vanishes. "They love me a lot, you know," he says, watching the girl walk away. "Poor things rely on me." He taps one cheek and then the other. "One will kiss me here, and another here. They're like this with me. We are like a family." And these days one particular member of the family has Mec wrapped around her finger.

He introduces her with a flourish. "Meet Qandeel Two! QB2! Miss Bushi!" he says when she arrives at the venue. She walks almost on tiptoe in her platform heels, gingerly taking one tiny step at a time as though she is afraid to fall over. Bushi is a small, doll-faced, twenty-two-year-old girl from Abbottabad. Her hair falls in tangles to her waist, and she has thick bangs that she caresses to the side every time she talks. She features in every video Mec posts on Facebook these days. There's Bushi lip-syncing a Bollywood song in the back seat of a car; Bushi at Muhammad Ali Jinnah's tomb in Karachi, pointing out his grave; Bushi wearing sunglasses as big as saucers, playing with her hair and stroking her necklace as she whispers, "I am Barbie doll;" Bushi in full bridal make-up at a salon, asking, "I'm looking hot, na?"

Mec likes Bushi to dress the way Qandeel did. He has even bought her the sunglasses she had. Sometimes he creates little skits for her videos, just like the ones Qandeel became known for. In one Mec sits next to Bushi and eats voraciously from a plate of food.

"Sirrrrrrr," she trills. "Sir, how did you like my food?"

The camera pans to Mec giving a thumbs up.

"That's it?" She pouts.

Mec flashes a peace sign.

She giggles, one hand with its long red lacquered nails covering her mouth. "Hmm! So delicious!"

In another Bushi sings the latest Coke jingle. Someone hands her a glass of water. She purses her lips and pushes the glass away. She wants a Coke, not plain old water.

The videos have hundreds of likes. "So innocent." "Nice movement of beautiful model." "When I see Bushi's videos, I remember Qandeel."

Mec's girls are less kind. "Prostitute." "You know she's been married two times?" They say she's managed to make enough money to buy her own home. "You know how much money she spent doing it up?"

If Bushi knows that the girls talk about her this way, she doesn't seem to care. She has been in the industry for three years and is now finally getting some attention. A video of her cooking skills racked up 2,500 likes on Facebook alone, Mec claims. "You know how many offers we got just based on that video?"

The comparison to Qandeel thrills Bushi. "I love it," she says. "Love," she repeats in a breathy voice. "She was so successful, but then . . . " She clicks her tongue and shakes her head mournfully. Bushi tends to behave like she is always being filmed.

But as much as she dresses and behaves like Qandeel, Bushi cannot come close to what Qandeel meant to Mec. None of these girls can. "Qandeel used to sleep at my side whenever she was here in Islamabad," Mec says. "I wouldn't even turn in my sleep. Totally still. I didn't want her to be disturbed. I didn't want her to wake. And I never wanted her to think any wrong things while we lay together. No funny business."

Qandeel shared an apartment in Islamabad with her sister Shehnaz, who had moved to the capital from Shah Sadar Din and found work at a beauty parlour. The apartment complex is small, with the sand-coloured buildings huddled close together. There is a small garden in the centre, the grass patchy and yellowing. The paint has crumbled off the walls in swathes. Empty plots ring the complex, and in the winter a chilling wind whistles through the stairwells. There is a high school and a Montessori nursery further down the road and a small market just a few minutes' walk away, with shops selling auto parts. Mec says he was the only one who could convince Qandeel to leave this apartment, to meet people. "She wouldn't even go to the market," he remembers.

Qandeel was content staying in her room for days. She liked to be alone, Mec explains. Years later, she visited the city for work and stayed at a hotel. Mec stayed with her but needed to go home to pick something up. Lock the door from the outside, Qandeel told him. I'm not going anywhere.

He had just reached his house when he received a frantic call from her. Someone was trying to get in. "They're knocking on the door!" he remembers her screaming. "Someone is trying to come in. Come back immediately!" She refused to hang up until he promised he would call the hotel's front desk. It was just the cleaners.

In her room she would write in her diary, watch videos or read things online and message Mec. She would ask him questions about the people she read about or saw on the news or in the videos. "Why are people talking about that person?" she would ask. "She didn't have a single friend, no friend, nobody," Mec insists. "She trusted me the most."

Mec likes to hold his phone out to anyone who asks him about Qandeel and scroll past hundreds, if not thousands, of messages from her. He affectionately called her Sonu. He strokes the screen. There are photographs of clothes and shoes laid out on a bed. "Which dress shall I wear?" the message reads.

His finger swipes down.

There is chatter about a possible date, an ex.

Swipe.

Snatches of songs, recorded late at night when she could not sleep.

Swipe.

"Happy Valentine's Day!" Small red hearts, a photograph of a rose.

"She spent three Valentines with me," he says. "She gave me a perfume."

Swipe.

They talked about her family and her marriage, he confirms. He knew about it all. It didn't mean much though. "I have two girls who have just joined me after fighting with their families," Mec says. "I know that once they are on TV, once the relatives can call up everyone they know and say, 'Our girl has come on television, you should definitely watch her show,' then everything will be fine. That's how it is. And once the *paisa* [money] starts coming in, everyone is happy. Then they can't wait to meet the girl again."

That's how it was with Qandeel, he says. They agreed not to tell anyone else about her husband and son. "We didn't hide anything," he bristles, "we just didn't talk about it. I know what these girls go through. I know what their lives are like. Now if a girl is going to sit in front of you and talk about her sick mother or her father who has cancer, or if she tells you, 'I go home and shoot up,' you'll say, keep her away from me."

With him, the girls get a chance to get out of their homes, to see what life could be like, he says. "People only see what's on the screen, right? What is it that they say about Qandeel? 'Bold thi, brave thi.' That's what they saw. She scared easily. You show me one girl here who was born with a golden spoon in her mouth. They are all struggling. It may be all glamour here, it may look good on screen, but these girls go home and eat the same daal roti as the rest of us."

I meet Khushi again, two months after she organized that fashion show, on 17 January 2017. Once again it's a day of new beginnings for her. "I'm done with modelling," she says. "I got out after that show." She has had to start again once more. She has a new job now at an up-market gym and is trying to become a personal trainer. It'll take her two or three months, but she's started chatting with women who visit the gym in the hope that they'll hire her once she's certified. Her friend, another model, makes 40,000 rupees a month teaching these women yoga. Khushi has heard of one trainer who made 300,000 rupees in a month.

When Khushi started modelling, she only told her mother and one brother. Her father believed the money she sent them every month came from a job at some company like the real-estate business she used to work for when she first came to Islamabad. Her mother agreed to stay quiet, but made her promise three things. "Don't stay the night with some man, don't do drugs or drink. You can die, you can starve, not have anything to send back home, but do not sleep with a man for money," Gulshan told her daughter. "The day you do that for money, I'm dead to you. If you send me money that a man has given you to stay the night with him, that money is *haram* for me." It had been hard for Khushi to keep these promises and still make enough money to send home every month.

The show that day had gone well, but Khushi had barely managed to scrape together enough money to make it happen. When she called one of her sponsors for the 50,000 rupees he had promised her, he told her she could have it but at a price. "Come get your cash," he said. "But that little friend of yours, what's her name? Sunny? You leave her here."

Khushi knew this would happen at some point. But she also knew that once she started selling her models, she would be no different to other women who had tried and failed to make a career of organizing shows in Islamabad. "They got greedy," Khushi says. "They would take two or three girls with them when they would meet any sponsor. *Bold si dressing karo* [dress sexy], they used to tell the girls. Wear tights. Leave with your money, without the girl, that's how it is done." These organizers would sell their girls, put on third-rate shows and pocket the rest of the money. "Their reputations are in the dirt now and no one will give them a single rupee." Anyway, Sunny found the amount offered laughable.

Khushi has not heard from Mec for more than a month now. "Mec isn't giving his models more than 3,000 rupees per show," she tells me. "Maybe you can pay your phone bill with 3,000, but there's not much else you can do." The last time they spoke, Mec told Khushi he had a show lined up for her to walk in. Each model would be paid 12,000 rupees by the organizers. Of that, Mec would give each girl 4,000. It was generous by his standards.

"I refused to do the show,"' Khushi says. "Maybe that's why he isn't talking to me." Her model friends told her she was a fool. Sunny no longer talks to her. You're ungrateful, Khushi was told. Most managers don't give their models a penny. "The show gets you publicity," they say, pocketing the entire amount the organizers hand over for the girls. 'What more do you want?' Others dole out 1,000 or 1,500 rupees to each girl. At least Mec doesn't do that, his girls say.

Of course, there are other ways to make money. It starts at the shows. A model might catch the eye of someone sitting in the front row. The girl can be found on Facebook, or the show's organizer can be pressed for her phone number. Sometimes there is a selection process. A show organizer can get in touch with a manager like Mec to request photos of models to take part in a show and be available "later." The girls can make 7,000 rupees each for the show and 20,000 for the party afterwards at one of the farmhouses on the outskirts of the capital. "Pay parties," Khushi explains. "If some low-level guy wants you at his party, he can get away with 10,000 or 7,000 rupees per hour. But if you get a high-level *ka bunda*—a landowner, a businessman—you can get double that."

The requirements are easy enough: sit with the man's friends, laugh at some jokes, a little dancing. "Whether you like it or not, you have to smile, you have to dance, you have to drink," Khushi says. "One politician worked out a deal with a friend of mine: four hours of partying or attending a wedding, with everything—drugs, drinks—but sex included. That's charged separately depending on what he feels like after the event." If the girl meets someone during the event who makes an offer, she's free to meet him afterwards and the politician does not object.

At the parties the girls are introduced as "my friend" or "Islamabad's top model." The girls network, they flirt. Each person at the party is an opportunity. The host might be called the day after and asked about the pretty girl in the white dress and gold sparkly heels.

A girl might get lucky at the party and make a *khaas* friend: that special someone who pays up to 150,000 rupees a month and installs her in an apartment or house. Some girls have several khaas friends and one of these friends might invite the girl to Dubai. "They go there for shoots," Khushi explains. "The ones in which you only wear a bra and panties." She grins. "The only time I was called to do one, I said, 'Give me a *crore* [10 million rupees] and I'll be on the first flight.' They never called back."

If Khushi were to break her mother's third and most important rule, she could do "night spends." Some girls beg their managers to pick them for these opportunities. "A friend of mine charges 20,000 rupees per hour," Khushi says. "Gold chains, branded dresses and shoes—you can afford all this with night spends, and even more if you keep yourself well groomed and maintained." Khushi's friend is very happy with her rate, but other girls compare theirs to make sure they aren't asking for too little. Some girls boast about their fees. These girls can pull in big sums, but they end up spending most of it in order to attract new customers. "We have to look perfect," Khushi explains. "Your hands, feet, hair, make-up, gym membership—all of it adds up." There is an emphasis on brands, with some girls shunning those who cannot afford designer clothes and shoes. They clearly haven't made it, they think.

If Khushi chooses to keep the promises she made her mother, she cannot live in Islamabad as a model. On paper, models here are paid per outfit for even the biggest of shows, and a new model can make 8,000–10,000 rupees per outfit, whereas someone like Khushi, with nearly two years of experience under her belt, can demand 15,000–20,000. A girl starring in a television commercial can get up to 10,000 rupees, and a "brand shoot" for a catalogue or magazine can get a model 25,000 at best. But without a manager, even one who would give her a fraction of these amounts, Khushi isn't booking any shows or shoots.

And the offers that are on the table are less than promising. "There's a really good opportunity here in Lahore," Khushi, a friend of hers said on the phone just a few days ago. He knew she was looking for work. "Why don't you come here?"

"For whom?" Khushi asked. "And how much per dress?"

"This isn't a per-dress kind of job," the man said. "It's more like per hour."

Khushi was confused.

"Can't you understand what I'm saying?" he said, annoyed. "Per hour. Two or three clients. Get on the first bus to Lahore and I can get you 90,000 rupees for a few hours, and lakhs [hundreds of thousands] for night spend."

"Three men? Together?" It was the first question she could think of.

"What's the big deal? I have girls who book five clients for a night. Together."

Khushi couldn't believe he was saying this to her.

"Here's the thing, Ali *bhai*," she replied. "I have six clients. My six brothers. Two are in Karachi, but don't worry, I'll get them to come to Islamabad. You just put your mother and your sister on the first bus here."

"Have some shame, Khushi," Ali snapped and hung up.

Until two months ago, Khushi had been making 80,000 rupees a month through modelling and small roles in television dramas. She would spend 30,000 of that to buy clothes, food, and medicine for her parents and load it into a car headed to Dhirkot. She had never told her father how she paid for everything, and he had never asked. But three months ago her eldest uncle received some photographs and videos on WhatsApp. The images of Khushi and clips of her runway walks had been pulled from Mec's Facebook page. "Your daughter dances in clubs," her uncle shouted at her father. "She works with people who supply girls. They do shows in the day and parties at night."

Khushi's father sent her a single message: "You need to stop all this. Either you keep me in your life or you keep this job of yours. Finish up everything and come home." She replied, "I'll come home. But who will pay for your expenses every month?"

She says she is fine with no longer being a model. She dreams of setting up her own small women-only gym. She's been receiving marriage proposals. If she were still in the business, she knows that no man would even consider her. "Every man likes to go to parties with a model on his arm, every man likes to flirt with these models, every man likes to chat for hours with these models, take selfies and make it their DP [display picture] on Facebook," Khushi says. "But no man wants to marry a model. That model could pray five times a day, but if she says to this man, 'I am going out to get some shopping done,' or, 'I need to meet someone,' he will think, Who is paying for her shopping? Who is she going to meet? If her phone is busy when he calls her at midnight, he will think, She's ignoring me, she's degrading me, she's talking to her lover. The girl could be talking to her mother, her father, her sister. But if her phone is busy, that's what the man will think. No man will marry that girl."

Since I last met Mec, Bushi has all but disappeared from his Facebook page. There is no mention of QB2 any more. I ask Khushi what happened to her. "Who knows? Some models' boyfriends will force them to leave the field. And some girls realise that there's only one of three endings to their story: either they marry some rich man *jo retire honay waala hai* [who is about to retire]. *Duniya se retire* [Retire from this world]. He dies, but leaves you enough to live off. Or they will marry someone who already has children and a wife. The man will make you his second wife, but will never give you the rights or love that he gives his first wife. The girls might marry these men out of desperation, because they're tired of trying to make ends meet. And others will never get married and they'll continue to model and eventually they'll be told, 'You're too old to model.'" Khushi shrugs. "I don't know which ending Bushi got."

"HOW I'M LOOKING?"

It is October 2013. During that month, thousands of hopeful singers flock to auditions for a chance to be on the first ever *Pakistan Idol*, the local edition of the globally popular competition, *American Idol*. Three judges have travelled to cities across the country to meet these young men and women. One man has brought dates for them, another flowers, and another sweets from Multan. "My family is a family of *paan* [betel leaves slaked with a scarlet paste of lime, areca nut and tobacco and folded into triangles] sellers," one contestant tells the judges. "My father was a *paan wallah*, I am a paan wallah, and God willing my son will also make paan." Best paan in the country, he tells them as he fans out the tightly packed emerald-green envelopes on a platter. "Khaike paan Banaras wallah!" he sings the popular Bollywood song at the audition before the three red-toothed judges. A labourer skips work for his audition. He cries when they turn him down. He is paid by the day and has earned nothing that day.

Some of the contestants, who have only ever seen the Indian version of the show, come into the room and try to touch the judges' feet. Isn't this what was expected? "Poor things don't know how to behave when they meet a celebrity," titters the eldest of the three judges, an actress everyone knows for her comedy roles. When one contestant prostrates himself before the judges, the producers scramble to pick him up. Some children come into the hotel lobby where the contestants are waiting. They don't want to sing; they are just happy to spend the entire day sitting on the red velvet seats inside the air-conditioned hotel.

Others don't have gifts and don't care if they make it through. "It's enough for us that we got to meet you," they say to the judges. Some take an aeroplane for the first time in their lives when they make it past the first round and are flown to Karachi, Lahore, or Islamabad for further auditions. Others haven't got over the thrill of being in a hotel and turning on the taps at any time of the day or night to see a gush of hot water come forth.

The contestants are in the running to win a car, a cash prize, and the chance to record an album, but everyone knows that the excitement of the show is the real prize. "We have to keep Pakistan's background in mind," the actress says when asked about the winner's prospects in a music industry that is all but dead anyway. Might as well give these people a generator, she feels. It would be of more use to them.

Ramsha, a fifteen-year-old contestant from Faisalabad, doesn't have any interest in the prizes. She sings songs from the Bollywood film *Aashiqui 2* and practises in the bathroom. She is going to Karachi for the next round of auditions. "I don't even want to be the main singer," she confesses. "I want to be a playback singer. I just want to be famous. I want that the world knows that I sing. I want to walk past someone and have them look at me and think, Oh she's that girl, the one from *Pakistan Idol*. I don't care about the prizes. Today you'll get a prize, by tomorrow it'll be gone. I want to be famous. That's why I'm here." At night Ramsha tries to sleep as her fellow contestants walk up and down the corridors of the hotel practising their scales.

Only twelve of the thousands of contestants from seven cities in the country will remain for the final round.

But ultimately, it is a clip of a young woman who doesn't win one of these coveted spots, a twenty-two-year-old in Lahore who goes by the name Qandeel, that gets all the attention. In the clip, she prances on camera in a pair of hot pink and black heels, an equally pink pair of tights and a green silk shirt. Qandeel snaps her fingers and dances and sits on the hood of a car bouncing her head to the music playing from her mobile phone. "I'm a professional model. I do modelling, shoots, brand shoots," she explains in a video recorded earlier at what appears to be her home. She sits cross-legged on a bed with an ornate headboard that has flowers and leaves carved into it. Her cheeks have been rouged and her eyebrows are swiped with too much dark powder. Her hair, parted down the middle, is pinned on each side with a schoolgirl's bar-rettes. "I love singing so much," she says. "It's not just a hobby but a passion. I feel I can be Pakistan's idol."

"What's your name?" asks the actress judge when Qandeel walks into the room for her audition. "Pinky?"

"Qandeel Baloch."

"OK, I thought maybe it's Pinky." She points to her outfit. "Everything is pink."

"You look so beautiful," Qandeel gushes. "I always see you on TV, but Mashallah, you look so beautiful."

"Feel free to praise him too, or he'll get offended," the actress says, gesturing towards the male judge.

"Oh there's no point praising men; it makes no difference to them," Qandeel replies.

"But I'm sure men must praise you," the third judge says.

Qandeel says she is nervous. She puts on a little girl's whining voice, and the judges cajole her to give it her best shot. But when she finally does sing, she is a natural. She isn't rooted to that oval plastic mat like the other contestants. She walks forward, beckoning to the judges with her arms, beseeching them with her words, closing her eyes as she sways. She stares straight into the camera. She isn't nervous; she is performing.

Later, the producers add some effects to the clip. One judge has smoke billowing out of her ears. When Qandeel hits a high note, there is a sound like a spring recoiling. The male judge buries his face in his hands.

When they tell her to leave, she strokes the hair falling from those two schoolgirl barrettes and gives a small smile and says in that little girl's voice, "Don't reject me, please." She pouts. "I want to sing a song some more."

The actress walks over to her and holds her by the shoulders and leads her out. The male judge pretends to cry.

"You fooled me," Qandeel wails to the cameras waiting outside. "I told my parents I'm doing this audition and they're so hopeful now. Now what am I going to say to them? They will just think, they rejected our daughter." She is on the verge of tears, her breath catching on each word.

"Don't worry, cheer up, OK?" the actress says, patting her shoulder. "We'll see you doing modelling some day." As she walks away, Qandeel covers her face with both hands and lets out a wail. The show's host pushes the mike towards her. She turns her back to him, doubling over as she sobs. Her shrieks echo in the hall. There is no one else there. The other contestants have gone away and it is now dark outside. The cameras follow her as she cups her face in her hands, the baby-pink-painted nails covering her eyes as she cries all the way out the door.

"Poor Qandeel has wept off all her *kajal* [kohl]," the voiceover to the clip would later remark.

Liars.

All frauds.

Watch it again. Do you see any tears?

What I did there was my acting. Everything was planned from the start.

It's all bakwaas [fake].

The audition clip is ratings gold. Qandeel is written about in one newspaper as 'one of the most memorable' *Idol* hopefuls. The reporter calls her Ms Pinky in the article, in honour of the hot pink tights and black and pink stiletto heels she wore.[1] "A spectacle to behold."

Her five minutes on *Pakistan Idol* rack up well over a million hits on YouTube in just a few days but fails to get her more work. She is becoming desperate enough to work for free. She takes on small events and functions in farmhouses, at estates on the outskirts of the capital, some shows in Karachi. She goes to every fashion show she can. Mec shows her off and wants to introduce her to everyone. They quarrel. This is just a waste of time, she complains. These people just want to take my picture; there's no money and no result. Later, when she is asked about those years, she will not go into detail about what she did to survive. You know what happens with girls, she would hint. You know what kinds of offers they make girls. You know how they try to misuse girls who are new to the industry. Talent is just not valued in Pakistan.

She loves being in front of the camera and having her photo taken. Mec jokes that the camera "becomes hot" from taking so many photos before she gets tired of posing. But she is still too fat. The weight doesn't come off, no matter how much she exercises. The samples that designers send for fashion shows are too small. Mec tells her he will keep trying to find dramas for her to act in, keep passing on her name and number to producers, but her chance to walk the runway is already over. There's a certain age, there's a certain kind of body, he explains. Focus on your singing and acting career, he advises her. Even when you're eighty years old, you might still be acting and you can definitely still be singing away like a bird. She knows he is right.

He remains one of the few people who has heard that naat of hers. No one is booking naat singers for their morning shows. They all want the same thing: put on those skinny jeans—or, for Eid specials, a bright shalwar kameez—and a pair of heels and sing a favourite Nazia Hasan pop song while shimmying—not too much, please, this is a family show—with the host.

I tried a lot. I didn't want to move forward in this industry the way other actresses move forward. Everyone knows what they get up to behind the camera. At least I'm better than that.

One day she meets a man named Jalal at a party filled with media types. He hosts a show on television where celebrities play games and compete against each other. She doesn't care about the show. When Jalal tells her he has represented Pakistan internationally as a black belt in tae kwon do, he is pleasantly surprised that a girl like her—an aspiring model or actress or singer; he isn't sure what she is—is so curious about his sporting achievements. I could teach you, he offers.

And so, three times a week, for up to two and a half hours each, she attends Jalal's classes, held at a mall in the capital. She wipes her face clean of make-up and puts on the crisp white shirt and trousers that all his students wear. The other models Jalal teaches are spoiled. If he scolds them even once, they don't come back. These girls have friends—men— loitering outside the class, waiting for them. He has no such complaints about Qandeel. He is impressed by her strength. Horsepower, he chuckles to himself when he sees her kick. When one of the boys in the class offers to take her home and makes a move on her, she uses that strength. "I really put him in his place," Qandeel tells Jalal at the next class. He would think of those kicks years later when he finds out she has been killed. He wonders why she didn't fight back. Then he reads in the newspaper that she had been given a sedative and feels proud that whoever did that had known she was a fighter.

She doesn't tell him she has wanted to learn to fight since she was a little girl. "I left my village to come to Islamabad," she replies when he asks her where she is from. He doesn't ask her anything else, and she never tells him about watching her brother practising his kicks and high jumps in the courtyard of their home in Shah Sadar Din.

She's trying her hand at acting. A television drama she has been chosen for falls through. Jalal sees another drama she stars in. She can't deliver dialogue at all, he thinks. She has a pretty face, but she can't act very well and she gets too emotional on sets. She sulks. Why is that girl's role bigger than mine? Why do I have fewer scenes?

Jalal suspects that she is struggling, and is proved right when she says she does not have the money to pay for classes. I don't have the money for my rent or any household expenses, she tells him. Please help me find a job. He can't do that, but he offers to let her attend his classes for free. Even when the modelling works out, she only makes up to

10,000 rupees for one photo shoot if she is lucky. Learn martial arts, he suggests; at least that's a skill you'll have if all other means of earning are closed off to you. He is thrilled when she is cast in an action production called *G4*. Her character beats up men. She is perfect for it. The project is cancelled.

After a year or so, she tells Jalal she is leaving Islamabad for Lahore. Nothing is happening for me here, she says. Everyone says I need to go to a bigger city and try my luck. She is sad about leaving the classes. Some of his students keep up with her and later tell Jalal that Qandeel is doing very well in Lahore. She is on TV often. She is making a lot of money. Her Facebook page is full of glamorous photos. Jalal is surprised to learn that she is doing so well. When she dies and he finds out that she had been supporting her parents even when she did not have the money to take a taxi to and from his classes, he will remember how there was always a general perception that she was a rich girl. She has even made a music video in which she preens like a Western pop star, wearing a tiny skirt and fishnet stockings. "Make me wet, yet be my lover," she sings.

The music channels said the video was not good. They told me, "It's too bold. The vocals are not good. It's too bold for us." They refused to air my video.

When she visits Islamabad, she makes sure to call Jalal. He meets her briefly, and, seeing that she is the bright centre of a buzzing new crowd, does not try to see her again. When she asks him why he is avoiding her, he tells her he does not like her friends. She laughs and tells him that if he ever wants to see her, she will chase away the whole lot of those strange, colourful characters.

She wants to go to Murree, a mountain resort town thirty kilometers northeast of Islamabad, because she has never seen snow in her life. She comes to Islamabad and pleads with Mec to drive her up there.

"I doubt there will be any snow now," he warns her. "It's not the season."

She insists. Her skin has reacted badly to the heat of Lahore and humidity of Karachi. A brief spell in the cooler green climes of Murree is exactly what it needs. Just a day or two, she promises Mec.

On the drive up there Mec laughs at her when she wants to stop and play with some children she sees on the side of the road. She crouches beside them and gives them fistfuls of candy and tells Mec she wishes she had money so she could pay for them to go to school.

With great difficulty, they manage to get a tiny room in a guesthouse in Murree. Most places are closed or booked out for the season. Qandeel plays with her phone constantly, taking selfies and recording videos. She is happy there. When they sway in a chairlift above the mossy hills and the gossamer mist brushes her hair, she feels as though she could reach out and touch the sky. She makes a video for her fans.

By the evening she is running a fever. They ignore it until it peaks at 104 degrees and then they have to find a hospital. It is raining hard and Mec has to return to Islamabad for a photo shoot. Back at the guesthouse, Qandeel tells Mec to leave and lock the door to their room from the outside. She wants to take her medicines and just sleep. She doesn't want any food.

When he is done with the shoot, Mec calls her from Islamabad. Poor thing could be lying in that room dead for all I know, he thinks. But she is awake and hungry. Come pick me up, she says. Bring something spicy with you, please. He gets a *karhai* [curry] made and drives for almost two hours to get to her. The door to their room has not been opened since he left. She looks much better. Let's get some coffee, she says after she has eaten. Having slept off the fever, she's been playing with her phone while waiting for Mec. She lies in bed and swipes through all the photos and videos from the trip. She uploads some of them to Facebook and Twitter.

In one video she is messing around with Mec in the market. Her eyebrows peek out above her big black-rimmed sunglasses and she has pulled up the hood of her Barca jacket to loosely cover her hair. She pushes up her sunglasses and tilts her head from side to side, trying to find her best angle. Mec, in a yellow shirt and sunglasses, leans in behind her.

"Ummmmm," she says into the camera. "How I'm looking?"

Mec grins.

"Tell me," she whines. A demand, the lilt of a petulant child: "How I'm looking?"

THE BLUE-EYED CHAIWALA

Not everyone seeks fame. Sometimes fame—the kind some people spend their entire lives courting—finds you. It is this kind of overnight fame that comes unannounced to a seventeen-year-old boy—a beautiful fair-skinned blue-eyed boy with a brooding stare—in October 2016 when he becomes one of the most recognizable faces in Pakistan. In just five days, two photographs of him on the social media site Instagram rake in more than 50,000 likes and thousands of comments. His fame spreads not just in Pakistan, but around the world. His "good looks" are featured on CNN,[1] the BBC notes that his "piercing eyes" have "thousands" of Twitter users "love-struck,"[2] and BuzzFeed describes him as "damn HOT" with "effortless high-fashion model looks."[3]

Very soon he is charming audiences on morning talk shows, being showered with offers to model and act, smiling and posing for countless photographs, and receiving a stream of marriage proposals. There have been many firsts for him this month: sitting in a chauffeur-driven car, flying in a plane, staying in a hotel, buying a suit. Before his new-found fame, he sold tea for a living in a market in Islamabad, and he would worry about how to earn enough to ensure everyone in his family—his father, his two mothers and seventeen siblings—had enough to eat. Now he dines at five-star restaurants.

What does he like to eat?

"Bhindi."

His name is Arshad Khan, and he has become known in Pakistan and around the world as the *Chaiwala*, or tea-seller. He is famous for having done absolutely nothing.

In 2015, Qandeel's "How I'm looking?" video created a blueprint for the kind of fame that viral stars in Pakistan could achieve. The question—with her intonation and accent—was parodied endlessly and mimicked not just by the average Pakistani social media user, but by some of the country's best-known singers and actors. It is impossible to know how many times the original video was watched—it has been copied and shared to hundreds of pages—but it led to Qandeel's inclusion in Google's list of the top ten Pakistanis searched for online in 2015.[4]

By 2016, the year Qandeel was murdered, there were more than 44 million social media users in Pakistan.[5] Facebook had the biggest slice of the pie, with 33 million users,[6] followed by Twitter with 5 million and Instagram with 3.9 million. Arshad Khan, like Qandeel before him, had joined the ranks of a handful of viral stars: men and women who become household names, their images or videos spilling over from social media sites into millions of conversations on apps like WhatsApp, shared and forwarded on a loop until mainstream media outlets take notice and feature them on the news or on talk shows.

Pakistan's most well-known viral stars include Taher Shah, whose "Eye to Eye" music video briefly trended globally on Twitter, while his second song, "Angel," racked up more than 2 million views on YouTube and Facebook in the first four days of its release;[7] Asif Rana, whose passionate 2015 Facebook announcement of a tiff with his best friend Mudasir became the stuff of a thousand memes;[8] and Shafqat Rajput, a barber in Bahawalpur who was filmed in 2017 applying flammable products to clients' hair and whipping out a lighter to set their coiffures on fire before trimming them.[9]

At the time his photograph was first taken, Arshad did not know about these viral superstars. He had never had a Facebook account. He could not read or write. His family and neighbours lived without electricity and did not watch TV.

Arshad was working at a *dhaba* (roadside café) in a Sunday bazaar in Islamabad's G9 neighbourhood when Javeria Ali, a twenty-six-year-old photographer who was on a photo walk in the market, spotted him ladling out cups of milky tea. He was wearing a turquoise shalwar kameez with a white scalloped trim around the neck. His hair was slightly tousled, with a few stray locks falling above his dark eyebrows, and his cheeks were peppered with stubble. He wore a black thread looped around his wrist to protect him from the evil eye.

Ali routinely shot portraits of street children, pushcart vendors and beggars, uploading the images to the Facebook page where she advertised her wedding photography services and classes for aspiring photographers. This portrait felt no different. She took three or four pictures of the chaiwala while his head was bowed, then he looked up for a split second and stared right at her. She got the shot. Arshad didn't even realise his photograph had been taken. Ali uploaded the photograph (captioned "Hot-Tea") to her Instagram and Facebook pages on 14 October 2016. It was soon shared on various blogs and social media pages, with users commenting on the tea boy's looks.

He had not seen his photograph on the news, and he didn't think of the girl with the camera until she came back to the market, this time with reporters and camera crews. He found out they were looking for him. He panicked.

Arshad lived in a slum in the city's Golra Sharif area and was entrusted with taking up to twenty of his neighbours' children to and from the market with him. The children did odd jobs or begged, and when they weren't trying to scrape together a few rupees got up to all kinds of mischief. When he saw the cameras and reporters, Arshad's first thought was that one of the children had done something bad, maybe smashed the window of a car belonging to someone influential.

His memories of the day are hazy. He remembers Ali telling him she had uploaded his photograph to social media and it had gone viral.

He did not know what that meant and remembers feeling fear. A long-ing to hide. His first instinct was to bolt. He recalls wandering around the city's Blue Area neighbourhood, thinking he might go to a friend's house and wait. His father kept calling his phone. One of the chaiwala's relatives sold second-hand clothes in the bazaar, and he had called Ar-shad's brother to tell him about the sudden commotion in the market. "I think Arshad has done something," he said. "The media people are here looking for him." Arshad was too scared to talk to his father. When he finally answered his phone, he said he would be home in ten minutes. After a little while, he stalled again. "Fifteen minutes," he promised. Hours passed. He wondered if the cameramen had found his home. Would they film his mother and sisters? He considered never return-ing to Golra Sharif. "I only wanted to hide," he recalled. "I wanted to disappear." He wandered the streets aimlessly until the sun started to set. This was the last time for the foreseeable future that he would be entirely alone.

The two days after his photograph went viral were a blur of interviews.

Arshad went to work in the market as usual, but the area around the dhaba was crammed with people who had flocked there to meet the Chaiwala. Arshad had never seen such a big crowd of people in his life, not even at a political rally. They didn't want to drink the tea he made; they wanted to take pictures and show him videos of news segments on him from around the world. They pressed against him as he spoke with one reporter after another. They asked him about his plans to marry ("I can't get married before my two elder brothers. I haven't thought about it"), and his favourite movies. He had only ever seen one movie, a Bollywood superhero film, in his life and had watched it on a knock-off mobile phone. He couldn't remember the name of the movie. They urged him to send a message to his friends and family, who were probably watching him on TV. "There's no cable and no electricity where they live, so how will they see my message?"

When a reporter asked him if he would like to work in films, he didn't think much of the idea and told him, "I'll work wherever I can and with whoever wants me. I'll work in films if I can." His family didn't like that answer too much, so the next time he was asked about films, he said, "I'll do good, clean, honourable work, and I haven't thought about doing films or dramas. In my family we don't do that and nor will we ever."

He was whisked away to a television station for an interview and made to wear a suit. Before he went on air he heard a member of the crew speaking Pashto, the language Arshad and his parents spoke at home. He pulled the man to one side and pleaded, "Can you tell me what is going on? How is everyone in the world looking at my picture?" He remembered how the media would descend on the bazaar for a few days every year or before Ramzaan and Eid and interview shopkeepers and vegetable sellers about rising food prices, and he thought that their interest in him was just like their curiosity about the cost of a kilo of tomatoes. It would wane after two or three days, he imagined.

On a cold evening four months after that day, I meet Arshad in an apartment—a makeshift office, says his manager Fahim, a place to "do deals and whatnot"—in a residential area in Islamabad. Fahim wears a tight black T-shirt, purple velour tracksuit bottoms, and slippers that squelch with each step on the tiled floor. Everything in the apartment is brand new. Someone has thrown the box for a thirty-inch LCD TV on to the small balcony outside one of the bedrooms.

Arshad is skinny, and his black suit and shirt look a little too big for him. The trousers are baggy and a pair of pointed black shoes with silver buckles peek out from under them. He is tired and not feeling well today. His whole body aches. He went to see a doctor and was told that for five days he needed to eat simpler food and only drink the *kahva* (tea) that he is used to. No sugary drinks or juices or fast food. His doctor says he is "mentally weak." His manager says he is just fatigued, but Arshad reminds them of his days hawking second-hand clothes, doing manual labour and construction work, and selling fruit and vegetables in the market. "This is no work for me," he says. "I've had to do a lot more than this. It's just a different kind of work." His only task for today is to record a video: a congratulatory message for *Kismat Connection*, a TV show that has just aired its hundredth episode. He's a celebrity now, and the producers of the show have requested a short video that they can air during the episode.

We go into the bedroom with the best natural light. The room is empty save for a folding table in the corner stacked with rolls of bedding and blankets. Arshad's social media adviser, Rizwan, works in real estate and rents out apartments just like this one. He darts in and out of our meeting while he tends to a group of prospective clients in the apartment's second bedroom. Arshad's team now includes a personal groomer, a photographer, a speech therapist, and a psychologist who, Fahim explains, teaches Arshad "daily life things" and "does therapy on how to live your life."

Fahim feeds Arshad the lines for the video. "Hi, friends!" he says. "No, wait, say, "'Hi, *doston*!'"

"Hi, doston," repeats Arshad.

"It's me, Arshad Khan," says Fahim.

"This is my Arshad Khan."

The more emotionless Arshad sounds, the peppier Fahim tries to make his lines.

Fahim gushes, "I want to congratulate Taher Ali Shah and the whole team of *Kismat Connection* that they have completed a hundred episodes!"

"I congratulate Taher Ali Shah sahib and the whole *Kismat Connection* team for completing one hundreh episondh," Arshad says.

"The whole team!" Fahim exclaims. "You need to sound excited. And say 'hundred.' Hund-rid. And epi-sote." When Fahim enunciates "sote," it sounds like someone has popped open a can of some fizzy drink. "Sote. Not 'sondh.' Sote."

"Hund-reh," says Arshad. "Epee-sondh."

They do one take and then another. Sometimes Arshad forgets the name of the man he is congratulating. Other times he forgets to sound happy. He repeatedly stumbles over the words "hundred" and "episode." He sounds morose.

"You need to sound happy," Fahim explains. "Imagine if you bought a new car. I would congratulate you, right? Now imagine that I'm not near you. Maybe I would send you a video, right? That's what we are doing here for Taher Ali Shah. He's done something really big. Something we are happy about."

"It's not like he's done some *umrah* [pilgrimage to Mecca]," Arshad quips.

Ten minutes later Fahim gets a phone call.

"Ep-pee-sone," Arshad mumbles to himself. "Ep-ee-sone."

Fahim leaves the room, asking me to try my luck. The door closes and Arshad turns to me. "What is this 'episondh?'" he asks. "Is it the fashion shows? Or those programmes that people do?"

Without a camera pointed at him, Arshad is a fast learner. Between takes he whispers the words in English to himself over and over again. He learns to say "hund-rud" and "epee-sode." When Fahim praises him for almost getting it right, he asks, "But what were the bits I got wrong?" Even when the sky begins to darken and Fahim turns his phone's torch on to continue filming, Arshad doesn't ask for a break or suggest they finish the video the next day. After twenty-five takes, Fahim decides that he can splice together sentences from the recordings and create one seamless video. Arshad claps his hands with relief. "We're done? What a nuisance."

Once the video has been wrapped up, Arshad slumps on a couch in the living room and stares at the new TV. A show on animals in the wild is on. "When Fahim has to teach me what to say and how to say it, I wonder how I'll ever do all of this," he explains, never turning his gaze away from a lion prowling on the screen. "I feel bad that he has to spend so much time trying to get me to do it right."

"OK, I'll explain to you what he means," Fahim interjects. "He is confident. He's not shy. He picks things up fast. But you have to remember the background he has. He didn't watch TV for even a day in his life. He didn't know who the people in the newspaper were. For him, words are just black-coloured lines. Now for someone like this to come into this world and to do these things is not easy. This isn't his language and he feels tension that why am I not getting it? Why can't I do it? I understand him, you see. I have an idea . . . " He snaps his fingers to get Arshad's attention. "Don't look there. Pay attention here." He flicks a button on the remote and turns the TV off. "So, as I was saying, when he tries to do something and he can't, then he feels shame. Right, Arshad?"

"Yes." Arshad nods. "Absolutely."

Arshad met Fahim on the third day after the media had come to the market. At this point, Arshad had been working in the bazaar for eight years. He had been at the dhaba for a little over two months and was making up to 600 rupees working three days a week. On the remaining days he picked up any work he could get. When the reporters and morning-show hosts asked him what he dreamed of doing, he said what any man who sees work as something provided by Allah so he can support his family would say: "When you're working for fourteen or fifteen hours a day, you don't spend your time thinking of dreams. And when you finally go to sleep, you're too tired to dream."

Fahim did not arrive at Arshad's home in a big car like some of the other hopeful agents and managers. He knew that Arshad's family thought that those who worked in showbiz were dishonourable, and films and television dramas were filth. Arshad's new-found fame scared them, and his parents told everyone they were worried he would be kidnapped.

"My work is like worship, for me," Fahim told Arshad at their first meeting. "The respect or humiliation we get in this world is in Allah's hands, and he has given me work that brings me respect. I can help you get work that gives you *izzat* [respect] too."

This promise buoyed Arshad as he entered a world utterly different to his own. "Before October, I knew my world and my work," he explains. "I knew everything about it. Now I'm in a new world, with new people. The way they sit, talk, dress—everything is different. My world has changed completely." He has made appearances at lavish weddings and met women who have wanted to talk to him and take pictures with him as they pressed their bodies against his. He sometimes thinks of the bazaar and how he would not even look at the women who came there, let alone dare to speak with them. He wonders how these women came to work in showbiz. If his sister ever wanted to become famous, if she wanted to work in show business like him, he would absolutely refuse to let her do so. It is no place for a woman, he feels. It can never be. On talk shows, when female hosts and guests sat next to him and talked so freely, his first instinct was to get up and walk away. He felt *sharam* (shame) and would try to end the conversation as soon as possible. He was aware that he did not sound like them. To this day he struggles to say words like fans ("phans") and Facebook ("Phasebook").

Arshad relies on Fahim and Rizwan to read his contracts. When a TV anchor asked him how he would give fans his autograph, he gave her what he thought was a perfectly logical answer for an illiterate person—"I'll use my thumbprint"—but the audience hooted with laughter and clapped and Rizwan had to spend hours teaching him how to scribble out a signature.

It has taken him some time to become accustomed to probing questions about his personality, his life before he became famous, his likes and dislikes. "No one had ever asked me before what country I would like to visit, what food I liked or what my hobbies were," Arshad explains. "I never wanted any kind of clothes or shoes or food. I knew what I was earning. I knew that I could have gone to any of these restaurants or shops and asked them how much something I wanted was. I wouldn't be able to afford those things even if I saved my entire month's salary. Then I would have felt sad. I never wanted to feel that way and so I didn't think about what I desired." But, slowly, Fahim and Rizwan's dreams for Arshad became Arshad's dreams for himself. Now he wants to act in commercials, films and dramas. He wants to model because it is easier for him to pose and wear beautiful clothes than to act. He wants to get an education and eventually open an institution to provide children, like the ones in his neighbourhood, with schooling.

All of this can only happen if his managers succeed in making him a star. Arshad has got what Fahim calls "over-the-night fame." In the ten years that he has been managing artists, Fahim says he's never seen anything like it in Pakistan. It usually takes years for people to get the kind of attention that Arshad has gained in a very short time. In the early days, when Arshad's schedule included up to a dozen interviews in a day and meetings with people throughout the day to work on deals, the team was sleeping only three or four hours a night, and he was mobbed by fans wherever he went. "This is a star's goal," explains Fahim. "Stars are used to this and it's what they work for. But Arshad never had these goals. He was tired and he got sick a lot."

It is important to Fahim and Rizwan that Arshad think of himself as a star. "If we just tell him what to do, then he's a worker," Fahim explains. "If you make a servant a king, then he'll never be able to maintain it unless he believes he is a king." Fahim simpers and cowers in his chair. "A common man will sit like this." He straightens his back, pushes out his chest and crosses one leg over the other. "But a king will sit like this."

They try to teach him the habits of a star. They encourage him to be demanding. Fahim estimates that it will take him five or six months to train Arshad to expect things to be given to him with the snap of a finger. "If he didn't do *nakhra* [make a fuss], I would make him do nakhra," he says. "If he is a star with us, only then will he be a star in the market," Fahim reasons. And once he starts behaving like a star, his fans will see him as someone to emulate and idolize. "A star's fans think that he is bigger and better than them," Fahim says. "Their idea of you is what they want to see. That's what you need to give them." And where the fans go, the industry follows. "If you're a producer, why would you choose Arshad Khan for your movie over someone else? Star power. That's why. The audience you can pull. The fans. If Arshad can guarantee that his movie will make 200 crore rupees, that's a safe bet for a producer."

However, four months after he was discovered, work has all but dried up for Arshad. In the last two weeks he has only appeared at a "meet and greet" breakfast and dinner with fans in Lahore—an opportunity for fans to take selfies with him. In January 2017 he starred in a music video with Muskan Jay, a singer and actress who was crowned "Mrs Pakistan" in 2016 in a Canadian competition. In the video Arshad played her love interest. He held Muskan close to him, hugged her and held her hands. A teaser for the video and a couple of photographs from the shoot were released online and quickly went viral.

The backlash was swift. Fans were not pleased. There were rumours of death threats from conservative family members. In an interview a few days before the video was released, Arshad apologized for the photographs. "Those photos were wrong, and no photos like this will come again," he said. "I don't want to work in films now. My family is getting angry about that."[10] Less than a week after the video was released, it was reported that Arshad wanted to quit show business. A member of Arshad's team claimed that he wished to return to his work at the dhaba.[11]

"That was fake news," Arshad says. "I never wanted to leave showbiz. It's all fake." He insists that while his family members are conservative—"namaazi," explains Fahim—they are happy for him and only want him to do the best work.

I ask Fahim if he feels the novelty of the Chaiwala is wearing thin. After dozens of interviews and appearances on almost all the popular talk shows and morning shows in the country, Arshad's rags-to-riches story has been told so many times over the last four months that it has lost one crucial element in a viral star's ability to draw a crowd: it is no longer surprising or unique. If Arshad wishes to forge a career on the strength of one viral photograph—if he wants the modelling contracts, advertisement offers and invitations to appear on talk shows—he has to continue to give Pakistanis something they have never seen before.

The average Pakistani social media user may scroll past dozens of viral videos, memes and photographs a day. Viral stars like Qandeel knew how to make those viewers hit pause. Qandeel's videos may have been scorned or dismissed as "attention-seeking," but she knew how to create content that sparked conversation. "Qandeel Baloch gave the selfie generation a catchphrase when she uttered those three words," declared an article naming the "How I'm looking?" video as one of the "10 notable quotes that defined Pakistan's entertainment scene in 2015." "The innocuous phrase was also quite revealing. [It] encapsulates our generation's need for validation online."[12]

Qandeel was aware that in order to sustain her audience's interest, she had to continue to give it something worth watching—people could laugh at her, be shocked by her, send her hateful messages or make fun of her, but that meant they were paying attention to her. "For popularity, you have to show yourself, you have to take your clothes off, you have to do nude photo shoots," she explained in an interview in 2014, well before "How I'm looking?" became her calling card. "To remain popular and 'in,' you have to upload strange photos of yourself on social media."[13]

But Fahim insists that Arshad isn't being talked about as much because he has become "exclusive." "Actually, we have decreased his appearances ourselves," he argues. He says that he has recently got enquiries about the Chaiwala from China, Malaysia, Greece and Dubai. "We want him to rest and relax. People think his fame has decreased, but we are making him exclusive. We don't just give interviews to everyone any more."

After the Muskan Jay video, Arshad's team has become cautious about the offers that it accepts. There are no more music videos for now. Fahim refuses invitations for appearances at parties. "Girls, parties—we keep him away from all that," he says. "I am scared that he'll get ruined." Arshad doesn't have a Facebook account, and he is allowed to have a mobile phone but can only play games on it. He doesn't take any pictures of himself or make videos or interact with fans on social media. His managers receive messages, calls and Facebook requests from women who want to propose to him or offer their daughters in marriage. Then there are the other, less tame requests and video messages. "I never show him those ones," Fahim says. "I don't want him to have those things on his mind. Whatever I think is good for a younger brother is what is good for Arshad."

Arshad still doesn't quite comprehend why his photograph went viral. How did one moment, one glance, change his life? "I still don't understand what it is in that photo," he admits. "People tell me that it's my face. Others say I have good-coloured eyes. But this is my kismet from Allah. This is Allah's doing."

Some days he still cannot believe he is the Chaiwala. "Sometimes I think this is all a dream and it can go away any minute," he says. "Just as Allah has ordained that the night takes away the day, He can take anything away from you in a minute. Things can come into your life suddenly, can also leave just as suddenly." He says he cannot imagine going back to the life he used to have before he became the Chaiwala.

Fahim and Rizwan urge me to stay for dinner. They plan to have a big, traditional meal of grilled lamb. But it's late and I refuse. As Arshad sees me out, he grins. "Forget this grilled stuff," he says. "The next time you meet me, I'll be a star. I'll bring you a live lamb."

Six months pass before Arshad is in the news once more. In July 2017 the National Database and Registration Authority (NADRA) states that Arshad and his family are from neighbouring Afghanistan and living in Pakistan illegally. A photograph has been shared on Arshad's social media pages featuring the Chaiwala, his hair curling past his ears as it had outgrown the cut he was given by stylists in Karachi, receiving his brand new identity card as a Pakistani citizen. But NADRA officials claim Arshad obtained the card using forged documents. The media contact Arshad's team for a comment. "Arshad Khan's manager Malik Fahim . . . found the NADRA claim shocking," an investigative story notes. "[Fahim] made it clear that he did not know Arshad prior to the Chaiwala becoming a celebrity."[14]

The photograph of Arshad smiling with his identity card is deleted from his social media accounts. Nearly two years would pass before Arshad appeared on television once more. In April 2019, he is interviewed on a morning talk show and the hosts prompt him to make tea and ask him to say a few sentences in other languages he might speak. He confesses that he can speak Punjabi, but not very well. "Can you say, 'This tea does not have enough sugar?'" the host asks him. Arshad repeats the sentence. The hosts are delighted. "This is the kind of stuff that will go viral!" they say. "No one has ever heard him speak Punjabi before." The interview fails to generate any buzz.

"GUYS, WHO WANT TO WATCH MY NEXT NASTY CLIP?"

The video from Murree has been viewed thousands of times. By the end of the year, Qandeel would be called an "insta-celeb." People are turning to Facebook and Twitter to find the "How I'm looking?" girl and they want more videos. They like to laugh at her.

Qandeel and Mec disagree over what she should do next. He takes her to every single event, books her for any show he can and introduces her to everyone they meet. Sometimes she complains that it is all a waste of time. People take photos with her at these events, but she isn't getting paid for them. She doesn't just want to make friends—she is looking for connections.

She stumbles across the Facebook profile of a man in Karachi, Mansoor, who was a model when she was just a girl in Shah Sadar Din. His Facebook feed is full of photographs taken at dinners and parties with girls Qandeel has seen on TV. She recognizes some of the names from his friends' list. He seems to have the connections she needs. She sends him a friend request. He is used to these requests from strangers, usually women, who hope that he knows all the right people and will be able to help them break into the fashion industry. In fact, it happens so often that he now has a policy of asking any girl who sends him a friend request on Facebook for her phone number to confirm whether she is indeed an aspiring model or actress and not some man trying to fool him. The ones who willingly give their phone numbers are legitimate. Qandeel sends him her phone number.

"Hi must talk to you," he texts Qandeel. "Call now."

She is travelling and is unable to speak with him just then. "Let me come too then I talk."

They continue to exchange messages and soon she is calling him "baby" and "*jaan*" (sweetie). When she tells him she is back in Karachi and feeling lonely, they meet for the first time and he takes her to a friend's house for some company. She messages him on WhatsApp late at night and asks, "What are you doing?" He is usually fast asleep. She likes Dubsmash, an app that lets users lip-sync phrases or songs, and sees that the video from Murree has also become popular there. She sees actresses and singers mimic her words in videos that they post to their social media feeds.

She uses Dubsmash to make a few videos of herself singing songs she loves. Mansoor's phone glows in the darkness of his room as she sends him each clip. "Put it on your Facebook timeline," she encourages him. She makes kissing sounds and calls him "jaanu" and "my darling" in the clips and pouts, "I can't sleep."

These are not like the clips that she now puts up on her Face-book page.

Guys, who want to watch my next nasty clip?

There, she is often mute and plays a variety of roles: sexy girl lying on her stomach, grinding against her bed while her fingers clutch a red teddy bear; ordinary girl drying her wet hair after a shower, her lips painted a glossy baby pink; sad girl stroking her cheek against the soft head of a white teddy bear and holding it close as she sighs and looks beseechingly at the camera to let you know "I mishhhh you;" angry girl bowing her head, furrowing her brow and blinking rapidly as though feeling the hot tingle of tears because "I'm angry with someone."

In other videos she coos, "Good morning," rubs her eyes and yawns.

She makes a video in which the lace curtains billow at the windows in her room as she lays her head on a white furry pillow and whispers, "This is how I like to sleep." She likes to line her eyes with a thick stroke of kohl, winged at the corner like the tail of a tick mark. "Goodnight," she whispers, looking into the camera on her phone, much of her face covered with the fall of her thick hair. "Sweet dream. Bye." She puts up a video in which she nestles against the curve of a man's body and hugs his arm between her breasts. She crops him out of the frame. "Did you guys know that today I don't have a teddy bear?" she says with a grin. She kisses the man's hand. "Instead of a teddy bear, there's someone else here today. Today I'm so much happy. You know why? Should I tell you?"

The commenters don't care.

"She was rejected in *Pakistan Idol* since than loose [*sic*] her mind."

"This guy is your pimp."

"You're a slut and I know it."

If people say something bad about you, judge you as if they know you, don't feel bad, just remember, "Dogs bark if they don't know the person."

"Horny bitch."

"You're happy he's fucked you without a condom."

"I love you."

"After fucking all girls feel v v v much happy."

"Finding a gun send me her address LOL."

I used to make funny videos just to make people laugh. People would abuse me so much I would wonder, What have I even done? When they say you are so bad, then you might as well become bad.

She is being noticed. Now, when she is invited on to the morning shows, she is singing less and talking more about the videos she puts up. "I saw your videos because one of my dear friends is a very big fan of yours," explains a host on one show.[1] "She used to post so many of your videos [on Facebook], so I thought I really needed to check out what was going on." She asks Qandeel about a video that has been shared more than 500 times on Facebook alone. In it Qandeel lies back on her bed, hot with a fever. "My head hurts." She sniffs. "My eyes are smarting."

"Perhaps it's because you were wearing so much eyeliner?" the host suggests.

"I love lining my eyes," Qandeel explains, "and I only use imported things. That was a Chanel eyeliner. Not local."

The woman hoots with laughter and begs her to show the audience how she complained.

"But my head really was hurting in that video," Qandeel insists. They don't care. She droops her head in her hands and sighs. "Ufffff, I'm running such a high fever. My eyes are burning."

"Marvellous!" the host cries. "Marvellous!"

The host shares a clip of Qandeel playing with a goat she has supposedly adopted as a pet. A little boy scampers past in the video.

"Who is that boy?" the host demands. Qandeel explains that he is her nephew.

The host laughs and says, "Oh, I was wondering if this would be something exclusive we could reveal—that you have a son."

Qandeel giggles.

It isn't just the morning-show hosts—the English-language newspapers have also taken note. "Who is Qandeel Baloch and what is she doing on my timeline?" asks an article published online by *Dawn*. "Facebook has a new bug and its name is Qandeel Baloch." There is curiosity. Who is this girl? Is she really this cartoonish in real life?

People think that I have become famous overnight. That I have won the lottery overnight. What I did on social media just clicked. They think I didn't have to work for this. I didn't have to struggle.

"I am the daughter of a huge landlord," she says in interviews. "I have property worth millions. I'm not desperate for money."

She makes the videos late at night, when she is sure that her whole family is fast asleep. They are just for fun. "I like to bother people, to point out things to them. I like to comment on some people or to give reviews on things. I do it from the heart. Not to be famous." Some people believe her. "This is exactly what happens when you're the brat of some rich man," one of the comments on her videos read. "These rich brats do stuff like this and bring shame to their parents and their country. She's just another spoiled rich girl."

Sometimes she calls Mansoor and whines, "I'm hungry." When he is free, he picks her up and takes her out for a burger or chips or chai, and they eat sitting in his car so that people do not bother her for selfies while she is eating. One time he is on his way to a dinner when she calls and says she is hungry, and he stops at a fast-food joint, buys her a pizza and pays to have it delivered to her apartment.

Mansoor knows that men are harassing her and want to sleep with her. She doesn't tell him about the kinds of messages they send her on Facebook, but remarks, "Every horny guy out there has some line for me. And none of them are worthy of me. They're all liars." Some of them start by complimenting her and telling her they are her biggest fans. Then they ask, "How much for a night?" She wants someone who will help her, who will take her out when she feels alone. Mansoor has grown to like her. He calls her "selfie queen." Qandeel isn't like the other models Mansoor knows. They are all sluts. She is not a slut, he says. She just wants to be in the limelight.

She is struggling to find work despite Mansoor's connections, and there aren't many offers for the notorious selfie queen to be the face of a brand or the star of a television show. Some people promise work in exchange for what Mansoor calls the "cast couch." But that is a trick; there is never any work. Mansoor feels Qandeel is fighting to survive. She is making some money from morning-show appearances, and for a few days she visits Dubai to do a photo shoot, but it isn't enough. She calls Mansoor one day and says that her brother is visiting and she needs some money. Can she borrow some from him? While he is trying to arrange that, he receives a message from her. Don't worry, she says. I've got it from someone else.

He knows money changes hands easily among the people he parties with. If Qandeel needs money, it isn't hard to get. Just the other night some girls came over to Mansoor's friend's house with a boy who "looked like a fag" and they danced for everyone and then people gave them a hundred dollars each. He likes that Qandeel never begs. When he eventually learned of her impoverished background, he would marvel. You really had to give her credit, he would say. Look where she came from and where she ended up.

Ahmed meets Qandeel on 14 August 2015, Independence Day, at a park in Islamabad. He is a reporter and is there to file a story on the day's celebrations for the TV channel he works for. There is going to be a musical performance in the park and Qandeel is one of the singers. Ahmed's cameraman points to her and suggests they interview her. Qandeel is tall in her shiny black heels, and wears a pair of tight moss-green jeans and a fitted white shirt. She has had her hair and make-up done specially that morning and looks beautiful in the colours of the Pakistani flag. Ahmed figures that a short clip of her performing is exactly the kind of colourful footage his producers want for an otherwise standard Independence Day package.

When the event ends, Ahmed is getting ready to leave when he sees that her manager's car has broken down. He offers to give her a ride back to the guesthouse she is staying at, and when they reach the guesthouse, she tells him that she is modelling in a show the next day. Does he want to come? And perhaps cover the show for the television channel he works at?

The following evening he goes to the show and stays until the end so he can drop Qandeel home once more. They are the same age—twenty-five—and they enjoy talking to each other and agree to stay in touch.

They have been chatting almost every day for more than a month or two when Ahmed calls Qandeel one evening and tells her he has just arrived in Karachi for work. She is at an event but gives him directions to meet her. For the next four or five days they meet frequently. Sometimes Ahmed comes to her apartment for a cup of tea. One day they meet after she gets her passport back, freshly stamped with a visa for Dubai. She is happy she will be travelling there again and shows him the visa. He spots the name on it and sees that it is not Qandeel. She tells him her real name. That name has shown up in her tweets ("Fouzia Azeem invites you to join their network!" "Fouzia Azeem would like to share a post with you.") but no one has asked who Fouzia is and she doesn't think she needs to remove the tweets. Ahmed doesn't give it much thought. After all, don't most women in show business change their names?

She mentions a brother who is in the army and stationed in Karachi, her sisters and their children, whom she adores, and her parents, who live in Multan. She meets them every Eid and takes gifts for the whole family. She lives near the seaside in Karachi, and she and Ahmed go for walks along the promenade and talk or ride the dune buggies that are rented out by the hour. One evening, as they walk back to her apartment from the beach, she suggests they check out a new shisha café that has opened up near her apartment building. Inside, a man spots her and says in surprise, "Are you Qandeel?" She seems nervous. She does not answer and instead shuffles behind Ahmed so the man cannot see her. Ahmed does not ask her why.

A month ago she was invited as a celebrity guest to judge a talent show at a university in Islamabad. "Cover yourself up properly," Mec instructed. "There will be boys there. You need to be careful." She stayed on the phone with him, and as the car got close to the university, she was excited to see a crowd of male students waiting. She turned her phone camera on and showed Mec. Some of the students took pictures of her. Others cupped their hands around their eyes and pressed up against the car windows. "Look at how they are welcoming me," she said with delight to Mec. He felt a jolt of fear. The boys had crowded so tightly around the car it could not move. "You fool, don't get out," he snapped. "Someone might hurt you." Some of the boys turned their backs to her and took selfies while she stayed inside the car with the doors locked. They refused to move. The university management told her she couldn't get out of the car and begged her to leave.

She takes to covering her face as much as possible when she is out in public on her own.

My name is Qandeel Baloch. I'm not the kind to get scared by you. Do whatever you want.

One evening, shortly before Ahmed is supposed to go back to Islamabad, he tells Qandeel he wants a tour of Karachi. He came by train and he has never seen the city's airport, but has heard that it is very big. He has only seen the chief minister's house, the high court and governor's house on television. Qandeel promises to show him all of it. "But if we take a cab, it'll end up costing us a lot," she says. She doesn't have a car, but she says she will figure something out.

When Ahmed comes to her apartment the next day, she has a motorbike ready and waiting. There are some small shops on the ground floor of her apartment building, and the men who own them like her. She can cajole them into running errands or doing odd jobs for her. She has managed to borrow a bike from one of the men.

For the next four hours, she sits snugly against him, her arms around his waist, her legs astride the bike as they sail through the city. She loves being on the bike and tells Ahmed she knows how to ride it herself. They don't get lost even once. The airport is indeed as big as everyone says it is. Qandeel points to the towering big-name hotels clustered together on one stretch of road, the small squares of light from a hundred rooms visible behind the blast-proof walls topped by barbed wire, and the concrete barricades designed to prevent bomb attacks. She shows him some of Karachi's famous restaurants, an old club that used to have a sign saying women and dogs could not enter, the gothic hulk of a building that looks like a church with an ivy-green roof, and the house—now a museum—that the founder of the country called home.

They disappear into the swarm of bikes on one of the longest, busiest roads in the city. Every light is green. There's no stopping them.

The wind surges against them like a great river and the streetlights stream past like a glowing ribbon. If the road had been a runway ending abruptly at a cliff edge, they could have soared into the air, two fugitives carried by the wind.

As Ahmed leans gently to either side and dips the bike to the left or right as he passes cars or steers a wide lazy arc past a roundabout, he thinks of the woman leaning against his back and how she looks just like another boy on a bike in her jeans and shirt, her face covered by a helmet. No one would ever guess that it was her, that it was Qandeel Baloch. At that moment she is not the girl in the shisha café or the girl on TV or the girl who makes everyone laugh with her broken English and fake American accent. She is none of the girls in the videos she posts. She is a girl none of the thousands of viewers of those videos have seen; she is herself.

When she can't sleep, which is often, she watches movies or YouTube videos and scans Facebook and Twitter to see what people are talking about. One night she is bored and decides to talk to her Facebook followers in an audio-only live session. They hear the wail of sirens and the sound of honking cars as she sings songs on request and answers some of their questions. Her phone keeps buzzing. She pleads, please stop calling my personal number. She apologizes for the noise. "I live near the main road next to the sea, where the McDonald's is," she explains. She is alone at home in the dark, lit only by the gleam of her laptop. "I've opened the windows because there's no electricity. So that's why you can hear the traffic."

She starts asking Ahmed what is going on in the news and what people are talking about. What is trending right now? Cricket? Politics? Football? She wants to make videos about things that people are discussing because this way they will also discuss her.

I act from the heart and I think from the heart. I'm not desperate for fame. Fame is chasing me, I'm not chasing it.

One evening she is feeling low and calls a friend in Islamabad.

She weeps on the phone. He tries to cheer her up. At this time the cricketer-turned-politician Imran Khan is making news as his second marriage has ended in divorce. Her friend jokes, "Chill out. Don't be so sad. Maybe you should just marry Imran Khan." In the morning he checks Facebook and sees that after they ended their conversation Qandeel posted a new video on her social media pages.

In it she is lying on her bed. She pulls up the front of her low-cut top. There is a black tattoo, one of the temporary ones she loves to put on her arms and neck, above her breasts. Her full lips are a bright red. She dedicates a song to Imran Khan. "I like you so much, and I love you so much," she says. "If Reham has left you, then there's still so many who want you. I am one of them. I want to marry with you. Will you marry me? Please?"

By morning she is flooded with calls from news channels. They have found a new angle in their relentless coverage of the divorce. Soon the video has been watched more than 830,000 times. A female television anchor calls her shameless.

These girls who call me bitch and whore and other names are the same girls who talk about respecting women.

She makes a few more videos. She gets more hits. On Twitter and Facebook she pleads with Imran Khan to accept her proposal, and people make fun of how she pronounces it — "par-posal." "I just want you to be mine," she tweets. "People tell me he will only keep you as his maid," she says in one interview. "But I would agree to that too. Anything for Khan sahib." She is back in the news. The Imran Khan angle works.

I always choose the wrong man. I don't have a special person. He comes in my thoughts and dreams. He's very good. He's just like Imran Khan. Other than Imran, I've never told someone, "I love you."

She knows that not everyone is happy with the videos. Mec scolds her for losing focus. Stay away from politics, he tells her. He wants her to stick to videos where she sings or dances or is funny, like when she asked, "How I'm looking?" He says she is being foolish and getting carried away by the attention.

In Islamabad men ask Jalal, her old martial arts instructor and friend, for her phone number. At a dinner her name comes up. He doesn't understand why everyone is talking about her. At home he looks up her Facebook page and sees the videos and photos. He feels ashamed. She is insulting herself. When he tries to talk to her about it, she gently brushes him off. "Sir, leave it be," she says. "I've understood these people. I know better. I'm happy. I'm getting what I want." She tells him she has finally figured out how to make money.

Ahmed sometimes tells her not to talk about certain things. It is too risky. People can get angry about any small thing, he warns her. But they will all say later that she did not listen to anyone, not Mec or Jalal or Ahmed or anyone who knew her.

Whatever you try and stop me from doing, I'll do that even more. I've been like that since childhood.

Two months later she sees on the news that the president has spoken out against the celebration of Valentine's Day. It's a Western concept, he says. On social media many are treating the statement with derision. The news is being covered internationally as well. She makes a new video. "They can stop to people go out," she says, "but they can't stop to people love." She says the same thing once more, this time in Urdu, with the exaggerated American accent she uses, as though she is not used to speaking the language. Just like any other rich brat who went to an English-speaking school. She continues in Urdu, "No matter what they do, they can't stop people from loving." She whispers the message again before adding a personal valentine message to Imran Khan.

She receives a phone call from a man who speaks with a British accent and says he is from an international news agency. He has seen the Valentine's Day video. He wants to talk to her about it. This is the first time she has been approached by the foreign media.

Initially she is suspicious. "What do you mean?" she keeps asking him when he tries to get her to explain something she has said or done. No one in the local media asks her what her work means. They only ask more and more frequently why she doesn't stop what she is doing despite the hateful messages. They ask why she wants *sasti shauhrat*—grubby, easy-to-get, cheap publicity.

It's no small thing to get sasti shauhrat. If it was so easy, then everyone would be famous.

When the reporter with the British accent runs his story, it is picked up in many countries, and she sees that the reporter has called her Pakistan's Kim Kardashian.[2] She makes a note to use that line in the future.

When she meets Mansoor again, he is worried. The Valentine's Day video is a very public middle finger held up to many conservative Pakistanis and clerics. In previous years the spokesperson of one of the largest religio-political parties in the country had declared the day "against Islamic culture." Such parties believe those who mark the day are from the "elite class" who ape Western culture. In 2002 co-education institutions in Karachi banned students from celebrating Valentine's Day for fear of reprisals from conservative or religious student groups,[3] and in many schools and colleges in the country the celebration of Haya Day (Modesty Day) is encouraged on the same date. In 2013 a handful of people gathered in Peshawar to burn Valentine's Day cards in front of the media while women in black burqas held up signs protesting against the custom, and the Pakistan Electronic Media Regulatory Authority (PEMRA) urged TV and radio broadcasters to be sensitive to "viewers' sentiments" on the day. "PEMRA has been receiving complaints from a large segment of society that Valentine's Day celebrations are not in conformity with our religious and cultural ethos and has, therefore, condemned its unequivocal propagation through media," a statement from the authority said. "Such events have been perceived as a source of depraving, corrupting and injuring the morality of Pakistani youth."[4] The year Qandeel makes her Valentine's Day video, a member of the Jamaat-e-Islami youth wing in Peshawar notes, "People who celebrate [Valentine's Day] are offending Islam. They are automatically discarded from our religion."[5] Mansoor suggests Qandeel think twice about what she is doing and saying on public platforms like Facebook. She smiles at him and asks sweetly, "Don't you want your friend to become popular?"

I am a moody type of girl. Kissi ki sunti nahin hoon [I'm not going to listen to any of you].

On 14 March 2016, four days before Pakistan plays India in the ICC World T20 cricket match, she uploads a video to her Facebook page. "If Pakistan wins, I will do a strip dance for the whole nation," she promises. "And that dance will be dedicated to our captain, Shahid Afridi. Just defeat India once, and whatever you tell me to do, I'll do it."

A few nights later, she uploads a trailer for the promised dance. She stands on her bed, wearing nothing but a bright green and yellow bikini and a white bathrobe stolen from a hotel. The robe has been pulled down and tied loosely around her waist. In the video, she cups her breasts and caresses herself. She sways her hips like a belly dancer while an Enrique Iglesias song plays on her laptop. She draws the robe close to her like a matador's cape and then flicks it back to reveal a smooth, uncovered leg. The "full film" will be released online if Pakistan wins the match, she promises.[6]

When Mec sees the video, he tells her, "People here don't let others live their lives the way they want, and you think you can do these kinds of antics? You're only going to get into trouble."

She calls Ahmed and weeps after she reads some of the comments on her Facebook and Twitter posts. He chides her. "Don't look at them," he warns.

She reads some of them to him anyway.

"Please shoot her wherever you find her."

"You ugly bitch. People like you should go die . . . fucking cunt."

"You have no shame so why are you even wearing this bikini? Take it off, you can earn some more."

"You uneducated bitch . . . you're giving Pakistan a bad name. Your pimp family won't even shoot you. Your father must be just like you that's probably why he doesn't say anything to you."

"You give the Baloch people a bad name."

"Shame on your parents."

"You want to read these things even when you know they're going to hurt you," Ahmed scolds her. "Why do you do it?"

I'm 99 percent sure that you guys hate me.

She hides her face in her pillow and sobs then stops to look again at the camera.

And I'm also 100 percent sure that even my shoe doesn't give a damn.

Qandeel's trailer goes viral. It makes the headlines not just in Pakistan, but in India too. She is called "Pakistan's hot new Internet sensation"[7] and "Pakistan's very own version of Poonam Pandey."[8] Pandey, an Indian model and actress, promised to strip for the Indian cricket team during the ICC Cricket World Cup in 2011. Qandeel would go on to repeat what Pandey said at the time, almost verbatim, when asked why she released the trailer—she did it to "buck up" the team. It was a patriotic gesture.

To become popular, you have to do a lot. It's necessary to do some bad things. You have to show yourself, take off your clothes.

An online campaign to shut down her Facebook page is launched. On 18 March 2016, Farhan Virk, a blogger and self-proclaimed social media activist with more than 100,000 followers on Twitter alone, makes a request: "Report [her] Facebook page and share this message. We can't see a retard like her shaming our nation. Keep sharing this message and reporting her page. We need to get it banned." Virk is often accused of operating fake Twitter accounts to spread rumours or impersonate politicians and celebrities. He has a significant social media following, particularly among supporters of Imran Khan's Pakistan Tehreek-e-Insaf party, as he frequently launches campaigns against those critical of the party or its leader. His message about Qandeel is shared more than 3,000 times on Facebook by his followers.

"We should have drowned in shame the minute we heard her say [she would strip]," Virk tells his social media followers. "In an Islamic state, what kind of thing is that to say?" He is a Pakistani, but Qandeel does not represent him, he complains, and people in India and other countries do not understand that. "Pakistan is not just the name of a country," he says. "To create Pakistan, two million of our ancestors gave up their lives, just so that the Muslims of the subcontinent could live their lives in an Islamic society, according to an Islamic way of life. Now you tell me—when you see her, what would those ancestors feel? Is our honour so lost that we call this freedom of expression or freedom of speech and ignore it?"

Today, the world might be available at the tips of any Pakistani's fingers with the press of just one button, but they must remember one thing: they are still rooted here in the land of the pure. "If this woman had done this in India, America or Britain, then we would understand it. Because in India, America or Britain two million Muslims did not sacrifice their lives to the country," Virk explains. He accuses her of dishonouring the Pakistani flag. The bikini she is wearing in that video is no ordinary bikini, he tells thousands of his followers. She is wearing the Pakistani flag. "Can your honour allow you to stomach that?" If you tolerate Qandeel today, then ten years from now every actress will be doing what she is. Virk's voice quavers. "And then we will hang our heads in shame and the people of India will mock us."

Pakistan loses the match, but the campaign against Qandeel's social media pages doesn't end.

There are so many problems in Pakistan, so why is everyone focusing on me? I'm just an innocent girl. Why am I being made a target of judgement?

Two days pass. Virk urges his followers once more, "We need to stop her from spreading vulgarity in our Islamic state." Those who do not want to join the campaign and report the page to Facebook probably "don't have mothers and sisters in their homes, they have other Qandeels in their homes." Those who report Qandeel's page post screenshots of their complaints to Facebook. "I am getting messages from Pakistanis overseas that due to Qandeel Baloch they are facing harassment," Virk claims. "Let's keep reporting her."

A letter is widely shared online: a cleric has issued a fatwa against Qandeel, declaring that it is forbidden to watch her videos or look at her pictures. The letter is later revealed to be fake.

On 22 March 2016 Qandeel's Facebook account is suspended.

She loses an audience of more than 400,000.

She is alone now. They had all warned her and she had not listened. Mec is furious. How long has it been since they last spoke? It feels like weeks.

Ten seconds was all it took to unravel what she has been working on for years. A ten-second video.

Soon after, she is invited to be on one of Pakistan's most watched talk shows, *Khara Such*. This is not like the morning shows, where she shares airtime with several others; the producers for *Khara Such* want only her. "This is social media," Qandeel shouts angrily in a promo for the interview that runs on television and online. "It's not someone's father's property. Everyone has the right to express their opinion on it."[9] The show's host, Mubasher Lucman, tweets this to more than three million social media followers. It is watched on Facebook more than 600,000 times, and the comments that follow are angry.

"Does that thing really deserve to come on mainstream media so bluntly?"

"Cheapsters like Qandeel Baloch must be brought into the open and insulted and, yes, molested."

"Women like these should be hanged if this country was made and separated on the basis of Islam and the word Baloch should be removed from the name of this slut."

Many viewers are unhappy with Lucman: "You will be just a pimp at least from my point of view," says one man. "Being such a respectable citizen of Pakistan, you should not invite such people and insult yourself and us Pakistanis," one woman writes. "Sick cunts both of you," says another.

A film director turned investigative journalist, Lucman likes to boast that his programme is the most banned show in Pakistan, frequently sanctioned by the government's media regulatory authority. In 2014 he was given a lifetime ban for remarks against the judiciary, but returned to television after apologizing in court. That same year he featured as a guest on his own show and threatened to quit television and leave Pakistan in protest over the government's failing leadership. His enemies, he says, want to silence him, and his show is a mixed bag of leaked videos, exposés of alleged government corruption and the odd interview with the disgruntled former spouse of some politician or celebrity.

Lucman opens his show that night with a few words about why Qandeel has been invited on to *Khara Such*. He says that he has overruled many members of his team who did not want to run this interview. They feel Qandeel should not be given the publicity that she seems to crave. But, "Social media is a reality that cannot be ignored," he says. "We can object to it, we can criticize it, but we cannot deny it. Because even we—the anchors, the columnists—look at the trends to see what the hot story is and what people are discussing the most."[10] For him, the reason for having Qandeel on the show is simple: "When something is being discussed so much, and when people have taken reactive measures to something, we need to ask her what she planned. Did she want this? What was her purpose?" If there is anyone in Pakistan who has not heard of Qandeel yet, they will know her name after her debut on this show.

On the show he asks her, "Qandeel, first of all, tell me how I should address you: as an actress, a singer, a model or a social media activist? What would you want?"

"I'm a singer and actress," she replies. She usually appears on these shows with a smile, often flirting with the host. But she is upset tonight. "People end up saying whatever they like, so . . . " she trails off.

She is hurt that she has been labelled vulgar. She has gone against her family to do what she is doing. Her family is not, as some of the commenters have said, a dishonourable family.

My family refuses to acknowledge me. It's because of all these things that are going on. They say you are dead to us.

Those who say she is dishonouring Pakistan are hypocrites, she says disgustedly. "When politicians go to *mujras* [dance parties] and watch girls dance for them, don't they realise then that this is a Pakistani girl? Where does their honour go then?" Isn't that more vulgar than anything she has done? "I am just very spoiled and stubborn," she explains. She says she is inspired by Indian women like Poonam Pandey, Sunny Leone and Rakhi Sawant. If they can make videos and upload pictures of themselves, why can't she?

There are those who claim she is not a Baloch girl. After all, what Baloch girl would promise to dance naked for the whole world to see? But she does not want to argue with these people. If they have made up their minds about her, there is nothing she can do. She doesn't care what they think about her. Everyone is just upset because Pakistan lost the match and she did not strip. They are furious about the trailer because it only gave them a peek of what they really wanted to see.

But on this show and the ones that will follow, she knows what the hosts want to hear. She can vent her anger for only so long. She must be contrite, and she must ask for forgiveness.

I only feel sad from the bottom of my heart that I put out a trailer for such a loser team. That's all I feel sorry for.

"I'm appealing to all of Pakistan," she tells Lucman. "Please forgive me. I made a mistake." She says it over and over again. She swears she will not put up any more videos.

There is no vulgarity in that video. I think it's hot. Watch it carefully.

I'll never accept that I was being vulgar. I think it's hot and very sexy.

When Lucman suggests that she stick to singing so she can become respectable, she says quietly, "I have no respect as it is. What respect will I get? You lose people's respect once and never get it back. It's gone."

On another show, a few days later, she is one of three guests alongside an actress and a religious scholar who is the head of a well-known madrassa in Karachi.[11] The host asks the scholar if in his opinion it is permissible for Qandeel to push the limits of freedom of expression in the way that she does. Should she really be allowed to make the kinds of videos that she does? Should she have offered to strip for the Pakistani cricket team? "So many evils are being born on social media," he replies. "She shouldn't have done this. It's obvious."

The actress chimes in saying that Qandeel is giving show business a bad name. It is because of people like her that girls from good homes think twice before wanting to become an actress or singer.

"If they are from good homes, then they should sit at home," Qandeel retorts. "Why do they want to come on TV?"

"I believe these kind of people are just bubbles," the actress continues. "When did they come? When did they burst and disappear? Nobody will know. They just vanish."

These female monkeys who curse me—do I go to their homes and force them to watch my videos? And then when their husbands complain and curse them, then they cry about "women empowerment."

Qandeel does not expect such women, these actresses, to stand by her. She learned this when she starred in a reality TV show the year before. She was sent to some village in Punjab with a crew of other aspiring actresses, models and singers to compete to be the ultimate "desi girl"—a modern city girl who can survive in a village and carry out tasks such as drawing water from a well or carrying bales of hay.

Did the other contestants know when they saw Qandeel pick turnips in a field and crack a whip over a donkey that she had grown up in a village not very different from this one? That she was playing at being a girl from the big city, and not a girl who had to learn to live in a village? She played the part well. In the very first episode she turned up in the village in her skinny jeans and stiletto booties—she could never go to Shah Sadar Din dressed like that—and tripped and twisted her ankle in the mud of an unmade road. Whatever they knew, those women called her "proudy" and voted her out. They did not want her there, Qandeel knows, because they realised she could win. Women rarely stand by her.

"A woman gives a man permission to misbehave with her," the actress on the talk show tells Qandeel. "And you are one of those women who do, from what I have seen of you and heard of you and heard you say." A woman like Qandeel can only be the bright light of some man's night, not the pride and joy of a home, she says.

Shut the fuck up.

The religious scholar tells her she has gone against Islamic law, the law of the country and Pakistani culture and manners. People like her want to see Western culture in Pakistan. "Our young men and women are being destroyed," he says. "We cannot allow it."

When the host asks the scholar if he would issue a fatwa against Qandeel's behaviour, she interrupts, "It's my conscience and I have to go to my grave and give Allah an answer for what I have done. So no one here can try to pass any fatwas on me. There's no need for that."

"I'm very happy her Facebook page was removed," the actress says at the end of the show. "In the future, if anyone tries to do something like that, they will think about the reaction first. The public, the people, will not be silent. They will say what is right and what is wrong. I don't think she should behave this way ever again. No one should follow her. People like her should just be made to disappear."

You're going to miss me when I'm gone. Kitnay gunday hain aap log waisay [You're so terrible], *double standard log. You like to watch me, and then you like to say, "Why don't you just die?"*

Will you be happy when I die?

When I die, yahaan pe koi aur Qandeel Baloch nahin aani [There will never be another Qandeel Baloch].

Aik sau saal tak Qandeel Baloch paida nahin honi [For a hundred years, another Qandeel Baloch will not be born]. *You're going to miss me.*

Qandeel wears a black tank top and a fitted black blazer on the show. When the programme airs, the channel has placed a blurred square where her cleavage would be had she been wearing something more revealing.

Jalal, her former tae kwon do teacher, watches these interviews and thinks about how much she has changed since he first met her. She has become so confident. The shows' anchors seem to be baffled by her. Sometimes he chuckles while watching her because she seems to be interrogating the interviewer, and not the other way around.

You think I'll go quiet if you close down my Facebook page?

Having observed her in his classes in Islamabad, he knows that she is quick to fight, easy to upset and sometimes shy. But now she also seems glamorous and self-assured.

They got my page banned. They are happy that I can't be bad any more.

During his classes she was happy while she was throwing punches, but would complain bitterly the minute she was hit. When he paired her up with a female student, she would argue. "I don't want to fight girls," she would say. "I want to fight the boys." But if she ever lost a point in these bouts, she didn't care whether her opponent was a boy or a girl— she would try to hurt them.

But I'm not done being bad. I'm just starting.

Jalal learned quickly that she was very sensitive. Sometimes she would break down and cry. She took defeat to heart.

Wait and see what I do.

But despite all that, Jalal admired her: she was a good fighter, and strongest when attacking her opponent. A blow might stun her, but she'd make sure the last punch was hers.

Now it's a fight between me and the public. Let's see who wins. I don't do these things happily. You could say that this is my revenge from this country.

THE HELPLINE

Nighat Dad is not an easy woman to find. The Digital Rights Foundation (DRF), an advocacy organization she founded in 2012, has just launched Pakistan's first cyber harassment helpline, and I'm in Lahore to see how it works. But the DRF office is located in a residential area of the city, and I quickly get lost within its winding, narrow lanes. I try to find my way by using the map application on my phone. Nothing shows up.

I think I have found the office at the end of a lane that curves away from a small patch of green where children in this neighbourhood come to play in the evenings. As I am about to ring the bell, a woman taking out the garbage opens the gate. I ask her if she works at the DRF office. She gives me a blank look and shakes her head. "There's no office in this lane," she says.

The gate next door opens, and a guard steps out. The house looks like any other on the street until you notice the thicket of barbed wire along the top of its boundary walls. The guard won't confirm or deny if this is the office for the Digital Rights Foundation or if Nighat is inside. He rests his hand on the gun holstered at his hip while I call her. She sends someone outside to fetch me.

This is my first time meeting Nighat. She travels frequently and we have only ever been able to speak on Skype. The first thing I notice is her easy smile. Her mouth is painted a bright crimson, and metallic-red hair sweeps across her forehead. A few forest-green locks peek out from under the shawl she has wound around her neck. She apologizes for how difficult it is to find the office. It is not locatable with any map app, and the people at the office do not chat with the neighbours. There are people who do not like Nighat and the work she is doing, and she does not want to make it easy for them to find her.

This morning Nighat is tired and only has a little time to spare before she has to leave for a presentation about the helpline at a local college. She thinks it's for two or three dozen people, but then receives a call from the woman organizing the event: the college has received a flood of requests once word got out that Nighat would be there. There are now close to a hundred attendees.

Since 2010 Nighat has been travelling across the country to conduct training sessions for Internet users—many of them women—who want to learn how to protect themselves and their identities online. At one such session one of the participants was a young girl from Swat, at the time under the control of the Taliban, who would go on to capture the world's attention when her then-anonymous blogs and her call for education for girls earned her a bullet in the head: Malala Yousafzai.

Nighat soon started to receive messages in her Facebook inbox from women who had attended her workshops. They were being harassed, blackmailed, or threatened online, and they were hesitant to approach a government agency, or their friends or family members for help. They were scared of being dismissed, judged or punished. In many cases they were unable to talk to a family member because they were forbidden to be on sites like Facebook in the first place. Many of those being blackmailed by current or former partners could not admit to their families that they were in a relationship—in one 2014 case a fourteen-year-old girl was blackmailed into repeated gang rapes when her boyfriend threatened to release a video he had secretly shot of them.[1] Word of mouth was slowly spreading that Nighat was the woman to approach if you were having problems with your online presence, or if your email had been hacked or your online security breached.

In 2015 Nighat was named one of *Time* magazine's "next generation leaders" for her work. She was suddenly one of the best-known digital rights activists in the region. The attention was a blessing for DRF, but it soon took a toll on Nighat. Her inbox was flooded with pleas for help from women across the country, and she felt increasingly helpless and exhausted, terrified of missing even a single message from a distraught stranger. When she mentioned this to a friend, her friend had an idea: why not share the load? Why didn't she start Pakistan's first cyber-harassment helpline?

By July 2016 Nighat had started to reach out to people who could help her set up the helpline and was mulling over how best to do it. Then news broke of Qandeel's murder. On 15 July, the day before her body was discovered in her home in Multan, Qandeel had posted a message on her social media platforms: "I believe I am a modern day feminist . . . I am just a women with free thoughts, free mindset and I LOVE THE WAY I AM . . . " In the days after her murder many reports in the international media would echo this description of Qandeel, praising her as a feminist icon. She had become a role model, "a one-woman revolution against religiously and culturally justified misogyny" (*Daily Beast*). In the Pakistani media some obituaries followed the same vein. She was no longer ridiculed or criticized, but embraced by the very people who had once scorned or ignored her. "Qandeel Baloch is dead because we hate women who don't conform," explained the cultural editor of Pakistan's leading English-language newspaper, *Dawn*. "Qandeel Baloch was an unapologetic rebel," lamented another journalist. There were slideshows of her photographs and listicles of "10 powerful quotes by Qandeel Baloch."

However, the online conversation was very different. In the week that followed Qandeel's murder, Nighat found herself targeted online for condemning the killing. Today she sits at her laptop, its cover scattered with stickers—Challenge Power!, Back Up Your Data!, and Queen in bright pink letters—and reads out some of the messages she received.

"You seem to be following her pathetic footsteps."

"Show your boldness and put off your clothes as Qandeel used to do."

"Do you want to spread pornography in whole country?"

"Kill yourself."

"After QB it will be ND."

These are some of the milder posts. Some of the activists Nighat knows were being trolled, receiving rape and death threats, and being slut-shamed online after they spoke out against Qandeel's murder by her brother. Many of Nighat's friends deactivated their social media accounts because they were intimidated by the messages they received after they expressed grief or anger over Qandeel's killing or shared any news stories that were favourable towards her. Three days after the murder, a story on the BBC detailed the kinds of threats that some female journalists were facing when they spoke about Qandeel Baloch. "I've been recently trolled on Facebook for posting a status update on how we, as a society, failed Qandeel Baloch," said Iram Abbasi, a reporter. "One user said I didn't have a 'good family background.' Another asked how I could come from a reputable family if I wore sleeveless shirts. For the same reason, another user said I was wearing 'dirty' and 'un-Islamic' clothing."[2]

On Twitter and Facebook newsfeeds were flooded with messages from Pakistanis who believed the murder, an "honour killing," had been just.

"Finally #QandeelBaloch murdered," tweeted one woman. "Someone had to do it. She was disgrace for the country . . . "

"Good news," wrote another. "She was just indecent and a dishonourable woman."

"She was going out of hand."

"She's certainly gonna suffer in hell. Her brother did well."

"Where there is no honor in killing, there are hoes like #Qandeel-Baloch. Honor killing is a good thing sometimes."

"Finally a good news after long time :p."

Qandeel's critics attacked her social media pages.

"Unfollow this account, she is spoiling Pakistan's name," urged one Instagram user.

"She was a vile human being no pride in herself and in Pakistan and with a body like that I'll be hiding it not displaying it," added another.

"This woman is a disgusting slut," one user wrote, accusing Qandeel and her supporters of pandering to the West. "People in Pakistan are desperately seeking to be like North Americans, mimicking their lives but you never will be. Embrace your culture, religion, and country. . . "

Another wrote, "People like this should be shot."

"I couldn't tolerate it any more," Nighat says. She was receiving calls from women who were worried about their privacy settings and what their friends, family members or work colleagues could see on their social media pages. They felt overwhelmed by the stream of hate speech targeting anyone who spoke out against Qandeel's murder. Nighat herself wanted to go offline. "I realised that if I needed to talk to somebody about the threats I was receiving online, I had no one to turn to," she recalls. "Who was I supposed to go to?"

She knew she could not delay the helpline any longer. There was just one problem: she had no money.

Nighat was a university undergraduate when she entered an online chat room for the first time. It was the early 2000s. Desktop computers were all the rage—by 2007 there would be machines in five million homes in cities like Lahore, Karachi and Islamabad,[3] and Nighat's brother-in-law, whom she lived with, had just bought one for the house.

By 1992 dial-up Internet was available in urban centres in the country, but it would be a few years before Internet service providers began offering low-cost packages. In 2000 only 133,900 Pakistanis were on-line,[4] and Nighat was one of them. The arrival of mIRC (Internet Relay Chat) software was a revelation: a whole world of strangers outside the tight circle of her family and school friends, all accessible whenever she wanted, and none of them knew her real name. At the University of Punjab in Lahore, where she was studying law, all the girls she knew were nervous about talking to boys—or rather about being *seen* talking to boys. For most of them, including Nighat, even the hint of some interest from a boy could lead to being yanked out of school. And many of the girls were the first in their families to attend university.

"I knew that if word got back to my parents that I was hanging out with some boy or talking to him, my education would be stopped," says Nighat. And so, on some nights, she would sit before the computer—which had been placed in her room—and her fingertips would hover over the smooth black squares of the keyboard as she waited to hear a dial tone, a whistle, a crackle and the staticky whine that let her know she was close, a few tries on a patchy connection away from being anyone she wanted to be. A woman with a made-up name who was free to be any ASL (age/sex/location). "When you heard that sound, when the connection was made, just like that, life would feel exciting," she remembers.

One night, some time after midnight or 1 a.m., she was in her room sitting at the computer, with her back towards the door. The lights were switched off and the door was unlocked. She was not allowed to lock the door to her room as her family didn't believe there was anything you needed to be doing in your room that warranted keeping others out. She logged on and opened up a chat window. She was curious about who was out there, and on that night, like other nights, the chat was a tepid interaction with someone halfway across the world. "Who are you?" she asked. "What do you do?" The conversation might last a few minutes before she moved on to someone else, or the person she was chatting with realised that she wasn't interested in anything more exciting than finding out the mundane realities of their life.

But that night she was not alone. There was someone else, standing quietly in the dark behind her. He watched her face, suffused with light from the screen, and saw her eagerly respond to someone on the other side. Nighat's elder brother, the breadwinner in the family, whom she had had to ask for permission to go to university—"What sense does it make for you to study the law?" he had asked, and then relented on condition that she went to classes wearing a *niqab* to cover her face and body—was standing behind her and reading the messages she was exchanging with a total stranger. Where had she even met this man?

Her brother exploded. "You have rubbed any respect we had in the dirt," he screamed. He slapped her. Her mother woke up and rushed into the room to find Nighat sobbing and pleading, "But what have I done?" Her brother was so upset, he started crying. Nighat's mother had no idea what was going on, but she realised the girl had done something that could bring shame on the family. She too hit her.

"From tomorrow, she will not go to university," Nighat's brother announced, his face wet with tears. "She's busy having affairs there." The next morning the computer was taken from her room. In the end she was allowed to attend classes, but she never used an online chat room again.

Nighat was born in Ratta Matta, a town of 30,000 to 40,000 people near Jhang in Punjab. Her parents, Mehar Allah and Nasreen, had also been born and raised there, like their parents before them. They were sharecroppers. After each harvest they would retain a small share of the crops they produced; the rest went to their landlord. They were almost illiterate; Nasreen had only ever read the Quran.

Some time in the 1960s, Mehar Allah went to Karachi. He was the first person in his family to leave the village for the city. He landed a job as a daily-wage labourer, hauling bricks and shovelling endless mounds of sand on to the site of a new building for a bank. It was hard work, and he missed his wife and children. Every day an army of labourers like himself worked round the clock as the creamy white tower, round as a stack of coins and ridged like a car tyre, rose against the city's skyline.

Once the building was completed, he was employed as a peon in a family-run textile business. Soon it was discovered that he had an excellent head for numbers, and moreover he was honest. He taught himself to write Urdu and worked his way up to clerk, poring over his employer's books. By the time Nighat was born in 1979, Mehar Allah had moved his family to the city, and in the 1980s he became a partner in the business.

He was determined that his children be educated and enrolled them in an English-speaking private school. "We went to a wonderful school called Little Foxes," Nighat says. She pauses. She realises that she has reverted to her childhood pronunciation of the school name, the name she and her sisters used when they had not yet learned to speak English. "Did I say 'Little Foxes'? I meant Little Folks."

The children were competitive and tried to get the best grades. They signed up for as many extracurricular activities as they could and took part in singing competitions. They were good singers—they got that from Mehar Allah, who could carry a tune and loved Siraiki poetry— their voices trained from years of performing and listening to wedding songs and hymns in Ratta Matta. Mehar Allah could never remember which grade any of his six children were in, but he attended the ceremony at the end of the year when they were awarded first, second or third place in their respective classes.

By the mid-1990s, Mehar Allah had started his own business, producing fibre canes, and had set up a factory in Lahore. He brought his nephews from Ratta Matta to the city and into the business so they did not have to herd goats and sheep for the rest of their lives. Mehar Allah also bought the land that his parents had tended and gave them their own home. For the first time their crops were entirely their own. But then Mehar Allah became very ill. He had always been a hard worker and had not taken care of himself. He suffered from diabetes and later temporary paralysis. The energy that had brought him from Ratta Matta to one of the richest cities in the country suddenly failed him. As he grew sicker, he wanted to be at home with his parents. He wanted to go back to the village.

It was decided that Nighat's elder brother would handle what was left of the business in Lahore, and Nighat went to live with her sister, who was married. Money was tight, so there could be no more private education, and she was enrolled in a government secondary school. It was a culture shock. The system was completely different to what she was used to: everything was taught in Urdu, including mathematics and science. She struggled to understand her teachers and did badly, often barely scraping through to the next grade. When the time came to apply to university, she realised she wanted to study English literature, but her grades were not good enough. On a whim, she decided to apply to the University of Punjab to study law. To her surprise, she was accepted.

By this time Nighat's brother, only four years older than her, was supporting the family. Mehar Allah and Nasreen would sometimes send their children gifts of flour, ghee or spinach from the village, but they could not pay for their education. Nighat's brother was more conservative than his father. Even though Mehar Allah had enrolled his girls in schools where they sat in classrooms with boys, his sister would not go to a co-educational university, he said. "My brother was paying for everything now and he held all the power in the family," Nighat says. "Everyone was dependent on him, and I needed his permission if I wanted to go to university." Initially, she had not been that keen on studying law, but the moment she was told that he did not want her to do so, she dug her heels in.

She refused to wear a full veil as her brother wanted her to. She would only agree to wear an abaya, a long, full-sleeved gown, and a scarf to cover her head. When I ask why she didn't just say she would wear a niqab to classes, and then remove it—after all, how would her brother know?—she looks surprised. The idea never occurred to her. "Why would I lie about it?" she asks. "I wanted to show them who I was. I knew that whatever I did would set an example for the other women in my family. I was the first one to go to university and study law—none of the men had ever done that."

In Ratta Matta, Mehar Allah's friends and relatives criticized him. Why are you sending your daughter to a university where she will study with boys? they asked. Why does she even need to study law? But Mehar

Allah had heard them boasting when their sons had come back to the village with a law degree, and had seen these boys throw their weight around because they now had a power that few in the village did: they knew their rights. Mehar Allah wanted to tell them all, My girl is also a lawyer. Three years later, he got his wish.

Nighat was twenty-four years old and a fresh graduate when her father received a marriage proposal for her from a friend. "The boy's family said they wanted to send me abroad to keep studying," Nighat recalls. "They wanted me to become a barrister." She didn't particularly like her suitor, but she had nothing to compare him to: she had never been on a date, and she did not dream of her wedding day like many of the girls she knew. Her father suggested that she get to know the boy, and he was given permission to call the landline at their home and talk to her. For six months they would have stilted conversations while Nighat's family members sat within earshot. They were allowed to meet only two times, even when they were engaged.

"It's difficult to talk to you like this," her fiancé complained. "I want to buy you a mobile phone." But Nighat was not allowed to have her own phone. It was the early 2000s, and only about 5 percent of Pakistan's population of 144 million owned a mobile; they were a status symbol.[5] Moreover, Nighat had only seen a mobile phone in the hands of men. However, she agreed, and hid the phone from her family, only using it to speak to her fiancé.

One day as she sat with her family there was an unfamiliar buzzing sound. It was coming from Nighat's bag. Her brother pounced, reached inside and pulled out the mobile phone. She had forgotten to turn off the ringer. Once again he told her she had brought shame on the family. She could not be trusted. She was not a good girl. Even today her voice is low and small, as though she is telling me a terrible secret about herself, when she recalls what he said to her that day. "I remember thinking, what is the big deal? What have I done that is so terrible? I'm only talking to my fiancé, and if he has a mobile phone, why can't I?"

She was married soon after. The promises about going abroad for her education had been empty. Her husband and in-laws told her she was not allowed to work. After all, what kind of woman would want to go to the courts and wait around for hours while strange men gawked at her? She whiled away her days watching TV in her cramped new home with her in-laws, cooking and cleaning. There was no computer and no need for a mobile any more now that the man she had been talking to on the phone was her husband.

When she was in her third year at university, some friends had talked to her about sex. She could not believe what they were saying. She told them they were lying. No one in her family had ever mentioned this to her and she had not used her precious time online to look up things like that. "It just didn't cross my mind," she explains. "I wasn't curious about it. I thought that you got pregnant by kissing." She insisted to her friends, It's the kiss. That's what does it. They laughed at her when she made a disgusted face and said she never wanted to get married. But now, a few months after the wedding, she found herself pregnant.

While her husband and in-laws were thrilled, she had never been more unhappy in her life. "I lived in a small room with my husband, I cooked and I mopped the floors," she says. "That was my life. I had no other purpose." One night at 2 a.m., a month after her baby was born, she woke to the sound of her husband's mobile phone ringing. He was fast asleep. She answered it. There was a woman on the line. "All my frustration from that past year just exploded," she recalls.

She woke her husband up and told him she was done with him. He was furious and, while tussling with her, tried to choke their baby boy. "I'm going to kill you," he shouted at her. "You are a bad woman. You have a terrible character."

In the morning Nighat's father came to the house. "If she stays here, I'll kill myself," her husband threatened.

"In that case I would have liked to leave her here, just to see that," Nighat's father said, picking up her bags. Holding her baby in her arms, she followed her father out of the house. It took her four years to get legal custody of her son, Abdullah, who goes by the name Bullah.

Back at her home, the family had gathered. They wept when they heard about what had happened, mortified that she would be a divorcée. Her aunts and uncles urged her to remain in *iddat*—the Islamically mandated forty days of seclusion for a widow or a divorcée. Her father asked everyone to leave. "There will be no such thing," he announced. The next morning, when he saw her, he asked, "What are you doing sitting at home? Get up, get out and find yourself a job." She went to the court and applied for her licence. She could finally practice law.

In court she would stand up to argue points only to have judges snap at her to sit down. She learned how women were treated in a system where, even as recently as 2016, only 5.8 percent of judges in the higher courts were women.[6] While she waited for hours for her cases to be heard, she saw how mothers were treated when they were allowed to meet the children who had been taken from them—weeping in the corridors outside the courtrooms as clerks, peons and lawyers stepped around them as they sat on the floor with nowhere to be alone with their babies. "I would look at these women and think, I'm a lawyer and I'm getting knocked out by this system. What are these women going through?"

Around this time she was employed by the law minister to manage his office in Lahore. The job was perfect in many ways. Her boss was usually busy in Islamabad and frequently appeared on television in religious programmes. He rarely had time to be in Lahore, and so Nighat could run the office as she pleased. But the best thing about the job was that she had her own computer and access to the Internet for the first time in her life.

She used the three years she managed this office to research and finish a course in Internet governance. By this time, 2007, 3.5 million Pakistanis had access to the Internet, and Nighat was interested in the ways these people, especially women, were using the World Wide Web. Who had the right to be online and who determined access to the Internet?

One day two women friends visited her at work. They were being harassed by men on the site Orkut, a social media that was popular among Pakistanis at the time. Is there any law against this kind of behaviour? they wanted to know. Should we just shut down our accounts or is there something we can do? Nighat didn't have an answer for them, so she started researching cyber harassment and looking into the laws governing Internet use in Pakistan. She helped her friends secure their accounts, boosting their privacy settings to avoid unwanted attention. They in turn told their friends about her.

One day Nighat's boss was in Lahore for the taping of the religious show that he hosted. He came to the office when he was done, and she brought some case files into his room, where he was sitting at his desk.

He looked at her for a while. "You've got a bit fat," he commented.

Nighat was taken aback. She stammered, "Yes, I suppose, a little bit."

"Come here." He beckoned to her. "Come sit on my lap. Let's see just how heavy you have become."

She stared at him. He repeated himself. "Come sit."

Nighat apologized and got up to leave.

"What did I just tell you to do?" he snapped.

A wave of fury rushed through her. "You should be grateful I didn't slap you for that."

Her boss sighed. "You should consider yourself lucky. I asked you nicely."

As Nighat was walking out, she heard him call out, "The other women lawyers do it for 500 rupees."

Nighat learned about a rights organization based in Lahore called Bytes for All, which focused on digital security, freedom of expression and gender-based violence online, among other issues. She applied for a job there, and was soon working with the organization tackling online harassment. She learned that since 2007 the Pakistan Telecommunication Authority had been spying on Internet and mobile phone users by using a technology that enabled it to read content in real time. Journalists, bloggers, rights activists and citizen journalists were at risk of being monitored, and many websites such as Blogspot or media platforms like YouTube were censored or blocked in the name of national security, religion or morality.[7] She began lobbying the government for comprehensive cybercrime legislation.

In 2012 Nighat began working as a consultant for UN Women. She frequently conducted digital security training for organizations and media groups, and a friend suggested that she set up an outfit devoted to this work. In October of that year, the friend purchased a domain for her. The Digital Rights Foundation (DRF) came into being, and Nighat would work at UN Women during the day and then spend her evenings working on her own organization's website. She wrote blogs and slowly spread the word about her work. It would be two years before she received any funding for this work.

DRF's first campaign was called Hamara Internet (Our Internet). The project was very close to Nighat's heart. In a country like Pakistan, where male users dominate online space, often outnumbering female users one and a half times, she observed how misogynistic tendencies slowly crept from the offline arena into online space. "It wasn't just about women facing harassment or threats online," she explains; many women were afraid to be vocal or to express themselves online, just as they were in the offline world. "Women were facing behaviour online that had a very deep connection to the offline space."

The Federal Investigation Agency (FIA), tasked with handling cybercrime in the country, reported that it received more than 3,000 cases between 2014 and 2015—with 45 percent of the cases related to harassment of women on social media platforms like Facebook.[8] In Punjab alone, where DRF is based, there were 170 complaints of cybercrimes against women in 2014.[9] However, not a single case was successfully prosecuted, and many women ended up reaching a compromise with the person they had lodged a complaint against. With little faith in the government agency's ability to handle a case, many women either choose to stop using the Internet or just keep quiet.

"[We want to] open up a new chapter in the struggle for women's rights in Pakistan by addressing the one element that many campaigns previously ignored," stated Hamara Internet's manifesto. "The Internet." The DRF team travelled to seventeen universities and colleges across Pakistan and trained more than 1,800 female students and teachers to protect themselves online. They taught girls how to lock their phones and create secure passwords. Girls told stories of being shamed off the Internet when fake profiles with their names or faces were created and used to send friends and family members explicit messages or vulgar photos; they received threats of rape and murder; they were stalked; their photos were copied without their consent, and their faces Photoshopped onto the naked bodies of other women.

In the first ever comprehensive survey of Pakistani women's experiences online, the DRF team learned that only 28 percent of the women they met as part of the Hamara Internet campaign knew about laws against cyber harassment. 70 percent of these women were afraid to post pictures of themselves online because they feared they could be misused. They were afraid to report harassment because it could tarnish their names or reputation or put them in danger. Many were forced to hand over passwords to phones, email accounts, messaging services and social media accounts to their partners or the male members of their families so that they could be routinely checked on.

As the DRF training sessions continued, Nighat started to hear from girls who had attended them. The messages would arrive late at night on her personal Facebook account and the Hamara Internet account. They were desperate. "If you don't reply to me in an hour, I'm going to kill myself," one girl said. These girls were being blackmailed, harassed or threatened online, and they did not know who to turn to. Often Nighat used her contacts in the tech world or within social media companies to try to resolve problems. She would also speak to the girls for days, counselling them or providing emotional support.

Other times, however, she had to be inventive with solutions. "Once

I received a message from a woman in Ireland who told me that a man in Pakistan, whom she had had a relationship with, was harassing and blackmailing her," she recalls. The two had been in a relationship for two or three years, and had exchanged photographs and videos. When the woman ended the affair, the man threatened to send her pictures to her parents and the priest at her church. Nighat contacted the FIA and explained what was happening, but they said they could not deal with an international complaint. The woman's only hope was to contact the Pakistani embassy in Ireland and ask them for help. When Nighat told her this, the woman threatened to kill herself. She was from a conservative Catholic family, and her family had no idea she had been in a relationship.

Nighat asked for the man's phone number. He lived in Rawalpindi. She took a deep breath and called him. "I spoke in English, with an accent," Nighat recalls. "I knew Pakistanis get impressed by that sort of stuff. I told him I was his ex-girlfriend's lawyer. I gave him details about where he lived, his job and so on, and said he was being observed. The next time he contacted the woman, the FIA would initiate a case against him. I knew all the relevant laws against this sort of thing and quoted them to scare him."

The man was terrified. He said he did not know there was a law against what he was doing.

"You might not have known about the law, but didn't you realise you were harassing this woman?" Nighat asked him angrily. He never contacted his ex-girlfriend again.

By 2016 she was feeling overwhelmed by requests for help from strangers. In many instances she was battling a legal system that did not support the women who approached her or understand the trauma caused by the harassment.

"I was contacted by a young woman a year ago who had received an offer of marriage from her brother-in-law," Nighat recalls. "He wanted her to be his second wife. The girl refused, and the man threw acid on her face. She fought a case against him, and he was jailed, but his cousins then began to blackmail her. They stole photographs of her and threatened to release doctored images online and among her family. She needed me to help stop them from doing so."

Nighat approached the police, but was rebuffed. "This woman was attacked with acid and you want us to focus on the theft of pictures?"

I meet the deputy director of the Federal Investigation Agency's cyber-crime wing, Noman Bodla, on a bitterly cold morning at the Islamabad office of the National Response Center for Cyber Crime (NR3C), which was established by the federal government in 2007 to curb "techno-logical abuse." There are five such cybercrime units across the country and that headed by Bodla has jurisdiction over Jhelum (at the northern edge of the Punjab province), Islamabad, Rawalpindi, parts of Kashmir, and Gilgit Baltistan. It is raining, and the unpaved road leading to the building has turned to mud. After visitors squelch past the concrete bar-ricades, they must provide their names and national identity card num-bers to a guard sitting in a small cabin, who notes down the details in a register. The black-tiled NR3C building has sand-coloured arches and small curved balconies. All the windows have been treated to mirror the world back on itself—today, shining slices of the grey sky. A guard stands at the entrance under an awning painted with a verse from the Quran: "Allah gives to those whom He wants."

The building is old and there are no elevators. Inside it is dark, with the only light coming from windows on each stairwell and bare bulbs in the narrow corridors. The ninety-nine names of Allah shadow all who walk through the corridors here, painted in blue as close to the ceiling as possible: the Omnipotent One, the Guarding One, the Dominant One, the Creator, the Reckoning One, the Watchful One. In Bodla's small office space, mostly taken up by a desk, a whiteboard the size of half a newspaper page has been mounted on the wall. On it a reminder is written in neat capital letters: HARD WORK BEATS TALENT WHEN TALENT DOESN'T WORK HARD.

Bodla had been in his position for a month when he realised that he was battling a force that he had never expected to go up against: Hollywood. "The movies have ruined things for us," he explains. "Everyone thinks we are macho men and we can do anything. They watch films where someone sits at a computer and with the press of a button, suddenly has access to all information. It's nothing like that." Bodla has received requests to recover stolen mobile phones and laptops, trace phone numbers and find children who have run away from home. "The complainant said that his daughter, who had run away, was on Facebook, and so he needed the cybercrime wing to locate her. Something could happen to them in a dream and they think they need to call us," he grumbles.

When the complaints are more suited to his job description—for instance, in cases of cyberstalking, online threats or abuse, or the misuse or theft of personal information online—most people expect a few quick taps on a keyboard will solve their problem. Bodla, who is in his late thirties, says that he was one of the country's first experts in the field of cybercrime. "I was studying all of this back in 2005 or 2006, when no one even knew about cybercrimes," he brags. As a digital forensics expert, his opinion is admissible in court, and he lectures law enforcement trainees and members of the judiciary about cybercrime.

Once a complaint is received at the NR3C in Islamabad—either through an online form, an email, a handwritten note or a call to headquarters—the complainant is asked to visit one of the five units with proof of any harassment or cybercrime. If the complainant does not live in a city with an NR3C office (located in Islamabad, Peshawar, Lahore, Karachi, and Quetta), they must travel to one of these cities.

Here their complaint is recorded and their name noted—there is no anonymity. All evidence of the crime, including screenshots, messages, photographs, or videos, must be provided to the officer dealing with the complaint. The material is not returned to the complainant but is filed away, along with thousands of other photographs and printouts, at the NR3C offices.

Once a formal inquiry is launched and the FIA has a warrant, officials can search and seize items such as laptops or mobile phones from the suspect's home. Sometimes a court order is sent to social media companies such as Facebook to request details about the suspect. "If we get those details—and that's a big if—then we are able to get an IP address and the suspect's name and location," Bodla explains.

Any evidence gathered in searches is sent to a forensic lab so that incriminating data may be extracted from it. Once the FIA believes it has sufficient evidence, it creates a report for its legal team, who see if there are grounds to prosecute. The legal team then recommends whether an FIR (First Information Report), the first step for a police investigation, can be registered. With the approval of the court and the director of the cybercrime wing—unless the complaint concerns nudity, child pornography or cyber terrorism, in which case the NR3C does not need to wait for the court's approval—an FIR is registered and the suspect may be arrested. "Normally, this process doesn't take too long," Bodla explains. "The complaint should be converted into an inquiry or the case closed within one month."

But there are exceptions. The suspect can be in another country. Don't forget that even "someone in Panama can cause so many problems for people here in Islamabad," Bodla says with a giggle, referring to a corruption probe against the prime minister after the Panama Papers were leaked, in which case the complaint is out of the FIA's jurisdiction. "In those cases the complainant has two options. Either live with it or wait for somebody to do the same thing from within the country." Even if the suspect is in another city, the complainant may have to wait while their case is turned over to the relevant NR3C office or until the local officials travel to the city the suspect resides in to further investigate.

As companies like Google or Facebook are not legally compelled to provide information to the Pakistani government, many complainants can only hope that they will cooperate by providing information about a suspect's IP address or by taking down photographs or messages that could put lives at risk, reveal hidden identities to the public, or cause distress.

In April 2017 Facebook revealed that the Pakistani government made 1,002 requests for data on the social media platform's Pakistani users in the second half of 2016—a steady increase since 2013, when the social media platform received only thirty-five requests for user data. According to the company's published policies, Facebook may "access, preserve and share your information in response to a legal request (like a search warrant, court order or subpoena)" if there is "belief that the law requires us to do so." Since 2015, Facebook has complied with 64 percent to 68 percent of these requests.[10]

In 2017, the Pakistani government appeared to be primarily concerned with the data of social media accounts that shared material deemed to be blasphemous, and it lobbied Facebook and Twitter to make it easier to track and locate users who had allegedly committed blasphemy online. In June an anti-terrorism court sentenced a man to death for reportedly making derogatory remarks about the Prophet Muhammad and his wives on Facebook—the first case of digitally perpetrated blasphemy in the country.[11]

While Bodla insists that the NR3C does not deviate from procedure when it comes to tracking suspects, a report in June 2017 by the *Guardian* revealed that the FIA detained social media users, including activists, journalists and a political party worker, for posting "anti-military" content online.[12] An FIA official who chose to remain anonymous told the reporter his agency could "interrogate and seize laptops and phones without warrant" and added, "We are authorized to detain anyone, just on suspicion."[13]

In other cases, however, the FIA has reportedly been unable to help complainants with relatively simple requests. In March 2017 a senator revealed that two fake accounts under his name were being run on Twitter, and despite letters to the FIA, the Pakistan Telecommunication Authority and the Intelligence Bureau, he had been unable to have the accounts shut down. "I was told that only Twitter administration could do that," Senator Raza Rabbani said during a session in the Senate.

Bodla estimates that in 2016 his office received roughly 2,500 complaints of cybercrimes. Of those, around 166 or 167 went on to reach the inquiry stage. And 61 of those cases led to the registration of an FIR. Many complainants choose not to pursue their case because they are unable to go through such a lengthy procedure, particularly if they do not live in a city with an NR3C office—in this case they must make repeated trips to the nearest office while their case continues. "Sometimes people back out of the complaint because they fear for their reputation or they feel social pressure to let it go," Bodla says. Between 2016 and 2017, some of the complaints resolved by the NR3C included instances of vulgar messages, the non-consensual use of photographs, publication of "objectionable content" and the creation of fake profiles. In March 2017 a woman was arrested for the first time for blackmail via social media.

When I ask Bodla what happens to complainants who are unable to bear the cost of travel to the nearest NR3C office, he admits that more cybercrime centres are needed, particularly for those who do not live in major cities. He says his office has requested the creation of fifteen more centres, in cities like Multan, Sukkur, and Gwadar. There has been no word on whether the request has been approved. He is irritated when asked about women or minors who may not have permission to travel to another city alone and who do not want to confide in their family about being harassed or targeted online. "The people who have those kinds of problems don't even come to us," he says. "I can't speak for them."

In the Hamara Internet survey, Nighat's organization learned that 15 percent of the 1,800 women surveyed in schools and colleges across Pakistan had reported a case of harassment to the FIA. Only 11 percent of these said they believed making a complaint to the NR3C would help. Some 53 percent of the women who had filed a complaint said the agency wasn't helpful at all.

Bodla says the only way to stay safe online is to follow two golden rules: never ever upload or share any pictures or messages, and remember that anything you share can never be deleted. When I ask how he intends to have a generation of Pakistanis plugged into Facebook, Instagram,

Twitter, Snapchat, and WhatsApp follow those rules, he admits that there is a need for "R and D" (research and development).

There are fifteen people, including five investigators, currently working under Bodla. Only one is a woman. The NR3C is required to have her present during raids, in case they encounter women in the suspect's home or need to arrest a female suspect. A male officer is more likely to deal with complainants, including women who need to report vulgar messages, doctored photographs, or intimate pictures, videos or messages shared without their consent. While organizations like DRF have called on the FIA to consider cultural norms in a place like Pakistan and have more women in the NR3C handle complaints, Bodla says that is not possible. "I have five investigators, and even if I wanted to address complaints to my female employee, she cannot handle all of them," he explains. When a woman calls the NR3C helpline, she cannot choose to speak with a male or a female officer—she must talk to whoever happens to answer her call. If the complainant withholds some material or the NR3C believes there isn't sufficient evidence, the case is not taken forward. Even if there were more female employees in the NR3C, Bodla argues, it wouldn't make any difference – after all, a complainant has to be prepared for any photographs, messages or videos to be seen in court if needed. "The complainants have to be aware that everything—nude pictures, videos or whatever—has to be on the record and perused in court. If they're not willing to do that, there's no case.

"I don't know why you think this is so extraordinary," Bodla says curtly. "If a woman was raped, would she bother going to a female police station? Normally men are sitting at the station, and they do the investigation. So what's the problem?" Those who say the NR3C needs more female officers are simply biased, he argues, and has a theory about such critics. "It's because there's a higher class of society involved in cybercrimes." He laughs. "The lower class would not be involved in using this Facebook stuff. They would bother about having enough food, not about using the Facebook for their friendships. The ones using Facebook or WhatsApp are the class that uses the Internet for their leisure time. And which class is able to have leisure time and access to all these fancy things? So that's why you think they should be treated in an extraordinary way?"

On my way out of Bodla's office I pass a man sitting on a wooden chair with a ripped seat by one of the windows in the hall. He has thrown open the window and dangles his feet outside. He's listening to the latest Bollywood hits on his mobile phone while scrolling endlessly through some social media feed. The music echoes through the corridor, which is lined with shelves crammed with papers. There are expense reports, budget notes, documents with the stamp of the director's office, and hundreds of brown folders, stacked as tall as a man, bound together with twine and bursting with sheets of paper, yellowing at the edges, some ripped or nibbled away by termites, so long have they been there.

In August 2016 the government passed the Prevention of Electronic Crimes Act (PECA), a piece of legislation criticized by opposition parties and rights activists as a tool to curb freedom of expression. The law includes punishment for hate speech and recruitment or planning of terrorist acts through online platforms (imprisonment for up to seven years and/or a fine), the dissemination of child pornography (imprisonment for up to seven years and/or a fine of up to 5 million rupees), cyberstalking, intimidation, harassment, or the non-consensual distribution of photographs or videos (imprisonment for up to three years and/or a fine of up to one million rupees), sexually explicit doctored photographs or videos and blackmail for sexual acts (imprisonment for up to five years and/or a fine of up to five million rupees), and the use of another's identity without permission (imprisonment for up to three years and/or a fine of up to five million rupees).

However, critics of the law, including Nighat, say the language of the act is vague and open to abuse. The section dealing with "spoofing," for example, would make it an offence to caricature or parody political leaders—this includes memes—resulting in imprisonment for up to

three years and/or a fine of 500,000 rupees. Section 10, dealing with
hate speech, warns against information shared online that "is likely to
advance inter-faith, sectarian or racial hatred" but does not consider
that material shared by religious minorities may offend those in a majority. In September 2016, a month after the act was passed, a Christian
man named Nabeel Masih was arrested and charged with blasphemy
for allegedly sharing a photograph of the Kaaba, Islam's holiest site, on
social media.[14]

While the section dealing with cyberstalking could help victims of
harassment, it could also implicate citizen journalists who use social
media to share videos or photos of wrongdoing or harmful behaviour.
The act gives the Pakistan Telecommunication Authority the power to
remove or block access to any content online "if it considers it necessary
in the interest of the glory of Islam or the integrity, security or defence
of Pakistan . . . public order, decency or morality."[15]

State Minister for Information Technology Anusha Rahman said in
2016 that the act could not be changed "on the whims and wishes of a
few NGOs," and she dismissed critics as having an agenda against the
government. "Every day, dozens of complaints are launched by those
who are targeted online," she argued in the National Assembly. "And
there have been cases where young girls have committed suicide, therefore, the government cannot let all this happen just like that." The matter was not up for discussion. PECA, its supporters insisted, was there
to protect the daughters of Pakistan. And were it not for the body of
a young woman, found hanging in her room at one of Sindh's largest
universities four months after the legislation was passed, it would have
been at least possible to believe this.

On 31 December 2016, a few days before classes resumed at the
University of Sindh in Jamshoro, a twenty-two-year-old postgraduate
student named Naila returned to the campus. She had travelled there
from her home in Qambar, about 300 kilometres away. At the time only
a handful of girls were at the hostel where Naila lived. The warden, one
of five students charged with watching over the hostel's residents, was

curious about why Naila had returned from vacation early. Naila said she was worried about her thesis, which was due soon, and wanted to have some quiet time to work on it. A student at the university's Institute of Sindhology, Naila was writing about the romantic poetry of the Sufi scholar Shah Abdul Latif Bhittai.

Marvi Hostel is home to 1,600 girls who live there for a paltry 3,500 rupees a year. They come to the university from towns and villages across the province and some also from homes in provinces abutting Sindh. Every year the university receives a flood of requests for accommodation. It is the only hostel for undergraduate and postgraduate girls on campus, and although enrolment has increased from 16,000 to 32,000 students in the last decade, no new hostels have been built to accommodate the growing numbers. There are up to 8,000 girls at the University of Sindh, and for many a place at Marvi Hostel is the only way they will be allowed to leave their homes for university. One official at the hostel estimated that sixty girls were often crammed into a space built to house thirty. Beds are squeezed in a few inches apart, and many girls share a single bed with friends.

Some time after 8 p.m. on the day she came back to the hostel Naila told the warden she wasn't feeling well. She wanted to see a doctor. It was past the time that girls were allowed to leave the premises alone, and if someone was ill, the warden had to accompany them. The warden told Naila that she would call a car and go with her to a doctor. Naila changed her mind. I'm just feeling a bit weak, she reportedly said. Perhaps I should order some food. Two burgers were delivered to the hostel. The police found the boxes in the dustbin outside Naila's room the next day, along with two empty strips of sleeping pills. The warden told four or five girls on Naila's floor to keep an eye on her, as she wasn't feeling well. The girls invited her to stay in their room, but Naila refused. She said she was fine.

When the warden did her rounds the following day, there was no answer from Naila's door. She thought she might be sleeping and tried to open the door. It was locked. The rooms on this floor all have a narrow window, almost level with the top of the door, and the warden pushed her hand through the bars of the window and pulled the curtain to one side. She stood on the tips of her toes and peered in. The room was dimly lit. The curtains of the other window were closed. She couldn't see Naila on her bed. Then she noticed the slightest movement, a gentle swaying in the centre of the room—a body hanging from the fan.

By the time the warden reached the provost's home, located on the other side of the hostel's grounds, she was panting and sobbing. She could barely speak. She kept clutching at her neck. She drank some water and then blurted, "A girl is hanging in the room."

A police officer was summoned. It took him two or three tries to break open the door. It had been locked from the inside with a deadbolt at the top. There was no other way into the room. The only other window opened on to a sheer drop to the ground.

The officer untied the blue and pink dupatta knotted around Naila's neck and lowered her body on to the bed below. A chair had been kicked to the side. The top button of Naila's black shirt, embroidered with hot-pink flowers at the neck, had been wrenched off. Her thesis was on the desk, along with her phone. There was no note. Naila's phone had been wiped clean of all messages, photographs, videos, or notes.

While the police were searching the room, the phone rang. When one of the officials answered it, there was only silence at the other end. The caller hung up and then quickly sent a text message: "Sorry, wrong number." But the number had been saved in the phone along with the name of the caller: Anis Khaskheli. The police would find that number frequently on Naila's call records over the last three months. "When we went to arrest [Khaskheli], he told us, 'I knew you would come for me,'" said Khadim Rind of the Hyderabad police at a press conference a week later. "'I was waiting for you.'"

Khaskheli was a lecturer at a school nearby. He had befriended Naila on Facebook a few months ago. "You will be amazed to know that this is a murder," Rind said sombrely at the start of the press conference. "Khaskheli trapped Naila for three months. He did it very, very slowly.

He spoke to her about love and told her he wanted to marry her. And then, when Naila said she was going to be done with her Master's and this was the time to marry, he refused." Naila, the police said, was not the only girl Anis was talking to at the time. "There are thirty other girls that we know of," Rind said. "Anis took nude pictures of them and he would blackmail them to get more pictures." The data recovered from Anis's phone was still being decoded. There could be more girls, Rind warned.

At the hostel the news was met with disbelief. Photographs of Naila, particularly one in which she is clutching a large mobile phone, were shared on Facebook among the students, along with tributes from friends and classmates. She was a pretty girl with a round face and a penchant for doing her hair in a beehive. She was "modern." She wore short kameezes, jeans and heels. She streaked her hair and dyed it for her brother's wedding. She liked to be fashionable. She was intelligent and had won awards for her work at the university. She loved Bhittai's verses and could rattle off his poems. Some of the girls refused to believe she could have been in a relationship with Anis. She may have killed herself because she was anxious about her thesis, they said. But those who have seen the thesis agree that it was well written and as good as any of Naila's other work.

Someone leaked a video of the police officer breaking into her room. In the video she is visible hanging from the ceiling.

Then the rumours started. Naila would share romantic poetry on her Facebook page and tag her professor in the posts. What kind of girl does that? Her family was uneducated and conservative. They wanted to marry her off as soon as she was done with university. She had pleaded with the hostel warden to help her find a job, so she did not have to return to Qambar. She killed herself because her family had insisted on an arranged marriage. But, as some girls pointed out, if her family was so conservative, would they really have sent their daughter to university in another city?

"She was proudy," one hostel official said. A haughty girl who wanted to be independent and shut the door in the warden's face when she suggested she might like to stay in a room with some of the other girls instead of sleeping alone on that last night. She killed herself when Anis, a "hanky panky playboy type guy," threatened to share her photos with others because "that would have ruined the image she had built of herself at the hostel."

There was gossip that Naila had four or five more SIMs in her purse, that she was one of those girls who didn't have just one boyfriend, but three or four. At the hostel some alleged these girls were "running a business." A bus ticket found in her room revealed that Naila had left her home in Qambar on the twenty-seventh, but arrived at the hostel on the thirty-first. Where had she been during those three days?

The rumours persisted. Naila had given the hostel officials an incorrect phone number for her parents, so they could not be contacted if she stayed out too late or did something against the rules. Some even said she was pregnant.

Deputy Inspector General Khadim Rind insisted that all photographs, videos and messages recovered from Naila and Anis's phones had been strictly safeguarded. "No one has seen them, other than the superintendent and myself," he said. "We used our own laptops to download the data and then we sat at home and made printouts of all of the communication." But there were some on campus, including professors and the officials at Marvi Hostel, who said they had seen the pictures Khaskheli had. In many of them, one woman said, Naila was naked. She seemed to be unaware that she was being photographed.

The university has tightened security at the hostel since Naila's death. The hostel provosts have created a network of "volunteers" who keep an eye on the girls. An old, unmanned gate into the hostel has been sealed. Any girl entering or leaving Marvi Hostel must now enter her details in a register at the gate and inform two women sitting there about where she is going. If she says she is going somewhere with her family, one of the provosts will wait outside the gate with her to see who picks her up. If a girl stays out past 9 p.m. she must write a letter apologizing to the hostel officials and her parents are contacted. "Many of these girls have left their villages or towns for the first time when they come here," explains a deputy provost. "Their minds are so fresh. They need a positive environment so they can stay on the right path."

But not everyone agrees that curbing the girls' physical movement is the solution to the problem. "I don't allow my daughters to even sit on a bike with their brother if they are leaving the house," says the university's vice chancellor, Dr Fateh Muhammed Burfat. "It's not about what I feel—it's the culture we live in. The person on the road has no idea that the boy you're riding around on a bike with is your brother. That is the environment that a majority of our female students come from. But then they arrive at university and see girls talking to boys or sitting on benches with boys in the gardens. The rich sons of landlords follow the girls in their cars or chase them, or they throw pieces of paper with their phone numbers written on them into the girls' laps. The girls have never experienced this. They can get confused."

On Facebook groups that have been shut down and re-created several times under different names, students can post anonymous messages about girls or boys they are interested in and provide their phone number. One page, with more than 5,000 followers, is called Sindh University Crushes and Confessions. "*Assalam-o-alaikum*, dear admin, don't show my name," reads one message. "My confession: there's a girl in the Physics department, I think she's in the first year, and she was wearing a black outfit the other day. You were sitting in front of me in the last seminar. You were preparing for the exam and I couldn't stop looking at you. You looked at me a few times. You must have understood by now who I am. Your eyes are beautiful. I like you. Please contact me."

Marvi Hostel does not have Wi-Fi and the network in the university does not allow access to Facebook or WhatsApp. While only some of the students own their own laptops through government schemes or awards, almost all have mobile phones with a 3G connection. "I am not running a jail here," says Dr Burfat. "I can't take away their phones, but the most we can ask is that they turn off the ringer and not take calls after a certain time. But if a girl is lying in her bed at night and chatting

with someone, how can we control that? Some of the girls are so secretive about their relationships, that even a friend sleeping next to her will
have no idea she's talking to a boy." A common trick, girls at the hostel
say, is to answer your phone with the words, "Yes, Mother?"

Dr Burfat says he has seen the pictures in Naila's case. "You would
not send such pictures to your parents, who you have known your whole
life," he says. "So why are you sending them to a man you have known
for three months? The girls here need to understand that they should not
do anything that would bring them shame. Today they are in the university, but tomorrow they will have to go back to their villages, right?
University life is one thing, but life in the village and what is accepted
there is completely different."

The provosts at the hostel know the security system is not foolproof
when it comes to keeping tabs on the students. "I can tell them when to
leave and when to come back, and I can tell them when to be in their
rooms, but once they turn on their phones, they could be anywhere they
want to be," a deputy provost says.

In 2016 DRF held a digital security training session at the university and also spoke to the female students about harassment and blackmail online. A month after Naila's body was found, the university held
another session: "Women protection and laws against women harassment." A professor who was at the event said that only two hundred or
so girls attended.

At the session Dr Burfat announced that a cell would be created at
the university where girls could report any harassment. "I am like the
father of all female faculty and students and will make sure that they
stay safe and secure," he told the students. One provost at the hostel was
sceptical about the cell or any platform to report harassment or cybercrimes. "You need a lot of courage to approach someone and show them
messages or pictures exchanged with your boyfriend," she said. "Only a
very bold girl, or a girl who isn't worried about the news getting back to
her family or being called a 'bad girl,' would come forward. For others,
it will take time. We just aren't there yet."

Sindh Inspector General of Police A. D. Khowaja also spoke at the seminar. He advised female students not to write anything on social media or in a message that they could not show to their brothers or fathers. No one would dare to blackmail them if they followed this advice, he said.

Some officials at the university argue that only the girls can safeguard themselves. "Look at this," exclaims a deputy provost at the hostel, waving her hand in the air. "Do you hear anything?" She claps her other palm to her hand. "Did you hear that?" She clasps both hands together and claps again. "Something can only exist when two people are involved." She waves one hand in the air. "One on its own cannot do anything. And a woman—a good woman—is like a mountain. You cannot move her for anything. Until she shows some weakness, no man can touch her or send her an inappropriate message or anything."

When the university re-opened in January, some of the girls were reluctant to return. They missed a few classes, but then slowly trickled back. Naila's room is still sealed. She lived here with four other girls and not a single one has returned to the campus or answered calls from the university officials. Their belongings are still in the room and their education incomplete.

"In the beginning, the girls felt scared to be in Marvi Hostel," says the senior provost, Aneela Soomro. "They would say they could hear voices coming from Naila's room and the sound of weeping or footsteps late at night. Some of the more mischievous girls started knocking on doors after midnight or making sounds just to scare people. But now I have girls coming to me and asking to live in Naila's room. It's an empty room and we don't have enough space as it is."

As for what happened in that room on the night she died, the rumours and stories continue to be told, and in July Khaskheli was released from police custody on bail. The case continues, but not many at the university are hopeful that the outcome will help them understand what happened or how to keep female students safe online. "To take your life is a very big step," a deputy provost says. "Why did she do it?

Why was she so scared? Only Naila knows what happened. No one else can tell you."

When I meet Nighat in Lahore in January 2017 the helpline has been active for close to a month. "I decided to start it up in the name of Allah," Nighat explains. "I figured I would find the funding." A few days after Qandeel's murder, Nighat wrote a tribute and published it online. And then she received a message: a global fund to support activists at critical junctures wanted to give her $5,000. A few weeks later another group got in touch. They offered her $20,000. And in November she won the 2016 Human Rights Tulip award for her work as a digital rights activist. The prize money: more than $100,000. "And just like that, I had the money for the helpline," Nighat says with a smile.

The helpline receives ninety-five calls in its first month. By the next month, the number has surged to 159 as word spreads. From Monday to Friday, 9 a.m. to 5 p.m., two women in their early twenties, Shmyla and Hira, answer the phones at the DRF office with a reassuring, "Assalam-o-alaikum, this is the cyber harassment helpline, how can I help you?"

The team received extensive training from a not-for-profit organization before the helpline became operational, and it has been a steep learning curve for Nighat. "I had this moment where I realised I've been doing things completely wrong," she says. "When I told the trainer about some of the ways in which I had to tackle complaints in the past, she was horrified." She made Nighat promise not to get "inventive" with solutions. It has not been easy to do so. "Initially, we had prepared a script with a psychiatrist and rehearsed it," explains Shmyla. "We were determined to stick to it. It went out the window pretty quickly."

The team does not ask for names or any identifying information, but callers usually quickly blurt everything out: real names, identity card numbers, the name of the school or college they study at and so on. They often insist, "I'm an educated person. I come from a good family." They are scared they won't be taken seriously. "They give us the information because they want to establish that they're real," Shmyla believes. "They want to tell us: I'm a real person. I'm not making this up."

Many female callers are desperate to prove that they did not invite the harassment and want to send DRF screenshots or messages. Other callers are embarrassed and wanted to talk in hypotheticals. "What if my friend sent pictures to her boyfriend?" one might ask. Some people are suspicious. They do not understand what DRF does and if they are affiliated to the government or police. All the callers have one thing in common: they need the problem to go away immediately.

DRF's job is to tell the callers about their rights when it comes to harassment and cybercrimes. They help them navigate the NR3C's system and explain the procedure—including how long it will likely take the FIA to deal with their complaint—and offer emotional support throughout the process of dealing with NR3C officials. "We have to encourage the callers to use mechanisms that are already in place," Nighat explains. "Only when those mechanisms are exhausted and the problem has not been solved do we try to fix it." She hopes that as more and more complainants reach out to the NR3C, DRF will be able to receive feedback about problems with the government's system, and then lobby for change. If callers do not want to deal with the NR3C or—particularly in the case of the LGBT or religious communities—are too scared to, Shmyla and Hira help them figure out a way to talk to friends or family members about the problem. In many cases, DRF speak to parents or siblings during a call as well.

There is one firm rule: no promises are made to callers and they are never told, "I'll fix this for you." In her first three weeks working at the helpline this took a toll on Shmyla. "My shoulders were always tense and I felt helpless all the time," she says. "I was snapping at everyone at home and my friends had started to wonder what was going on with me. I wasn't behaving like myself." When she spoke to Nighat about this, Shmyla realised what the problem was. "I knew the callers wanted to hear, 'Don't worry,' and I just couldn't say this."

One particular phone call is difficult to forget. "I picked up the phone and there was this girl sobbing," Shmyla recalls. "She was hiding in her bathroom and calling me. She was younger than me. She told me, 'I'm calling you as a last resort.' She had been in a relationship with someone and he had photographs of her. He would tell her to send him more pictures, and if she would refuse, he would threaten to share the ones he had online. The demands would change. He would say, 'I want you to come on Skype tonight. If you don't, I'll show the pictures to everyone.' He knew where she lived and she was terrified that if she didn't give him whatever he wanted, he would share the photos with her family."

Shmyla told the caller she had enough evidence for a case. She knew where the boy lived and his real name. The girl needed to go to the NR3C. Shmyla tried to convince her to confide in her sister, and have her accompany her to the NR3C office. "I never found out what happened," Shmyla says. The girl never called back. "At the end of the day, I have to treat this as another job," Shmyla explains. "It's very hard to do that, but I'm beginning to realise that I have to."

She brings empathy into her interactions with callers as much as she can. She won't promise them a solution, but she tries to reassure them by talking about other similar cases. She wants them to know they aren't alone. She tells them what they are feeling is normal and they shouldn't berate themselves. She breaks down the NR3C's procedures and possible responses. It makes her feel useful when she can help build an evidence file for the NR3C, tell callers what steps to take and how long they can expect the FIA to take with their case.

One complainant who has stayed in touch with the DRF team has been dealing with the FIA for a year and travelling every month to the NR3C office in Lahore to pursue their complaint. As only a small fraction of callers are able to undertake that kind of journey, DRF is now considering creating a network of volunteers or lawyers across the country who can accompany women or minors to cities with an office. In May 2017 a news report claimed that the NR3C office in Lahore, where DRF is based, had yet to clear a backlog of 6,000 cases registered in six months.[16] The office had only seven personnel, and some of them were not trained to handle complaints, with simple forensic analysis that could be completed in ten to fifteen minutes taking months, the report added.

"I had one case where the NR3C officials kept hinting that the complainant should drop the case," Shmyla says. "They would say things like, 'Evidence can be lost, you know.'" She encouraged the caller to insist on a formal complaint and then provide DRF with the details of the FIR so that they could see if the officials had worked up a strong enough case for prosecution.

The most commonly received complaints at the helpline are the creation of fake profiles, blackmail and the non-consensual sharing or manipulating of data such as phone numbers, photographs or personal information. In the overwhelming number of these cases, the complainant cannot afford to wait for weeks for the NR3C's response.

One man called the helpline on his sisters' behalf, in order to ask for help in taking down Photoshopped pictures and fake Facebook profiles that shared the girls' phone numbers and promised callers "anything you like." The girls' family, from a small town in Punjab, was being ostracized as the news spread. "I understand that this is not their fault," the man said. "But how many people am I supposed to explain that to?" The girls were unmarried. Who would want to marry them after this?

"We can tell those kinds of callers that we'll provide them with emotional support and psychological help, but they don't always want that," Hira says. "When something is spreading like wildfire online, they don't want to know how to cope with it—they just want the problem to go away. When I can't help them with that, I begin to wonder, Are we even doing anything substantial? Will we ever be able to?" In such cases, or when a caller's life is at risk or they cannot easily travel to another city with an NR3C office, DRF will tap into personal contacts and connections within the government, law enforcement agencies or NGOs and companies such as Facebook and attempt to have the material removed immediately.

Hira says such cases have made her realise that she is not completely happy that the helpline exists. "I'm more frustrated that there is even a need for something like this," she explains. At such moments, the simpler cases—someone needs help to deactivate their social media page or change their password after their phone has been stolen, or they cannot read English and need help navigating Facebook's privacy settings—are a relief; a quick shot of motivation to keep going.

Nighat still gets messages in her own inbox from women who are desperate for help, but these have slowly decreased to two or three a day. Now she no longer feels panicked if she is not constantly checking her phone. The DRF team has run extensive social media campaigns about the helpline, which has received local media coverage, and its number has been shared at every opportunity. Nighat has had time to pause and reflect on what else needs her attention. She even took her first vacation with her son recently, and when we Skyped, she looked happy and well rested. It was a brief respite from a job where her personal and public lives cannot help but seep in to one another—after all, she even lives at the DRF office, sharing two rooms on the first floor with her sister and son.

"The work is personal for me," she explains. "With every achievement, I feel like everything that happened to me, all the bad stuff, all the struggles, are slowly erased from my memory. I tell other women about what happened to me. I'm not from a privileged background. My struggle is that of any ordinary woman here. Women like me fight battles on two fronts: one for others and one for ourselves. There were many times when I wanted to give up, when I wanted to leave this work and just do something else. But then when I get messages or hear from women who need my help, they bring me back to the work."

Today, when Nighat reflects on her time at university and the days when she did not have permission to use a computer, she thinks of the room on the ground floor of her home where the walls are painted a cool deep green, and of the two women who wait for their phones to ring so they can help create a safer space online for anyone who wishes to be there. "I'm bringing up an army of women," she says. "They may not have any background in this work and they may not know anything about digital rights. But I'm here to train them."

In January 2017, after they found out about Naila, Nighat and Shmyla wrote a searing open letter to the minister for information technology, Anusha Rahman. They reminded her of her promise to protect Pakistani women online through the Prevention of Electronic Crimes Act of 2016. "A law which was enacted in the name of 'protecting daughters of Pakistan' couldn't save the precious life of one daughter, namely Naila," they wrote. "As you must have realised by now, Naila was driven to end her life when she was constantly threatened and intimidated. There is no support system out there for women to seek help; no emotional guidance on how to deal with gender-based threats and cyber harassment." They criticized the NR3C system and pointed out that Naila would not have had access to an NR3C office in Jamshoro. "By assigning the task of enforcing a law relating to cyber harassment, stalking and bullying to a highly centralized federal agency with regional offices confined to Rawalpindi, Islamabad, Lahore, Karachi, Quetta, and Peshawar, the Ministry is failing to reach women like Naila Rind." The minister did not acknowledge the letter or the criticism.

There are days when Nighat feels overwhelmed by the limits of the helpline. When she hears about cases like Naila's or thinks about the constant stream of abuse and threats that Qandeel Baloch faced online every day, she feels she has taken on more than she can handle. But then Nighat reminds herself of her father and the building in Karachi that he helped to create all those years ago when he first moved to the city. For four decades, that building, where Mehar Allah worked tirelessly every day in order to earn enough to bring his family from their village to the city, was the tallest in Pakistan. Nighat knows that it takes time to build great, enduring things

"I'M GOING TO DO SOMETHING THAT GETS EVERYONE WORRIED"

She likes to joke that she often stays up until dawn because . . . well, do you know what happens when someone thinks of you? You get the hiccups or you cannot sleep. And do you know how many people are thinking of her late at night? By now she has more than 43,000 people following her on Twitter and 800,000 on Facebook. She has started using Instagram. It's no wonder she's tossing and turning and playing with her phone while everyone else she knows is sleeping soundly. She whiles away the time reading comments on her social media pages.

"You're a she-male and we know it."

What the fuck? That's funny.

"Fingering *karti ho tum*? [Do you finger yourself?]"

What is fingering?

"I offer you five lakh [500,000] rupees for one night fucking."

Oooof, that's bad.

"I wanna masturbate, show your boobs."

Gandi baat. Don't talk like that.

"Doggy style please."

Everyone want to fuck me.

"Shame on you."

Why? What have I done? What should I feel shame for?

"You actually deserve to b born some where in a house of slut who can fuck even only for a ride."

Same to you.

"Don't comment on this bitch because she is a lame ass retarted whore she can even lick the poop of a donkey. If I find this woman alone, I would kill her right on spot and would hide her haram body."

You watched my video. Did I tell you to watch it? Go listen to a qawwali [devotional music]. If you're so pious, why are you watching my videos? Can't sleep without watching some porn and you're here lecturing me?

They always say the same stuff. The curses have lost their bite. Come on, she encourages them in her videos, say something different to me. They respond by sending her pictures of erect penises.

Interviewers are baffled by her and can't understand why she still makes videos and puts up pictures. "We can't even show our viewers some of the comments you get on your videos," says one talk-show host. "You're a girl and you get these remarks and comments—don't you care? You still continue to do what you're doing?" What kind of woman would not care?

Here's what she has learned: it's just words. And when she doesn't read the comments, those words don't exist. She doesn't want to care about what people think of her.

If I took these people seriously, I wouldn't be alive right now.

Their words are like the barks of empty-bellied mongrels on the street that bare their teeth and drool at you as you drive past in your car. They can't touch you. Dogs bark, but who responds?

Not all of the comments are hateful. Some of her fans send her private messages on Facebook.

"I think everyone has the right to live and no one has the right to criticize anyone and besides all that you are doing great."

"I saw your video. Plz don't cry like this because you have true followers who won't like to see that . . . be happy, people love to talk and bark, so you ignore and you do what you think is right. U r so gorgeous pretty girl in the world ok so plz be happy."

A girl named Ayesha writes to her from India. "You are very beautiful. Don't be sad. Find happiness in yourself. Don't listen to the useless things others say. All the best for your bright future."

Love me or hate me, both are in my favour. If you love me, I will always be in your heart. If you hate me, I'll always be in your mind.

It has been a month since she uploaded the trailer for the striptease, but even now that's all interviewers want to talk about. And so, in April, when she is invited to be on a talk show called *Ajeeb Sa* (*Kind of Strange*), which has a humorous angle, the host asks funny questions and the overall tone is not serious, she says yes. It might be fun.

The host, Raja Matloob, likes innuendo and makes sly jokes about his guests. Every time he cracks a joke, there's a burst of canned laughter and a giggling chimpanzee pops up on the screen. The show is shot in Lahore, but the producers say it isn't a problem that Qandeel is in Karachi. She's not the only guest on the programme—she will be sharing airtime with Mufti Abdul Qavi, a cleric from Multan, and the producers will just split the screen in two. Mufti Qavi has been a regular guest on talk shows, particularly *Ajeeb Sa*, since his spat during a live interview with the actress and model Veena Malik made headlines in January 2011.

"We're going to do some fun questions," Matloob tells her during a commercial break. "Some games-type questions, OK? So that we can put out a good image."

"OK," Qandeel agrees. She glances up from her phone and smiles at him. "But if a bad image comes across, I don't have any problem."

"Since when have you been so innovative?" Matloob asks her early on in the show. "Have you been like this since childhood, or have you recently become so enlightened?"

"I don't know about innovative," Qandeel replies. "But since childhood I have been bold like this, blunt like this, and hot and sexy like this."

He asks her what she likes to eat.

"Oh, I'll eat just about anything," she replies.

"Really? How many have you eaten in your life?"

Qandeel knows he is making a crude joke about how many men she has performed oral sex on. She pretends she hasn't heard him.

Matloob asks her about the videos she makes late at night. Why does she want to be a social media celebrity?

"I chose social media over electronic media," Qandeel explains. "I'm not desperate to come on TV and be on these shows. I have self-respect." (The snickering chimp pops up on the screen.) "I'm a girl from a Baloch family, and Baloch have a very strong sense of self-respect," she continues, with the chimp and a burst of canned laughter punctuating her words. The producers run some of her videos. They have been blurred. You can only see a pixelated writhing body in some.

She is bored with talking about the promised striptease, but Matloob doesn't want to let it go. Every time he says "striptease," the producers bleep out the word. "So what if I had done it?" Qandeel asks. "Is dancing bad? And I would have stripped in my own way. They should have seen how I stripped. But our nation just got terrified. Oh my God, what's going to happen? Oh my God, what will happen? Maybe I would have stripped, maybe I wouldn't—I would have expressed my happiness about the team winning the match in my own way."

She tells Matloob she wanted to leave Pakistan for a little while after that video went viral. "I was getting a lot of threats," she confesses. He doesn't ask her about the threats, and she does not expand. "I'm still getting threats now," she adds. The chimp pops up on screen, giggling behind a paw held to its mouth. She thinks of the mongrels baring their teeth at her. "The people of this nation are like the tail of a dog," she says, using an Urdu proverb. "A dog's tail will never become straight; it'll always be crooked. I even asked the people for forgiveness, but I still get abuse. I won't keep asking for it."

It is time for the second guest to come on. "We will ask him if the way Qandeel tried to express her happiness for the cricket team was right," Matloob announces.

The camera cuts to Mufti Qavi in Multan. He is sitting before a pale green wall. He is bearded, and his beard has been trimmed to a neat point. He wears a plaid waistcoat over a beige shalwar kameez and has a dark velveteen *karakul* hat on his head. Mufti Qavi is a member of the Ruet-e-Hilal committee, the group of scholars and clerics tasked with sighting the new moon at the start and end of Ramzaan in Pakistan. For thirty days every year, millions across the country wait for the committee to announce the first fast of Ramzaan. Then, at the end of the month, when the committee sights the slivered crescent of the moon, three days of feasting for Eid follow. "I'm going to be in Karachi for the moon sighting," Mufti Qavi says to Qandeel within minutes of being introduced to her on the show. "So Inshallah we will be meeting each other."

"Many people have condemned and criticized Qandeel and her videos recently," Matloob says in his first question to Mufti Qavi. "They say that vulgarity and nudity are being spread through her videos. What do you think?"

"Qandeel has been blessed by Allah to be a Muslim," Mufti Qavi replies. "And all her talents and abilities have been gifted by Allah. So if she shows off her abilities, then she knows that she needs to keep Islam's teachings in mind when she does."

Matloob tries a more direct line of questioning. "Mufti sahib, people say that videos that are made in the bedroom need to stay in the bedroom. Do you think bedroom videos should be leaked?"

The cleric gives a long-winded answer about Islam's teachings about modesty.

Matloob isn't getting what he wants. The cleric isn't taking the bait. "Mufti sahib, is wearing a bikini a sin?" he asks.

Mufti Qavi holds forth about how women should dress modestly.

Matloob turns to Qandeel, "The offer that you made Shahid Afridi, would you make the same offer to Mufti sahib? Is it valid for him too?"

Qavi does not seem to know about Qandeel's video. Everyone else is in on the joke, but the doddering cleric does not have a clue that he is talking to a woman who promised to dance naked in front of millions of viewers. "I am certain that the way her name is beautiful, her behaviour is also beautiful," Mufti Qavi says.

Even Qandeel smirks.

Matloob gives up. He drops the light tone. Mufti Qavi isn't responding to his questions the way he had expected. "Do you know how many homes you have destroyed?" he asks Qandeel.

"Why don't you people start teaching viewers how to pray during your shows?" she retorts. "Why do you call me on your show if I have sinned so greatly?"

"We call you on the show to ask what is mentally wrong with you that you do these things," Matloob replies. "Can you show your family what you do? Can you show your parents? What about your brothers? If someone goes to your father or your brother and says, 'Look at this video of this girl,' how would you feel?"

Qandeel is taken aback. She is quiet for a few seconds then asks, "Why are you getting personal with me?"

Matloob ignores her question. "You have put these things online that so many thousands have seen—"

She interrupts him. "Not thousands," she corrects him with a smile. "Millions."

They continue to argue. A few minutes later, Matloob asks Qandeel about her family once more. "Can we watch your videos with family? Can you? Can you show the videos to your brother? And if someone shows him the videos, how would he feel?" He tells her that no Muslim girl, no girl from a good home, would behave like she does.

Mufti Qavi steps in. He is gentle with Qandeel. He chides her almost like an elderly uncle. "If there are videos or photos that she cannot look at with her children or her parents, then she should know that this is against decency and honour," he counsels. "We don't need to put a fatwa on her; she should ask herself that—can you look at those photos with your family? Are her actions according to Islam? She can decide what to do."

Neither Qandeel nor Matloob could have predicted that response. She is used to being scolded on live television by clerics. Matloob is hoping for some of that ratings gold. Even when she is no longer there to defend herself, these men will still be asked about her on talk shows.

But that day Mufti Qavi does something no other guest on a talk show with Qandeel has done. He asks her to sing something for him so he can see how beautiful her voice is. He requests a song in Arabic.

As the show wraps up, Matloob tells Qandeel, "You should meet Mufti sahib in Karachi. But promise me that when you do, you'll show him the bedroom where you make those videos." He insists, "Show Mufti Qavi the bedroom where you make the videos. Will you promise me that?" In the final few seconds of the show, Matloob says once more, "It's your right to show him the place that you show hundreds of thousands of people."

Qandeel doesn't seem to mind. She finds it funny. When the Pakistan Electronic Media Regulatory Authority condemns the Qandeel and Mufti Qavi episode of *Ajeeb Sa* for vulgarity, Qandeel defends Matloob online. She liked being on his show. She had a good time. And everything he said? They were just words. Just jokes.

She tweets a link to the episode and addresses Mufti Qavi: "Thank you, Mufti sahib! I am proud that people like you are there to represent Islam."

"People have started loosing [*sic*] interest in you," reads a comment on her latest picture.

Is it true? She tries the old tricks. She now uses hashtags to drum up interest in her photographs and videos: #unique, #kiss, #loudandproud, #boobs, #hotpicture, #shameless, #lesbian, #bigbooty, #assup. She scours Twitter to see what people are talking about. There is a video criticizing the Board of Control for Cricket in India for excluding Pakistani cricketers from the Indian Premier League. It's perfect for a new video for her fans in India.

She puts on a silky leopard-print shirt and stretches out on a soft leopard-print blanket on her bed. She has a selfie stick now, and uses it to prop up her phone to record the clip. "Are you afraid of Pakistani cricketers?" she mocks the BCCI.

She makes another video about cricket, but this time it's for Shah Rukh Khan. People are saying his cricket team, the Kolkata Knight Riders, might win the IPL (Indian Premier League). She wears a little black dress, the one she likes to wear to parties and events, the one that sheathes her arms and chest in lace. It shows off her cleavage and her breasts. She has stopped using kohl to line her eyes. She is trying a new, softer, more refined look. She no longer plucks her eyebrows to thin streaks. None of the girls do that any more. For the Shah Rukh video she puts a skinny wreath of fake flowers on her head. Some of the girls like to do that for their selfies. She promises Shah Rukh Khan that if his team wins, "I'll celebrate it, and celebrate it such that people will be shocked . . . I'm going to do something that gets everyone worried." She smacks her lips to her hand and blows the camera a kiss. "Love you all."

She falls in love with Indian cricketer Virat Kohli. She likes to draw out the "oh" until it sounds like a sigh. He has been making headlines for his relationship with actress Anushka Sharma. "Seriously, I feel that he should leave Anushka Sharma and should think about me," she says, lying back on her bed. "Virat, I love you, baby," she tells him. "Please, please, please, please, please leave Anushka. Please." She whimpers. "Please."

She puts up a video of herself in a jacuzzi and dedicates it to him. She wallows in the steaming water wearing a dark purple halter-top bikini, holds up her selfie stick and tells him, "Virat, I love you, baby." Someone opens the door behind her and walks in. They close the door but stay out of shot. The video cuts to the next shot, in which she emerges from the water and pushes back her soaked hair. "Virat, I miss you, baby." She blows a wet kiss. She has really fallen for him, she says.

To be "in," it's necessary to put up all sorts of strange pictures on social media.

She retweets all the media outlets that run a story on these videos. By May 2016 there are rumours that she might be a contestant on the Indian reality-TV show *Bigg Boss*, a spin-off of the British *Big Brother* series. She is thrilled. She shares every story that hints that she might be in the show. The Virat Kohli video is being noticed. "The famous Pakistan model who proposed [*sic*] Virat to be a part of *Bigg Boss*?" tweets a Hindi news site. Qandeel retweets it. She reaches out to the reporter who had called her Pakistan's Kim Kardashian. "Post some news about *Bigg Boss* in a positive note," she texts him. When a local newspaper asks her to confirm the *Bigg Boss* news, she states, "I have certain terms and conditions. Once those are met, I'll release a statement." When she is asked if she has applied to be on the show, she is scornful. "Why should I fill out a form? Those are for common people, not celebrities!"

There is gossip that she has been offered a role in a porn movie.

"Qandeel Baloch set to break Sunny Leone records," she tweets.

She gets a call from a woman named Amber who says she works for the BBC. Amber wants to interview her. The year before, Amber, who is based in Pakistan, met a colleague from London. "Have you seen the videos of this woman?" the colleague asked her. "She talks about how she's feeling and how she can't sleep?" Amber didn't know about the videos and looked them up.

In the first one she saw, Qandeel was moaning about having a fever. She watched another. Qandeel was complaining that she couldn't sleep. Amber had to see more. What else would this girl do? Amber showed the videos to her friends and they shared each new one on their Facebook pages and made little Dubsmash videos imitating Qandeel. Nobody in Pakistan does this kind of stuff, Amber thought to herself. She watched the videos and laughed at how the girl talked. Sometimes, Amber and her friends were bored by the videos, but then something in the latest one made them sit up and take notice.

Now, after watching so many of her videos, Amber wants to meet

Qandeel. She pitches a story to her editors in Islamabad and London. This woman represents a digital revolution in Pakistan, she tells them. A social media revolution. She is challenging Pakistani notions of what women can do. Her editors aren't impressed. What's the big deal? They are just videos.

But no one is making these kinds of videos in Pakistan, Amber insists.

The story is turned down.

The striptease trailer really helps Amber. After she sees it, she makes her case again. The editors finally agree to let her work on a story about Qandeel, but for now it will only run on the BBC's Urdu platform.

Qandeel doesn't know about any of this. She keeps Amber hanging for a little while. She doesn't reply to her messages. She doesn't commit to a meeting. She has never done a television interview with a foreign news outlet. Amber wants to film the interview at Qandeel's house. She wants to know more about her. Qandeel hesitates. She is in Lahore, she tells Amber. She doesn't want to do the interview there. The BBC can wait until she returns to Karachi.

Amber keeps messaging her. She is surprised: why does Qandeel need to be convinced to appear on a segment devoted to her on one of the best-known media platforms in the world? But the interview will only be done on Qandeel's terms. She wants it to be filmed at a hotel. Amber doesn't insist on visiting Qandeel's home. She figures she can interview her again, perhaps a few months down the road.

Qandeel asks her old friend Mansoor to come with her. He tells her to take a taxi if she needs a ride to the hotel. It's not that, she explains. I want them to meet my friends. My decent friends. Please come with me for support. He tells her he can't make it.

During the interview she wants to be seen in the hotel gym and she wants to swim. She is the only woman in the pool. All the men cannot help staring at her. She swims up to the camera and, once she is close, emerges from the water to give a loud smacking kiss. Her bright orange wetsuit clings to her as she steps out of the pool and stretches out on a lounge chair. She wants to do the interview by the pool. She agrees to sing.

Some time after this interview airs, Qandeel hears from Mufti Qavi. "I promised I would meet you," he reminds her. He is going to be in Karachi before the month of Ramzaan starts in June. He sends her details of his itinerary. She is travelling and says she cannot meet him. He persists. He is going to be in Karachi to appear on a TV show some time later in the month. She agrees to meet him, but then, on the day they are supposed to meet, she tells him she is not feeling well. The third time he gets in touch, he says he will be in Karachi for a few days in the last week of June. He is appearing on another TV show. She apologizes for not being able to meet sooner. He wants to have iftari, the meal to break the Ramzaan fast, with her. She wants to meet in the afternoon instead. She calls him and they meet at his hotel on 20 June.

They are in his room. She makes a video using her selfie stick. She draws the curtains closed and tells Mufti Qavi she likes to smoke Marlboro Lights. He is on the phone, seated on a sofa behind her. He tells her to be careful. She must not take any photographs that make either of them look . . . Well, she should know what he means. She assures him she will keep that in mind.

She takes a few pictures. After all, she is the selfie queen. Her followers on social media will be anxious to see pictures of her with Mufti Qavi. Would he mind . . . ? She leans in next to him and snaps a photograph. He has taken off his glasses. He is not smiling. She puts on his karakul cap. She arches an eyebrow and stares into the camera, her mouth open in a perfect O, feigning shock. Mufti Qavi stands next to her. His mobile phone is pressed to his ear and he is mid-sentence. He is no longer wearing his waistcoat, and his hair is slightly tousled. "Yayyyy," Qandeel captions the photos on Twitter. "Having memorable time with #mufti Abdul Qavi."

When she sits next to him, after she has recorded the video she needed and snapped some more selfies while wearing his karakul hat, he tries to kiss her. He wants to hug her. She laughs and tells him not to do that.

"I know," he says. "You can't trap a girl in the first meeting. As our relationship develops, we will become more open with each other." He tells her he isn't fasting—for her sake—and isn't bound by any of the restrictions placed on a man who is keeping the fast. They share a Coke and some tea he has ordered for her, and he takes a few drags from her cigarette. When we share things, it increases the love between us, he tells her.

He promises to help her meet Imran Khan. She still loves him, doesn't she? Mufti Qavi is the head of Khan's party's religious wing, he says. She wants to shoot a small video of him promising that he will take her to meet Imran Khan.

Mufti Qavi wants to marry her. They can keep it a secret, and he is willing to give her anything in exchange, he promises. Imran Khan is too old for you, he insists. Forget him.

He keeps trying to kiss her but stops when she chides him, but then he tries again. Several times people knock on the door, but he gets rid of them. He tells Qandeel he knows just how to seduce a woman; what a man could do to give her pleasure.

Wow, Mufti sahib knows how to romance, she thinks.

Qandeel puts the videos and photographs on her social media pages. The videos are played over and over on the news. The photographs go viral. The story about the sexy young model meeting the Muslim cleric is a hit. "Qandeel Baloch claims Mufti Qavi hopelessly in love with her!" declares the headline in one newspaper. "When Qandeel Baloch met Mufti Qavi: a guideline on how NOT to learn Islam," says another.

A very public row takes place between Qandeel and Mufti Qavi. Who is telling the truth about the meeting? Mufti Qavi tells everyone that Qandeel called him first—she insisted on meeting and coming to his hotel room. She wanted to be alone with him, he said.

She says he is lying. "I thought there would be some betterment in [meeting him] for me," she tells reporters. "I party a lot, I thought it would be beneficial to me if I spent some time around someone who is religious. He called me." A few weeks later, she remarks to an interviewer off the record that Mufti Qavi was actually interested in setting her up with a friend of his.

Amber's BBC editors in London sit up and take note. They want to run Qandeel's BBC Urdu interview again, close to a month after it first aired, but this time the editors do not need to be convinced that she is worth the airtime. The interview is given a spot on the network's main platform, accessible to millions around the world, not just on the BBC's Urdu site. The editors go back and forth once more—not to discuss whether the story deserves to be told, but to ask themselves if it is still safe to air the interview because Qandeel is now pleading with the government to provide her with protection against the threats she is receiving from Mufti Qavi's supporters.

Later, Qandeel's parents will tell the media about the day their daughter called them and said she had been terrified alone in that hotel room with Mufti Qavi. She told them she had slapped him and tried to get away. And then when he looked at her, his eyes turned dark with rage. He looked like a ghoul and she was scared he would grab her. She couldn't even imagine what he wanted from her. What he wanted to do to her.

THE MUFTI

"**I** know it's not right to have your palm read . . . " Hina says. But there is something about her brother that's important to know in order to understand him—in order to understand all that had happened between her brother and Qandeel Baloch—better. When he was younger, Hina's elder brother Abdul Qavi was taken to a skin doctor for some ailment. The doctor also dabbled in palmistry and liked to look at his patients' hands and tell them whatever he could see. He uncurled Abdul's fist and ran his fingers over the faint spidery lines on the boy's palm. He is unusual, the doctor told Abdul's parents. He might have even said extraordinary. Abdul is intelligent. But there will be many who are jealous of this. There will be many who are against him, who will not like how intelligent and extraordinary he is. Just as the sun rises to its peak, so too will Abdul. And just as the sun reaches in its flaming ascent the point known as *zawal*—a time when some Muslims believe it is forbidden to pray and others say it is the moment when the everlasting fire in hell is kindled afresh—so too will Abdul's life have a moment of zawal. A time of misfortune.

Abdul's sisters saw that he was careless with his tongue, that he was too trusting, too naive. "My father would tell us, 'Explain this to your brother. He says things in jest and he does not realise that every person is not his friend,'" Hina says. She teaches women how to read and understand the Quran, and in Multan she is known as *Apa* (elder sister) among those who flock to her classes. "This is one of the first things the Quran teaches us: how to hold your tongue. But my brother lacks this ability. When people know that about you, they will try to exploit this weakness. Even now, even after everything that has happened, he will not change. Whatever happened to him was a trial from Allah."

But Allah looks out for His beloved ones, she says. "It is Allah's grace that has saved my brother." After all, it is at times such as a trial, when your heart is hurting and you feel forsaken, that you are drawn closer to Allah. That is what happened to her brother after he decided to meet Qandeel, Hina believes. That woman was a test of Abdul's faith. She ushered in a time of great uncertainty and bad luck for Abdul—the zawal the doctor had foreseen all those years ago.

Abdul Qavi and his three sisters were born and raised in Multan, as was his father and his father before him, and so on for decades. His family can trace its lineage in the city back 300 years, he says. The fifty-nine-year-old cleric still lives there with his wife, his three daughters and their children, in a small house located at the back of the Darul Uloom Ubaidia, the madrassa that he runs in Multan's Qadirabad neighbourhood. "Look for the street that is crowded with the halva and milk sellers," he said when giving me directions to his home. "You'll know you're near me when you smell sweet wafts of halva. Let that be your guide." And if you get lost, he instructed, just ask any man on the street where you can find Mufti Abdul Qavi. Everyone here knows him.

I do get lost. I cannot find the halva sellers. And no one—not shopkeepers, guards, traffic policemen, rickshaw drivers, men idling on the side of the road, men squatting on donkey carts—knows Mufti Abdul Qavi's name or where his madrassa is. When I finally find it, the place smells of nothing. The madrassa is located in a lane off a small square. A man leans against a cart laden with fish. They have been gutted and laid open to the sun as the blood congeals on their gleaming scales. A milk seller places a plastic dummy milk bottle as tall as a man outside his shop and paints its creamy white surface with a menu—cardamom milk, milk with crushed almonds, cold milk soda. A billboard for "Gorgeous Beauty Saloon & Institute," sun-bleached black and white with tinges of green, has been fixed above the milk shop.

The swinging glass doors to a shop selling "Multan's famous *sohan* halva here since 1970" are closed. There is no one inside and a barber has set up shop on the kerb. An old man sits on a high chair before a table with a mirror propped against an electricity pole. He stares at his reflection as the barber tilts his head, clutches his tufts of greying hair to hold him steady and strokes a razor down the side of his jaw.

The madrassa, flanked by a shop where a boy is slapping pats of dough inside a hot tandoor, has a faded date painted at the entrance: 1862. Inside, visitors are welcomed with a sign that reads, "This is a school for those who seek knowledge; the streams of knowledge that flow from here shall never run dry."

"All of this," Mufti Qavi says, drawing an arc with his arm from the milk seller to the boy with the naan to the madrassa established 155 years ago and the two mosques—one set up by his uncle—further down the lane, "this whole street is ours." When Qandeel was murdered, there was talk about Mufti Qavi's connections with the village where her family still lives. There was speculation that his photographs with Qandeel had tarnished his reputation in Shah Sadar Din and that he was furious about that. But Mufti Qavi rubbishes these claims. "I have nothing to do with that place," he wants people to know. "But my great-grandfather was married to a girl whose family was from there." The girl's father had been the prayer leader at the village mosque. That connection meant that people from the village had gone to Mufti Qavi's ancestors to study the Quran and receive religious guidance. "Everyone who is running a madrassa or mosque there, or anyone who prays there, has likely been taught to do so by my family," he says. He only returns to the village now on "happy or sad occasions."

Mufti Qavi spends his days in the offices abutting the madrassa.

The two-storey building is centred around a courtyard used as a parking space. The first floor has rooms to accommodate any guests of the madrassa. Mufti Qavi's office itself is small and carpeted, with a few dark green shelves stacked with books. The walls have been painted a sickly pale green with a glittery sheen as if glass has been crushed into the paint. The colour is streaked in some places and chipped in others, revealing slate-grey concrete beneath. The room doesn't get any sun, and the bright white phosphorescent lights stay on until Mufti Qavi leaves for the day. There is no privacy. The windows do not have curtains, and the door stays open all day. He points out that there is no guard at the gate or the entrance to the office. Mufti Qavi wants his visitors to know that he has nothing to hide. Anyone can look into his office. Anyone can walk in to give Mufti Qavi a box of mithai as thanks for solving a particular issue or to fold a wad of notes—rent for the properties he owns in Multan, he explains—into his hand, and he will pause briefly in the middle of whatever he is doing to say "salaam" before continuing a conversation or helping someone who has come to him for advice.

When he speaks, his visitors know not to interrupt. He sways gently back and forth and projects his voice as though addressing a gathering or standing at a lectern rather than sitting in a room that can accommodate six or seven people at best. When he becomes impassioned, his voice rises like he is trying to drown out someone else's words. If his phone rings while he is speaking, he will answer the call but keep the caller on hold until his sentence is complete. Only then will he turn his attention to the call. Once he has had his say, he will hang up with a quick "Peace be with you." Callers rarely get to question or argue with anything he has said.

Most of the space in the office is taken up by a low, hefty slab of wood topped with a sheet of glass. Mufti Qavi sits at this "desk" cross-legged on a small raised wooden platform with a bolster at his back. When meeting journalists, attending an event or taking part in a television show, Mufti Qavi likes to wear a waistcoat and his karakul cap. Today he wears a grey waistcoat and a cap threaded with embroidery. His beard is clipped to a precise point under his chin, and when he smiles his cheeks lift in two cheery, plump points, and his small eyes, often difficult to see behind the light that glints off the glasses he always wears, narrow into slits. His hair and his beard are an even black. There is no grey, no salt and pepper. His nails are neatly trimmed and his hands smooth and pale. There are no creases in his cream-coloured shalwar kameez. But when he sits at his desk on that wooden platform you see his feet. The soles are ash-grey, the skin is calloused around the toes and his nails broken and jagged.

He is particular about the placement of books, stationery and papers on the desk, sliding them across the glass until the corners of all the books are aligned with the edge of the table and the papers lined up next to the books before he speaks or acknowledges visitors. And they in turn must be seated in a particular way in this room. Visitors accompanying someone, or those who want to sit in on a particular meeting to glean some religious knowledge, must sit on the floor directly opposite Mufti Qavi. Men who come to Mufti Qavi for guidance or religious instruction must sit to his left, while women go to the right.

"Come closer." He beckons to me, pointing to the carpeted floor on his right side.

He clicks his tongue. "Closer."

He pats a spot that is within arm's reach of him. "Come on," he cajoles. "More closer."

There's a reason for this seating arrangement, he explains, and the story tumbles out. Akbar, the Mughal king who was married four times, had yet to have a son. Two of Akbar's wives were Hindu and two were Muslim. Now, to cut a long story short, one of the Hindu wives gave birth to a son. Of course, many Muslim clerics today—not Mufti Qavi but many others—say that Hindus and Muslims cannot get married, and so you can just imagine what they would call a baby born from a union between a Muslim and a Hindu, a word that Mufti Qavi would not like to say in front of me, a woman whom he has just met but whom he looks upon as his daughter, but of course we all know what that word is, but anyway back to the story. Whenever Akbar's Hindu or Muslim subjects came to visit him, Akbar would have the Hindus sit to his left, and the Muslims to the right. When one Hindu objected that the king was treating the two groups differently, a wise vizier helped Akbar out of a potentially sticky argument by explaining, "The king has seated his Hindu subjects to his left, so that his heart faces you."

Mufti Qavi loves this story. When women visit him with their fathers, brothers or husbands and appeal to him for help with domestic issues—and he is often on their side, you see, and scolds the husband who beats his wife or the father who wishes to forcibly marry off his daughter the moment she hits puberty—no one can claim that Mufti Qavi is biased towards them. For his heart, he says, quoting the vizier, looks upon the men.

"Now, come closer," he says. "You see, I don't like to speak loudly. Everyone in my home knows this—from the children to the wife. If I must call someone, I just—" he claps his hands together like a magician "—do this. I don't like loud voices at all. Now, say in the name of Allah, and . . ." He folds his hands and rests them on his stomach. He bows his head and closes his eyes. It's hard to tell if he is praying or if he would like you to know that you have his utmost attention. "Ask me anything," he encourages, his eyes shut.

Mufti Qavi is clearly used to having an audience. His appearance on Raja Matloob's show with Qandeel was not his first or last on national television. In January 2011 he had been on TV with Pakistani actress Veena Malik, who had been voted off the Indian reality TV show *Bigg Boss*.

Malik had spent eighty-four days in the *Bigg Boss* house before she was evicted. As an article in the English daily the *News* noted, "When the show started off, hardly anybody in India knew of [Veena Malik]. But by the end of the first week, she had the audience agog."[1] Malik struck up a friendship with an actor named Ashmit Patel, and was not afraid to be seen "openly fondling him on screen and sitting in secluded corners . . . having long, intimate discussions," the article stated. They kissed and hugged often and there were rumours that they had had sex while in the house together. Malik dressed in skirts, shorts and high heels on the show, and in one episode wore a bathing suit as she joined the other residents of the house in the pool. This did not go do down well with the audience in Pakistan.

In January 2011, fresh from her sojourn in India, Malik was invited on to a talk show on Express News to defend her actions in the *Bigg Boss* house to Pakistani viewers. "There is an allegation against you, made by a segment of Pakistani society, that you brought dishonour upon Pakistani culture in India," the host Kamran Shahid said to Malik. "Your dresses and your actions, as well as your interactions with people there, did not represent the ideological foundations of Pakistan, its culture or its people. As a cultural ambassador of Pakistan, do you regret your actions—if these allegations are true—or do you think the allegations are baseless?"

Malik said she did not set out to represent Pakistan, nor could she have acted as a cultural ambassador on the show. "I was there to represent the Veena Malik of Pakistan's entertainment industry," she argued.

"So what you're saying is that the entertainment industry is vulgar and encourages nudity?" Shahid countered.

Before Malik could explain herself further, Shahid cut to the night's second guest, Mufti Qavi. "Mufti sahib, I'm going to stay neutral," Shahid said, "but you on the other hand have an opinion about all this." Mufti Qavi told Malik that her actions had saddened his heart and the hearts of millions in the country who liked and respected her. Allah had blessed her with beauty and grace, he said, and showing off that beauty and grace was permissible, but within certain parameters. "After all, Allah loves beautiful things," he lectured. "But if [Veena Malik's] conscience is alive, she needs to look at her pictures and ask herself if what she has done is right or wrong." He would give remarkably similar advice to Qandeel five years later during their interview on *Ajeeb Sa*.

Malik said her conscience told her she had done nothing wrong. The argument swiftly escalated. Mufti Qavi told Malik he was hurt by what she had just said. "No Pakistani can sit with his daughter and look at those images of you," he said, his voice rising. The host tried to get Mufti Qavi to be quiet, so that Malik could respond, but the cleric shouted over him, "Whenever she has a son, he will not be able to look at these images of her. Her father and her brother could never look at them."

"If you want to come and talk to me about Islam, then you should know that you are not permitted to even look at me right now," Malik responded. She ran her fingers through her wavy chestnut-brown hair. She was wearing a low-cut sleeveless black top and she leaned forward as she addressed Mufti Qavi. She wanted to know how he could praise her beauty and grace when, according to Islam, he could not gaze at a woman who was not related to him. "You should be punished for that," she said. Instead of lecturing her on Islam, Mufti Qavi should turn his attention to other problems in the country, she suggested. "Go and look at what the politicians are doing. What about bribes and robbery? What about murders in the name of Islam? Why are you picking on Veena Malik? Because I'm a woman? Why me? Because I'm a soft target."

Mufti Qavi tried to reply, but Malik would not let him. She told him to "focus on the clerics who rape the children who come to study in their madrassas." Mufti Qavi asked her to refrain from attacking him, but Malik would not be stopped. "If you follow the Prophet Muhammad (PBUH), then you would know that he was a man who stood up in respect for women," she scolded him. "He would not call them dishonourable . . . Just because you're a mufti, you think that you can accuse a woman of anything and pass a fatwa on her whenever you feel like it?"

Shahid did not intervene as his guests continued to shout at each other for nearly twenty minutes.

"I speak on behalf of all those who say that your behaviour was so horrifying that to call you a Pakistani or to call you a Muslim would be an insult to Pakistan and an insult to Islam," Qavi told Malik. However, a few minutes later, when she asked him which actions in particular had angered him, Qavi admitted that he had never watched *Bigg Boss*. "I did not watch your programme, but millions of Pakistanis who did say that your behaviour was an insult to Pakistan and Islam," he hastily added.

Malik won. Qavi looked like a fool—a man who had passed judgement on a woman's character when he did not know very much about her at all, and who did not hesitate to call her behaviour blasphemous or insulting to Islam in a country where such an accusation can be punished by death.

Their exchange was widely reported locally and internationally, with many praising Malik for taking on the clergy. Audio of Malik's retorts during the show was even remixed into a viral song featuring the line, "*Mufti sahib, ye kya baat hui*? [Mufti sahib, what is this?]"[2] The line entered pop culture as a meme. An opinion piece in the English-language daily *Dawn* maintained that Malik's "articulate, proto-feminist defence on television garnered unexpected support from the liberal intelligentsia," while Mufti Qavi was derided as a "hapless cleric (who claimed not to have seen what he was happy to comment on)." A blog for the same newspaper argued that the episode had been "brilliant because in an hour it summarized everything that is wrong with this country and our mindset."

For many Malik was the star of that show. What they didn't realise, however, was that producers at television channels across the country realised that in Mufti Qavi they had a potential ingredient for a hit show—one that might not be critically praised but would be watched and talked about. The Malik–Qavi spat had been a ratings success. "When did Mufti Qavi the cleric who just ran a madrassa become Mufti Qavi the media darling?" asked a local journalist in Multan. "It was on that show. Before that, people didn't know his name. He was just one of dozens of clerics here and he would only be invited on talk shows sometimes to talk about the sighting of the moon or some other religious matter."

The words that Veena Malik taunted him with—when he spoke of her beauty and grace—drew many, especially journalists in Multan, to Mufti Qavi. They believed that he was only being honest in praising a beautiful woman; he was not pretending to be a religious scholar immune to the pleasures of the material world. And even though those journalists do not want to be associated with him today, then they praised him as a "liberal *maulvi* [cleric]." Initially, he was embraced by the media fraternity in Multan as someone who was approachable. He was available at a moment's notice for a press conference, a live call or a show. "Everyone in the media knew which maulvi was always ready to be on TV," explained one reporter. "And he could talk about everything from politics to transgender rights, and he didn't just drone on with a lecture like some of the others."

Mufti Qavi gave good TV: he got into arguments, he could be charming, he was witty and cracked jokes with his fellow guests. He was entertaining. In 2015 he made an appearance on a talk show with a glamorous, mouthy transgender rights activist named Almas Bobby.[3] He flirted with Bobby, who was wearing a bright red and gold sari, and joked that they would get married. "I have a very open mind and an open heart," he said as she playfully swatted his arm. He only wanted 35 rupees dowry, but he needed to go home and ask his wife for permission to get married to her, he said. The audience, mainly women, giggled and clapped, and Bobby swooned and clutched Mufti Qavi's shoulder.

Some said his behaviour was not appropriate; others liked seeing a cleric let loose. "Why should we expect our maulvis to always be sitting in the mosque, stroking their big beards and holding prayer beads in their hands?" asked one of Mufti Qavi's friends. "Why can't a cleric have fun?"

Many journalists and producers who booked him for prime-time shows said that Mufti Qavi was knowledgeable—he knew how to make an argument and he was well read. "Whatever you wanted him to give a fatwa or an opinion on, he could do it," said a reporter. "Other religious scholars didn't want to sit with women on live TV or talk about women's issues. But we knew that if you made Mufti Qavi do it, you'd have a hell of a show."

Mufti Qavi would stay in touch with reporters and send them his itinerary any time he travelled. That way, they knew exactly where he was if they needed him at a studio or to be available for a call. Soon he was the first name that came to mind when a cleric was needed to chip in on any topic. Journalists in Multan like to tell how every second or third day you could see a television van parked outside Mufti Qavi's home. His knowledge of Islam and his frequent appearances on TV as the representative of the majority of Pakistanis served as a short cut to influence. There is a rumour that that he was a member of a secret WhatsApp group of senators, who would turn to him for advice or suggestions on political matters. He was invited to officiate at marriages between some of Multan's richest families, including those of high-ranking officers in the army.

Many journalists and reporters in Multan say that their professional relationship with Mufti Qavi gradually turned into a friendship—or at least a relationship where they felt comfortable confiding in him and asking him for counsel. One reporter explained that many men would go to Mufti Qavi to talk about things that they felt too ashamed to approach anyone else with. He encourages "frankness"—it's a word he uses often—and when he has an intimate discussion with someone, he likes to brag about their "frankness ka level." When those journalists who had befriended Mufti Qavi heard what Qandeel said about their meeting, when she accused him of being too "frank" or inappropriate, they believed her. "Maybe the things he was saying were new for Qandeel," one of his friends said, "but for us, it was not surprising at all. We knew he was like this." However, Mufti Qavi has since learned to take certain precautions—at one point in our meeting he asks me to turn off the tape recorder so that he may ask me something "while being frank."

"Mufti sahib is able to make you feel comfortable and draw you out," the reporter explains. "He is the kind of cleric who is also human. He doesn't hide under a cloak of morality. He tries to see where he can create paths for you—and your desires—within the ambit of religion. We could talk to him about boyfriends, girlfriends, or relationships outside of marriage." And besides, this reporter said, Mufti Qavi seemed to be that rare thing: a cleric "who loves to talk about sex." He didn't make religion feel removed from modern life.

"We would spend evenings with him and ask him all sorts of vulgar questions," one reporter said, giggling. "No, I don't want to say what the questions were. I'm feeling shy. But when we asked him these things, he didn't judge us. Any other cleric would have cursed us." This reporter once played a prank on Mufti Qavi. He visited him to record a short interview for a piece on relationships between students and teachers after there had been a highly publicized case of harassment at a local school. When Mufti Qavi's opinion had been recorded, the reporter pretended to turn off the camera but actually kept recording and asked him a question about the religious angle when it came to girls dating their teachers. He wanted to catch the cleric saying something scandalous. "He gave me an excellent answer," the reporter said. "He opened up his books and showed me examples and used logic to talk about the issue. If you want a modern version of Islam, he's the guy to go to. He is the true preacher of liberal Islam, and in Pakistan there are very few clerics you can say that about."

Mufti Qavi's interviews appealed to religiously moderate Pakistanis, and he discussed women's rights when few clerics were doing so publicly. "Religious scholars need to be in line with the needs of the world and the time they're living in," he tells me. "We need to learn to speak in English. We cannot just rely on Arabic. We should speak well in Urdu. Perhaps we should even know how to speak Chinese. Because we don't just need the education we get in madrassas. We need maths, science, geography and so on. There must be religious education and regular education. Our children—and especially our girls—need this."

He is irritated by those who try to make Islam seem unyielding. During our meeting he receives a call. A man has just lost his wife and wants to know whether it is permissible for him to touch his wife's shrouded body at her last rites. "This is just against intellect," Mufti Qavi clucks when he ends the call. "If my wife, who has been with me for fifty years, leaves this world, can I not hug her? Can I not kiss her? She's a piece of my heart. Some maulvi has told this man that to even look at your wife's body is haram."

This, he exclaims, is the difference between Mufti Abdul Qavi and everyone else. This is why, he insists, other clerics criticize him. It has nothing to do with his TV appearances or his behaviour. "They are angry that Mufti Qavi has made them redundant," he says. "I have wiped out the work they did for a hundred or two hundred years. I have eroded the influence they enjoyed here when they gave people opinions like this." He tells me that if he hadn't been a religious scholar, he would have carried over this tendency to question popular opinion and rules in another profession. "I am revolutionary," he explains. "If I was a professor, a politician or a businessman, I would still be revolutionary. Because what you have to understand is that 'Mufti Qavi' is the name of a revolution."

By 2016, Mufti Qavi had perfected the persona of the affable, fun-loving cleric. It's easy to see why the producers of *Ajeeb Sa* liked having him on. A month before the episode with Qandeel, Mufti Qavi had been on the show with an actress named Sheen.[4] When Sheen told him she was a fan of Imran Khan, he said he could introduce her to the politician. In 2013 he had been made president of the religious-affairs wing of Khan's Pakistan Tehreek-e-Insaf party and often arranged meetings between religious scholars and the party's leaders. It was the same offer he would make to Qandeel.

It's hard to conceive of another cleric answering the kind of questions put to him that night. "Do you like to go on long drives?" Sheen asked him. "Are you able to?" Later, "When is the first time you lost your heart to someone?" It was easy to make light of Islamic injunctions with Mufti Qavi and make jokes that other clerics might find offensive. During the same episode the host asked Mufti Qavi if it was permissible to contract a *nikkah* [marriage] with a woman over the phone. What about through a group chat on WhatsApp so that you could have the requisite two witnesses?

Mufti Qavi had earned himself a reputation as a misogynist from the Veena Malik interview but then began to portray himself as a champion of women's rights. Five years later, as he sat with Sheen, Mufti Qavi had learned to temper his responses when asked a question about women or women's issues. "What if your parents want you to marry someone and you want to marry another person? Is it disobedi-ence to refuse?" he was asked on that episode of *Ajeeb Sa*.

"Not at all!" Mufti Qavi replied. "According to Islam, women are utterly independent when it comes to their choice of who to marry." He was no longer afraid to be ridiculed for his love of beautiful women. He described himself as "*zinda dil*"—one whose heart is passionate. "When-ever I travel, I look around to see who is the most beautiful woman on the aeroplane or in the airport," he said on *Ajeeb Sa*. "You see, the Holy Prophet (PBUH) said that when you see someone who is beautiful, you ask them to pray for you. Because if Allah has blessed them with beauty, then he will also listen to their prayers. Allah is beautiful, and he loves beauty. So, if I see a beautiful woman in an airport, I make it a point to go stand in the same line as her. And in the aeroplane I look for the most beautiful air hostesses. I like to ask them to pray for me."

"Have you ever been involved in a scandal?" the host asked.

"I have done things in the past that could have resulted in me get-ting stuck in a scandal, but Allah is Sattar, and that means 'one who veils sin,'" Mufti Qavi replied with a grin.

The Multan bureau chief of a television station who has known Mufti Qavi for around two decades explains, "If you had met him earlier, be-fore all of this, you would have wanted to meet him again and again. You just have to remember that he's an ordinary man who knows more about religion than you or me. He's no angel. But one thing's for sure: just like any ordinary man, Mufti Qavi has the devil inside of him too."

I told Mufti Qavi I wanted to know what had happened in that hotel room when Qandeel Baloch met him in Karachi in June 2016. In inter-views since then his version of events has changed with each retelling.

He knew the photos didn't look good. He should have never let her wear his cap. That's what ruined it all, he confided in a friend. The cap. As for his waistcoat—he had merely taken it off because he needed to do his ablutions for prayer. When he came out of the bathroom in his hotel room, Qandeel was already wearing his cap and wanted to take a photo.

The story changed. She was not wearing a dupatta to cover her head and she felt bad about it, so he offered her his cap. No, she asked him if she could borrow his cap. Well, actually there had been a few people in the hotel room with them—his followers in Karachi—and when he saw these guests to the door and returned to where Qandeel was sitting, she was wearing his cap. Either way, it didn't look good.

She had perched on the arm of the sofa he was sitting on. He counselled her to remain respectful, and she chided him, "Mufti sahib, your heart must be veiled." It was important that their hearts were filled with modesty, she felt. The rest did not matter. She needed to take some pictures with him. Just as he had fans and followers, so did she—and hers were online and they would want to see proof that she had met Mufti Qavi.

"This was all part of the plan," Mufti Qavi now says with a sigh. "I should have stopped her but I didn't want to seem rude." The plan, he says, was for Qandeel to sell the photographs to the highest bidder among Mufti Qavi's "enemies."

The day after the photos went viral, Qandeel and Mufti Qavi were invited on to Mubasher Lucman's talk show, *Khara Such*. "Mufti Qavi and Qandeel's photographs are all over social media," Lucman said at the start of the interview on 21 June 2016. "And both of them, for various reasons, have been in the news many times. It seems Mufti Qavi likes to be in the news, and since Qandeel is in showbiz, she enjoys it as well."[5]

Mufti Qavi seemed to be wearing the same waistcoat and cap from the day he had met Qandeel at the hotel, while she wore a black shirt that left her shoulders bare, and held a wrap around herself, fidgeting with it often as she tried to cover her shoulders or her chest.

For the previous twenty-four hours Mufti Qavi had been ridiculed in the media. He had been referred to as "the Qandeel Baloch of maulvis." "When Qandeel Baloch met Mufti Qavi: a guideline on how NOT to learn Islam," mocked a story in the English-language daily *Express Tribune*. "Qandeel Baloch claims Mufti Qavi 'hopelessly in love' with her!" announced *Pakistan Today*. Almost every channel ran a story on the meeting between "scandal queen Qandeel Baloch" and the cleric.[6] The video Qandeel had shot in which Mufti Qavi promised to introduce her to Imran Khan was played over and over again.

Even after everything that has happened, Mufti Qavi wants people to know that the thing that saddens him the most is that he was only trying to help Qandeel. "I've never told anyone this, but I spoke with Imran Khan's secretary," he says. "I spoke with a close friend of his. This friend picked up my call immediately, you know. We talked in great detail. This person who is so close to Imran Khan said that he would meet Qandeel a few days after Eid."

Mufti Qavi also has friends in India and tells me he promised Qandeel that he would speak to them about getting her on to *Bigg Boss*. And that he had called the owner of one of Pakistan's most-watched television channels and pleaded with him to give Qandeel a chance to perform a naat on any show. After she was killed, the police questioned him about phone records that showed he had called her three times right after they met. He was only calling her to let her know about Imran Khan, *Bigg Boss* and the naat, you see. "Now you tell me," he says with a sigh. "If I call someone my *beti* [daughter] and help her like this, why would I do whatever she said I did?"

On Lucman's show neither Qandeel nor Mufti Qavi mentioned these phone calls. Qandeel insinuated that Mufti Qavi had tried to proposition her—he "made me an offer," she said demurely. Lucman wanted to know why Mufti Qavi met Qandeel alone and what they did in the room together. "Let me explain one thing to you very clearly," he said to the cleric. "Until I get answers to my questions, this programme will keep running." The show overshot its time by an hour and a half as Lucman's guests squabbled about what had happened in that hotel.

Qavi said that Qandeel had confided in him about her family life and told him about her father, who was unwell or injured. This was a detail about Qandeel's personal life that had until then never been revealed. Lucman did not ask Qandeel if it was true or how Mufti Qavi could have known something like that if Qandeel had not told him.

Lucman invited the deputy secretary general of Imran Khan's political party, Imran Ismail, to weigh in via a phone interview. "Mufti Qavi does not hold any office in the PTI; he never has and, God willing, he never will," Ismail said. "I will ask Imran Khan to never let people like Mufti Qavi in the party. What he has done is a stain on the name of Islam. It's very clear what his intentions were when he called an unmarried young woman into his hotel room alone."

Mufti Qavi grinned widely.

"Mufti sahib sits on TV shows and satiates his lust with the things he says," Ismail continued. He mentioned the interviews about beautiful women. "How would Mufti sahib feel if some man spoke to his wife or daughters this way? There is no better way to disrespect a religion than what he has done." Ismail's next few words were unprecedented. "Mufti Qavi needs to apologize," he said. "Whatever Qandeel Baloch is doing, at least she is doing it in front of the whole world. There's no hypocrisy, whether it's right or wrong . . . but Mufti Qavi is a scholar of Islam and he has a nation following him and he did all of this."

Few Pakistanis would ever have seen a cleric shamed on national television in this way, and even fewer would have seen a woman like Qandeel praised over a cleric.

"Even now," Ismail continued, addressing Mufti Qavi, whose face remained fixed with that grin, "you have a smile on your face and there is no trace of shame for what you have done."

Today, to me, Mufti Qavi explains why he did not appear worried, angry or ashamed during that interview. He did not raise his voice or attempt to silence his critics. He was serene and for the most part smiled pleasantly as if he could not hear the things that were being said about him. He says he knew Qandeel had been paid to appear on Lucman's show and how the host wanted him to behave. He was supposed to shout and argue and lose his temper. He had expected the things that were said about him. He was prepared. "I wanted to show that none of it affected me," he explains, chuckling. "Those people on the show just wanted to create hatred for men of religion. They wanted to show, and may Allah forgive me for saying this, that I am some kind of—" he lowers his voice "—sexy man of God."

The day after the Lucman interview aired, Mufti Qavi was removed from the Ruet-e-Hilal committee. The PTI issued a notice saying he had been stripped of his membership of the party. Once more he was just another maulvi who ran a madrassa in Multan.

Qandeel tweeted the news and mocked people with "fake faces."

Mufti Qavi headed back home from Karachi and wondered what he would say to his wife and sisters when he saw them. He felt embarrassed. He had lost everything that he valued. Everything he had achieved in the last six years had been erased by two or three minutes of video and a few questionable photographs. He felt forsaken.

His car pulled up to his house. As he got out, he recounts to me, he felt his phone vibrate in his pocket. Once, twice, three times. In the space of three minutes, a string of five text messages arrived. They were from Qandeel. Even today he can recite the messages he says she sent him.

"I am sorry Mufti sahib, what happened was bad it should not have happened."

"It's all my fault."

"Please forgive me if you can."

"Whatever happened to you was not right I'm really sorry."

"The one who forgives has a big heart."

He walked into his home with a great big grin on his face. This was Allah's grace. Just when his faith had been tested and he had wondered why such misfortune had come his way, Allah had sent him a small sign as if to say, You will be victorious.

After all, if he had really kissed and hugged Qandeel and said he wanted to marry her, if he had really done something wrong, then why was she the one apologizing? Even today Mufti Qavi keeps photocopies of those text messages—blurry pictures taken of the phone—to show to journalists, friends and family. He says he has lost the phone he originally received the messages on.

In the days after the Lucman interview aired, Mufti Qavi received dozens of phone calls from admirers and well-wishers all over the world. They told him not to worry; they would always support him. They said terrible things about Qandeel. The names they called her are too terrible to repeat. They made his heart tremble. Mufti Qavi will utter those names if you ask him to, but only if you also accept the sin of saying such words. "*Gushti*," he says, spitting out the word. Whore. They knew the names of the men she visited at night, his followers said. We'll have her picked up, they promised Mufti Qavi, and then just see what we do to her. Some of them told him exactly what they planned to do to her.

The police later told him that thousands—yes, thousands; he has many followers, you see—of phone numbers that showed up on his call records matched the ones on Qandeel's records.

"Now what can you say to these followers, these passionate men?" Mufti Qavi asks. "If Imran Khan can have followers—" he thumps his desk in indignation at the suggestion that clerics might not have thousands of zealous followers who promise murder "—then why can't Mufti Qavi?" Thump. "After all," he asks, "aren't you my follower now that you have come here to meet me? Now that I've told you everything about myself and how I care deeply for women?"

The day Mufti Qavi is lowered into the ground, thousands of those followers—especially women—will come to his home, he promises. They will tell his wife and sisters, Your brother was our brother and our father. He knows it. And to those who say he should not behave inappropriately with female followers, "There are two kinds of people in this world. One will dig a well in the middle of the road so that any traveller who drinks from it will send him their blessings. But another man would close up that well because he fears someone could fall into it in the dead of night. Now, both those men will get Allah's blessings." So, if Mufti Qavi calls a woman his daughter and she kisses his hand and feels some relief or if she whispers her problems in his ear, what is wrong with that? It may not be what another cleric would do, but that doesn't make it wrong, does it? "It's just a form of worship for me," he explains.

Mufti Qavi walks at a quick trot to his home. He crosses the courtyard outside his office and enters a dark, narrow lane with pools of water from leaking pipes. The lane opens on to another courtyard, and Mufti Qavi strides to the far right corner and calls out for his wife. He wants a quick bite to eat. Inside his home, his sisters sit in a room where charpoys heaped with bedding are wedged in close to each other. His wife is in the kitchen heating naan bought from the shop next door. She is small and squat and her eyes are limpid and bulbous, one darting to the side while the other fixes you with its gaze. "Did you know that one channel ran a piece of news saying that my wife was going to have a press conference to speak out against me?" Mufti Qavi says, chortling. "I told them, 'Go to my home and find my wife. She will either be cleaning my home, cooking my food or washing my clothes.'"

His sisters received text messages in the days after the photos with Qandeel went viral. "We are going to reveal the truth about you," one said. "You pretend to be so good. Go and look at what your brother is doing."

Ordinarily, Ramzaan is a happy month in this household. The family gathers for the night prayers, breaks their fast together and then meets before dawn for the start of the fast the next day. That year the women of the house wept and prayed together and asked God to help the careless Mufti Qavi out of his bind. Did Qandeel have another video? they wondered. Did she have more to show? Now they hear that a documentary is being made on Qandeel, and they worry that Mufti Qavi will be given a "lifelong negative role." God forbid someone suggests that he had a hand in her murder. There were stories in the newspapers about Mufti Qavi's connections with a man named Abdul Basit who drove Qandeel's murderer away from her house in Multan that night. While some allege that Basit is Mufti Qavi's nephew, others report that they are cousins.[7] But Mufti Qavi's sisters say this is a case of mistaken identity. They marvel at the sheer coincidence of the fact that one of their nephews is also named Abdul Basit.

They wonder about what happened between Qandeel and their

brother. "When Allah will call us to his court on the Day of Judgement, then all will become clear," his sister Hina says. But Mufti Qavi is impatient to end the conversation. He has another court to attend to—what he calls the "Islamic court" he rules over in his office.

He hurries back to his office. Several men and a woman sit inside. The men to the left, the woman on the right. She holds a squirming infant in her arms. Her husband uttered the words "I divorce thee" three times during a fight, and under Islam a marriage can be annulled by doing just that. He wants to take it back. The baby whimpers and wriggles as the woman answers Mufti Qavi's questions about her marriage: Does her husband beat her? Has he ever told her to get out of their home and never come back? The matter is dealt with swiftly. The divorce is annulled and the couple reunited with Mufti Qavi's blessing. It's time for the next petitioner.

A man comes into the office with a little boy bundled up in a shawl. A stray dog, likely rabid, bit the child. The man carries something in a paper bag. He spreads a newspaper before Mufti Qavi and the contents of the bag spill out in a dusty heap. It looks like white sand but is gritty rice flour. Mufti Qavi mutters a prayer. He then takes the child's hands, places them gently on the surface of the flour and covers them with his own hands. We sit in silence as he whispers prayers. He lifts the child's hands and brushes the flour off his palms. The man scoops the flour back into the paper bag. He will take it home and ask his wife to make dough with this flour. Then he will pinch some dough between his fingers and pull it apart. He will see hair in the dough the colour of the rabid dog's fur. He will know then that Mufti Qavi's prayers have worked and the dog's poison has been drawn from his child and transferred into that flour. Sometimes there are two or three short hairs in the dough; other times people have reportedly found a dozen or more bristly sand-coloured hairs. The man is instructed to bury the dough in the ground. His child will be cured. If there is no hair in the dough, the child was never at risk.

The child's father presses a box of mithai into Mufti Qavi's hands.

The cleric is pleased. He pries open the box. "Have something sweet," he offers as he plucks out a yolk-coloured *laddu* (sweet).

For now at least this "court" brings him joy while he waits for the world to forgive him and forget whatever happened with Qandeel Baloch. He wants to write a book about the practice of honour killing. He wants the world to know that he believes a woman like Qandeel, killed for honour by her brother, is a shaheed, a martyr. His sisters tell him he should stop talking about this book.

There are no more TV appearances these days. The invitations dried up shortly after the Lucman interview. A reporter who came to interview him claimed that Mufti Qavi was furious with Lucman. "You never know where a bullet can come from any day," the mufti said. He did not realise he was being recorded. The reporter says he sent the tape to Lucman in order to warn him. Mufti Qavi's journalist friends don't suggest his name to producers any more.

Sometimes his friends say that his name has been ruined and his reputation irretrievably lost; other times they tell him to have faith. They assure him that the entire episode with Qandeel was in fact a struggle between two powerful media companies. Mufti Qavi was a regular guest on a popular religious show on one channel, and the other channel wanted to bring that show down. Qandeel was planted. She had been told exactly what to say and do.

When news broke of Qandeel's murder, Mufti Qavi had been invited to talk about her on the same channel where he had first been introduced to Qandeel on the talk show *Ajeeb Sa*. "We belong to Allah and to him we shall return," he said in the interview. "But I also have a message for those who are watching and listening right now. In the future, before you falsely accuse a man of doing something, for God's sake think about the consequences. And when a man has been accused, it is a blow to the hearts of all his followers, and their every sigh is an appeal to Allah. He may grant their wish."

"I'M TELLING YOU THAT MY LIFE IS IN DANGER"

The idea for the show is simple: in each episode the host gives viewers a peek into the lives of well-known Pakistanis. Political leaders, musicians, former and current prime ministers, lawyers, actors, models, dancers, athletes and filmmakers let the cameras into their homes and introduce their friends and family members to the host—a man named Sohail, who puts on a slow, sing-song voice for the interviews and likes to say that in fifteen years he has interviewed practically every Pakistani worth interviewing, and those he hasn't will also eventually make their way on to the show.

Episodes have previously featured Benazir Bhutto and her husband Asif Ali Zardari, Imran Khan, the actresses Meera and Reema and musician Shahzad Roy, and the show has been shot in other countries including Spain, Sweden, China, Norway, and the US. Budding politicians like Benazir Bhutto's son have promised Sohail that his first local talk-show interview will be with him.

For the show's annual Eid special, the producers could have any guest they want, but that year they want Qandeel. She has thousands of followers online—her Facebook page has been restored after briefly being taken offline following a deluge of complaints—she has been mentioned in the National Assembly (as the butt of a joke, but even so her name has been spoken there), and it is impossible to count how many people have watched her videos as they are copied and shared on multiple platforms the minute she uploads them. And the whole business with Mufti Qavi is even more of a reason to feature her on the Eid special, which always attracts a significant audience. She is the talk of the town, as Sohail says. Although he does not reveal exactly how many people tuned in to that episode, he knows that it was in the millions. Yes, millions. More than any of his other 500-plus interviews.

Qandeel demurs when the producers ask if they can shoot the interview at her home in Karachi. She insists on doing it in Lahore, where Sohail is based. They guess that her home isn't like some of the others that have been featured on the show and she is embarrassed by it. She wants a ticket to Lahore, accommodation at a five-star hotel and plenty of time for outfit changes to show off the wardrobe she wants to bring with her. And she has requested a pair of swimming goggles. She would like to be filmed in a pool, just like in the BBC interview with Amber, and she doesn't own a pair of goggles.

On the day of the shoot Sohail is nervous about how irritable Qandeel seems to be. She is on edge, quick with a comeback or an argument. He overhears her on the phone, talking gently to her father, and asks if he would like to be featured on the show. Does he live in Lahore? But she refuses. Sohail will realise later when he sees that the man is lame and old, wears a dhoti and a kameez and mumbles why Qandeel did not want him to appear on the show.

Between takes she scrolls through messages on her phone and shows them to the crew. When she shows Sohail a text message from a man who is accusing her of not being Baloch, he cautions her, "The higher you fly, the more people will try and yank you down towards earth." She mentions to Sohail that she has quarrelled with her brothers. They are threatening her and she isn't sure if she will go back to Multan to see her parents over Eid. Later he wishes he had asked her more about this, but she mentioned it so casually that he hadn't thought it was a big deal. It certainly isn't an uncommon complaint from women in show business in Pakistan.

Sohail concludes that she is just another attention-seeking woman who likes to talk about her problems. She wants sympathy. He knows what some of the actresses he has interviewed think about Qandeel. They gossip about her and raise their eyebrows at some of her photos and complain that what she is doing isn't right. She is "low," they say, by which they mean common. When Qandeel tells Sohail that she is going to star on *Bigg Boss*—but don't mention it to anyone—he thinks that if this is true, it is very likely she will make a name for herself, and the offers for films or Bollywood projects will inevitably follow. And then those actresses will stop saying horrible things about her—in public at least.

The episode opens with Sohail walking up a driveway towards a sprawling farmhouse with lush green gardens, miniature bridges over gurgling streams, a swimming pool and a lone horse which wanders into the frame. He introduces Qandeel as Pakistan's "social media queen," and as he puts his hand out to shake hers and greets her with a salaam, she throws her arms wide open as if to give him a big hug. He baulks. She cackles. "What? Did that scare you?"

As they walk to some chairs in the garden, Qandeel's stiletto heels sink into the grass and she stumbles. She is wearing a wig—a sleek chestnut-brown bob parted on the side so it covers much of her face— and large tinted sunglasses. She is not in the Western clothes her followers are used to, but wearing a shalwar kameez with a dupatta. After all, the episode is scheduled to air on Eid.

She changes into a wetsuit for the swim, and is handed a large towel the minute she gets out of the water, and then they drive to a hotel in the city, where she puts on leggings and a fitted top for the gym. When she is done with her workout, a waiter brings her a tall glass of chilled orange juice. She is filmed walking out of the hotel trailed by a few well-dressed men and women who look like members of her entourage but are in fact hotel staff.

Back at the farmhouse, three men—friends? fans?—have been stationed at the gate, their arms full of bouquets of red and white flowers for Qandeel. A shiny black four-wheel drive waits in the driveway. Qandeel changes into a deep-purple sporty peplum top and tights for a dance session with a choreographer. The men with the flowers join them in a large dimly lit room and watch her writhe and do some belly-dancing moves while vacant-eyed trophy heads of hunted deer on the wall look down on them. Sohail knows that some of the shots from the dancing segment will have to be cut because the dancing is a little too . . . well, you know. This is a family-oriented show.

The producers want to show her working out, dancing, and partying with her friends, but there are no friends or family she wants them to meet. In the end someone invites Sohail to a dinner, and Qandeel and the whole crew tag along. In the show it looks like a dinner her friends have thrown for her. When the show airs, some of the present people are annoyed with Sohail. They did not want to be seen—much less on national television—with a woman like Qandeel.

Qandeel changes for the dinner. She puts on a pair of black trousers and a grey shirt and twists her long hair—the brown bob is gone—into a topknot, and is taken in a brand-new white car. Some of her friends and family members watch the show and wonder where she got the money for the cars and the house with the swimming pool. On the drive over to the dinner Sohail presses her about how she earns her money, and she says simply, "I don't depend on show business. I have side businesses, some online businesses, some trading on the side . . . It's enough that I live my life very well."

She tells him about her sister Shehnaz in Islamabad, her school days in Multan and her brother who is in the army. It is the first time she has spoken about her family so candidly, and a journalist in Multan watching the episode, whose ears prick up at the mention of a brother in the army, later remarks to his friend, "She's going to get into trouble for that." She is leaving tantalizing clues about herself for anyone who wants to dig into her past.

Qandeel comes across as honest—maybe a little too honest, as parts of her interview are cut out because the producers don't want to get into trouble for obscenity—and she does not seem to filter her thoughts or give measured answers to questions. At one point she even seems to forget she is being filmed and says, "What the fuck?" and then she giggles with embarrassment. They will need to beep it out.

Five days ago, after her meeting with Mufti Qavi was broadcast on practically every news channel in the country, an Urdu-language newspaper based in Multan managed to find out her real name. A reporter even discovered that she had worked as a bus hostess. He had picked apart the threads of the story she had woven—the story of Qandeel Baloch—for her social media followers. The paper had printed pictures of her passport and national identity card. Now everyone knows her real name: Fouzia Azeem. The news is online and has been picked up by mainstream English and Urdu media outlets.

During the interview with Sohail, her first major one since her real name was revealed, she downplays the story. When he briefly touches upon it and asks her to confirm what her real name is, she reminds him, "Well, now the whole world knows it." She airily tells him that everyone in her family calls her Qandeel, and has done so ever since she was a little girl.

Did the people who put out that story think that they could hurt her by telling everyone her real name? By telling everyone where she comes from? She is certain she is being targeted because she has humiliated Mufti Qavi. She was trying to show people what a fake person, a fake scholar who uses religion for his own purposes, looks like. Now she is being called an impostor, a "fake person" simply because she changed her name when she entered show business. "Message to my country's people," she writes on her Facebook page. "Just be aware of such fake people who have two faces and who are cheating people in the name of religion." She adds, "Qandeel Baloch is not two faced as like such people. What I am my fans know me [sic] #DoubleStandardPeople #Hypocrite_Fake #No_Support."

I'm literally feeling alone in the fight. I tried to reveal the true faces but actually I'm banged for that. I should not take such steps.

She has heard that Mufti Qavi has been removed from his post on the Ruet-e-Hilal committee, a position he loved to brag about. She doesn't take pleasure in his humiliation. She feels bad for him, but something tells her that he will bounce back from this stronger than ever.

Mufti Qavi deserves worse than this.

She does not want to talk about Mufti Qavi in public any more. Only people in show business seem to be pleased with the scandal. She received a phone call the other day from an event planner who wants Qandeel to be the show-stopper in an upcoming fashion show. Everyone has seen the photos and videos from the Qavi meeting and everyone is talking about her, the planner says. But Mansoor warns her to be careful when talking about religion—not everyone is pleased with how she has been talking about the cleric. There are no more gleeful tweets from Qandeel ("Now this is called halal selfie ☺☺"). Instead, she proclaims on her Facebook page: "I'm too upset with what has happened in the past couple of weeks and I here by [*sic*] announce that I do not have any issues with Mufti Qavi, whatever has happened between both of us is PAST now." She makes an apology: "I respect my religion and this issue is portraying Islam in a wrong way which is surely not acceptable for me." So when Sohail asks her about Mufti Qavi during his interview she will only say that whatever has happened is God's will.

The day after the shoot she calls Sohail. She wants to tell people about the text messages she has been receiving and how angry she is that pictures of her passport and identity card were printed in a newspaper. She wants to hold a press conference. Can he tell her how to go about it?

He sees her the next day on TV in that same sleek brown bobbed wig as her press conference at the Lahore Press Club is carried live by many channels.[1] She wears a modest shalwar kameez with a dupatta and purple-tinted sunglasses that make it impossible to see her eyes. Is she on the verge of tears?

She sits at a table with a bouquet of microphones fanned out in front of her. "I have called you here today because you must have seen how there has been so much said about me on social media and the media," she tells the reporters. "I have one question: why is Qandeel Baloch being maligned? What have I done? I am, by the grace of Allah, a Muslim and a daughter of this nation." She also wants to address what she has been saying about Mufti Qavi. "I don't think that all muftis are bad, and not all ulema are bad," she explains. "Being a Muslim girl, I respect all the clerics because they keep Islam alive . . . but it is people like Mufti Abdul Qavi who disgrace Islam with what they do behind closed doors. I have no quarrel with other clerics. I respect them. I didn't set out to humiliate Mufti Abdul Qavi. Whatever has happened is God's will." Her voice quavers. "But after this whole incident with Mufti Abdul Qavi, I've got so many threats, so many threats that I cannot sleep at night," she says. She is getting calls from numbers in Afghanistan, and threatening emails and messages. "My sources have told me to go underground," she reveals. "I am a prisoner in my own home."

She is afraid of the strangers who are getting in touch with her. She fears for her life and for her family. She wants the government to provide her with protection. "If something happens to me tomorrow or something happens to my family, then the [government] will be held responsible," she declares.

The reporters press her. There are many women in showbiz, one says to her, and they aren't getting these kinds of threats. Perhaps it is because they don't get up to the antics you do. You say that you have showed us Mufti Qavi's real face. Who are you planning to expose next? Sohail watches the press conference and admires her for having squeezed in both an interview and a dramatic press conference on her trip to Lahore—paid for by his producers. He doesn't worry too much about the threats that Qandeel mentions. After all, she seemed like an attention-seeker, didn't she?

I'm telling you that my life is in danger and you're accusing me of a publicity stunt? I can't say anything to that.

When she gets back to Karachi, she meets her old friend Mansoor, and he takes her over to a friend's house. She often breaks her fast with this friend in the evenings. He scolds her for the videos and photographs with Mufti Qavi and says she does not understand the danger she is putting herself in. Stay with me for a few days, he offers. It's safe in my home with so many guards and people around all the time. She refuses and says she is planning to go to her parents in Multan for Eid, as she does every year. She also says she wants to leave Pakistan for a little while, perhaps with her parents, after Eid. She jokes that he has not given her *Eidi* [gifts of money given on Eid] yet. As she is leaving, he hands her a hundred dollars. He does not understand why she is going back to Multan now. It isn't safe for her. "They'll get you killed," he says unhappily, but perhaps she is too excited about the crisp green note to pay attention or ask him who exactly "they" are.

Things are not going according to plan. On 8 July she released one of her boldest works yet—she starred in a video for a song called "Ban." The producer and director have worked with some of the biggest names in the music industry. They told her she would become an international artist once people saw the video. She could even go on tour in Canada. Look at the other women who have made these videos. Look at how their careers have taken off—they're hosting talk shows, commanding great sums of money for appearances in other videos, and some of them have even put out their own songs. She wants to be more than just a social media star, right? They know she understands that a flash of skin will always get people talking. And doesn't she want to change what people are saying about her? Give the people something that can drown out all the other stories and rumours.

She falls out with Mec over the video. He didn't want her to do it. He told her he didn't like what they wanted Qandeel to do in the video. The director was ready to pay 300,000 rupees for Qandeel, but then she went behind Mec's back. She didn't know about the offer on the table and ended up accepting half the amount. She is given a free hand to do whatever she likes—clothes, hair and make-up, dancing. She wears a bobbed black wig and colours her lips a glossy hot pink. She brings her tinted sunglasses and the black lace dress from her video for Imran Khan. Her blue and pink bra peeks through the lace as she bends over and pushes herself against the singer, a kid in his late teens who likes to style his mop of hair in spikes.

Fine, the wardrobe is cheap. I agree it's cheap.

With every thrust of her hips, the kid sings about her dangerous "thumkas" (hip thrusts), how sexy her moves are. She likes the lyrics, especially the line, "Baby, please don't do it again." She changes into a black bodysuit with sheer stockings and stiletto heels for some of her solo shots. She wears a low-cut pink babydoll dress with a push-up bra and tries to twerk. She sucks her finger. She isn't happy with the twerking. She isn't sure how to do it. She turns away from the camera and squats and thrusts her hips in and out, in and out, and then gazes over her shoulder and lightly smacks her ass.

Fine, I don't know how to dance.

In between shots she sits on one of the props, hunched over and hugging herself as she watches the cameramen and lighting guys set up.

But look at my confidence. How would I rate this video? 10/10. Why not? I broke a record in Pakistan. No one has done this before.

She isn't happy with some parts. She asks the producers to delay it, to take out some shots, but they refuse. Why is she so worried? Nothing in the video will be a problem, they assure her.

The video is watched more than 5.5 million times on YouTube alone. It is too risqué to be shown on television. But between Qandeel's social media following and the production company's, who needs airtime? The video is released on Facebook and YouTube with a cheeky disclaimer: "This video can shock, offend and upset people. Are you sure you want to watch it?"

Mec is furious with her. He refuses to share the video on his Facebook page. She tries to make peace. She calls him and weeps and complains about the shots she did not like. He scolds her. She doesn't know how these people work. How they can secretly film you or fool you. She is still so naive. Let it go, she pleads with Mec. Let's have a clean start. I swear I'll listen to you now. She says that many times in that last month, every time she does something that lands her in trouble—Let's start afresh—and each time Mec believes she really does want to.

It doesn't matter. No one is talking about the video any more, not since a man appeared on TV five days after "Ban" came out. He told everyone he was Qandeel's ex-husband and was sitting next to a small, full-lipped, serious-looking boy. The boy is her son, Mishal.

Ever since that newspaper revealed her real name, she has had bad luck. There are now two court cases against her accusing her of not being Baloch and threatening her with a fine of five crore rupees if she does not stop using "Baloch" as a name. Just dogs barking, she reassures herself. She receives a phone call from a man who says he is close to her father. His name is Safdar Shah. He tells her his house is right next to hers. She doesn't understand what he means. In Shah Sadar Din, he says. Your home in Shah Sadar Din. Who is this man? she wonders. He says he is a lawyer and so she asks him for advice on the legal cases. Are they serious? Could something come of them? And is there any law which could stop her using "Baloch" as her surname?

Safdar Shah likes to tell Qandeel with indignation that if the daughter of a rich man can go to India and act in films there, then why can't the daughter of a poor man from some no-name village do the same? When he mentions this for the fourth time in their conversation, she retorts that perhaps he should forget about these other actresses and think about Qandeel Baloch, who is the number-one top model in Pakistan. He chuckles.

People in Shah Sadar Din are burning with jealousy, he tells her. They can't stand how successful she has become. It doesn't matter to her. She is setting her sights higher—a career in politics might be in her future. Perhaps in Imran Khan's party. Shah is very enthusiastic about this idea. She is curious about who has been feeding information about her life in Shah Sadar Din to the media, but she is not scared—after all, the stories keep her in the headlines, and who doesn't want that? She likes being in the limelight. Let the dogs keep barking.

But then she sees her little boy on television.

Her phone will not stop ringing.

"I am in Multan," she messages Mec. "Handle all these calls, please. Need your support. I am very much alone. Everyone against. Even my family. What should I do? No one can understand me."

He tells her to stay away from the media. Ignore the calls and requests for interviews. Don't say a word.

"Can you please handle all these people?" she replies. "The cases. I need a lot of support."

Later, "It's very hot here."

There is a picture of her being shared online and shown over and over again on the news. In it she stands with her husband and his mother in a field. She remembers that picture. She hadn't wanted to stand close to them. Her gold bangles had clinked as she crossed her arms and held herself. People start posting that photo in the comments section of anything she shares or writes on her Facebook page.

An entertainment reporter from one of the English-language newspapers calls her. She tells him about how her husband would beat her and how she has not seen her son in years.

No one tells me, "Qandeel, you have gone to war against a society, against a kind of place where men think women are as lowly as their shoe. The kind of place where it's so common for a man to hit a woman, that if some man doesn't hit his wife, people call him beghairat [dishonourable]." Why don't people see that?

She cannot stop crying. The reporter is irritated. Does this woman ever stop being such a drama queen? He had admired her for the stunt with Mufti Qavi, but really this is too much. But he needs to keep the conversation going. He needs something, a nugget of information that will make his story stand out from all the others. He tries to sympathize with her. It must be troublesome that you cannot meet your child any more, he offers.

"They will kill me," she replies, sniffling. "I can't go back." How dramatic! She just wants to be in the news all the time, doesn't she? He does not ask her who "they" are and she does not say. "I took a divorce because I wanted to study further and work, but I was forcibly married," she explains.[2]

The reporter wants an exclusive face-to-face interview. She tells him she is in Multan, and when she comes back to Karachi she doesn't plan on doing anything for a month or two. She doesn't want to speak to anybody. She wants to file a custody case for her boy.

The reporter ends the call, walks back into the newsroom and tells everyone the drama queen is crying again and saying the same old things about threats to her life. Remember all those videos where she sniffled and complained about a fever or a headache, or the time she wailed and sobbed after Pakistan lost the T20 match against India? This story about the husband is just another excuse to make a video. The reporter files his story. It instantly goes online, and everyone in the newsroom is delighted because they have never seen such high traffic. They covered the Mufti Qavi meeting and her "Ban" video when it came out, because they know that anything to do with Qandeel Baloch brings a tide of readers to their website.

The numbers on the story about the drama queen's husband will only be surpassed by those for the piece about her death two days later.

On her visits home she does no work. She sleeps for most of the day. A lady comes to the house to rub mustard oil in her hair and massage her body. Qandeel dyes her hair on the trip, peering into a small mirror above the sink in the only bathroom in the house. She gets a call from Mansoor. He tells her some of his friends want to meet *the* Qandeel Baloch. They are planning to hold a party on a boat this week. Come with me, Mansoor says. She tells him she is in Multan. When I come back, she promises, we'll go on a cruise together.

She does an interview over the phone with a man who hosts an online talkshow.[3] He takes a few calls from listeners. One man asks her why she does not use her fame and celebrity to do something good so the people who curse her and call her names can then have something to praise her for. "I definitely plan to do some positive work, but these days there are so many issues I am dealing with," she replies. "There are the court cases . . . the controversies that won't leave me, and then on top of everything, my brothers want to kill me."

The caller interrupts her. "But you are planning to do some work which will bring glory to Pakistan?"

The host does not ask her about her brothers, and she does not mention them again.

She likes to sit with her mother and massage her feet. She feels happiest when she is doing this. Her father has come down with a cold. She plays Abida Parveen songs for him on her phone. Her younger brother is there as well. After they eat dinner together, he offers to go out to buy the milk that her mother gets every evening. He pours swirls of sweet ruby-red Rooh Afza syrup into the chilled glasses of milk. Her phone's battery dies. She goes to her room to charge it. She gets a phone call.

At last! Some good news.

She texts Mec, "I am very much happy." She is out of credit on her phone. Send me some balance, she tells him. I have something to tell you. She calls him promptly when the credit comes through. Why didn't you let me call you if you have no money on your phone? he chides. But she wants to be the one calling. In the future, years later, she wants to remember that she had called him and told him her life was going to change.

He asks her if everything is all right, and if she is still having problems with Mufti Qavi.

She tells him that has been cleared up. Promise me something, she says.

What promise?

Promise me you'll come to Karachi with me.

Mec says he can't travel at the moment. He has too many events lined up.

Are they more important than me? She pretends to sulk. When she finally gets him to say what she wants to hear, she tells him she has received a phone call from the woman who organizes the entertainment and fashion industry's biggest annual awards show. This year they want Qandeel to open the show, she says to Mec with a squeal. With Ali Zafar! One of Pakistan's best-known singers! The organizer's daughter had shown her Qandeel's photographs and videos. People—women—in showbiz have been talking about her. Some are envious, some are in awe, and others are disgusted. But there is a great deal of respect after the incident with Mufti Qavi. For so many years people in the industry have been judged by the religious conservatives and scolded on live TV shows or been subjected to fatwas about everything from how they dress to their personal lives and the films they star in. Now, finally, one of their own—yes, they could accept her as one of them—has thumbed her nose at them all. She has guts, they grudgingly accept.

Mec has to come with her to Karachi. She won't go without him. Forget everything else that has happened. Now she will start again, and she will do things differently. No more secrets—everything she has hidden for years, the life she has pretended to live, all of that is finished. She has known it all along: if you have strong willpower, nothing can keep you down. Life taught her lessons at an early age. It has not been easy to become a woman who supports herself and her family. She will tell everyone exactly how she did it.

Maybe she can even start some organization, some agency to help girls who have the same dreams as her. She will make sure that they do not have to go through what she did. Do you know what she is? What she is becoming? A girl power. A one-woman army. An inspiration to those ladies who are treated badly and dominated by society. Everything is going to change now. There will be new tricks, or perhaps none at all. After all, she is no longer just Qandeel Baloch. She is also Fouzia Azeem. Will Fouzia Azeem make videos and take selfies and tell Imran Khan she loves him? What will Fouzia Azeem, the woman who escaped an abusive marriage, the woman who supported her family, the woman who has a child, have to say?

There will be more work, more countries to visit, but can she leave the country if there are two court cases pending against her? Perhaps she should ask Safdar Shah to look into that. Get a passport for yourself, she instructs Mec. We're going to have many travels together. She is going to make it as a singer. She will do concerts. Concerts in Dubai! She wants to be back in Karachi as soon as possible. She wants to book her flight first thing in the morning. Will Mec make sure she is up early tomorrow? She has been told to get back to Karachi as soon as possible to choose her wardrobe for the awards ceremony.

He promises to call in the morning to wake her.

Promise you'll come with me, she insists. I'll send you a ticket as soon as I'm back in Karachi.

He promises.

The next day, 16 July, a Saturday morning, Mec keeps his word and calls Qandeel. There is no answer.

Silly girl. She must have stayed up late again, and will now sleep until the afternoon.

He had sent her a message the night before. "I am so happy. May you remain happy. I'm always praying for you. My heart is so happy."

I think I'm afraid to be happy, because whenever I do get too happy, something bad always happens . . .

It is 10.30 a.m. She has not called him back and is not answering her phone.

He messages her: "Good morning. Have a nice day."

THE MEDIA AND THE MURDER

Malik Azam started working for the *Daily Pakistan* newspaper's small Multan bureau in 2010, and his first story for the paper is still one of his favourites. He got a tip about a piece of land owned by the government that was being encroached upon by a minister. When the story ran, an opposition political party jumped on it, and soon the news was being discussed on talk shows and written about in other newspapers. The province's chief minister took note, and Azam says he soon received a phone call. "They asked me where I'd found the information," he recalls. "I led them to it, and then, just like *that*—" he snaps his fingers "—the encroachment was finished. Today there's a hospital on that land."

It was everything he loved about journalism. "The stories you see these days," he says, shaking his head. "Everyone is chasing the government's soft stories. Even the biggest media groups are just doing PR. I want investigative journalism. The salary doesn't matter. The resources don't matter. It's all about your will. How strong is your will? How far can you reach?" The best stories reassure him that "at least I have done something."

"The best stories uncover truths, no matter how cleverly hidden," he feels. You may have have read Malik Azam's "best story," even if you don't know his name or read the *Daily Pakistan*. It was the story of a girl from a small village in Punjab who changed her name and hid her identity and became one of the most scandalous women in Pakistan.

There are only a handful of men in the *Daily Pakistan*'s Multan office on the day I visit to meet Azam. He speaks softly and starts our conversation with "Bismillah" (In the name of Allah). His hair is greying at the sideburns, and he has a bushy handlebar moustache. His forehead is lined, and when he ponders the answer to a particularly tricky question, he often furrows his brow, the lines deepen and his eyes look sadder than they usually do. Every day he spends more than an hour commuting to and from work. He is running late on the day we meet, but even so, when he arrives he looks freshly shaved, is wearing a perfectly ironed shalwar kameez and apologizes profusely. He is not in the habit of being late. He insists on offering me lunch to make up for it, but then, slightly shyly, wonders out loud what a woman from Karachi would want to eat in Multan. Perhaps pizza, like his daughter enjoys?

The *Daily Pakistan* newsroom is a bare-bones space, a bit run-down and dark. There are no windows, and stacks of old newspapers are heaped in corners and under tables. A young boy scuttles between the desks with a steel tray crammed with hot cups of tea. Someone plays a recording of Quranic verses on their computer and turns the volume up until the room is filled with the recitation. "Which of your Lord's favours will you deny?" the verse asks. The men will shortly lay reed mats on the small balcony outside the office, next to the stairwell, and gather for prayers.

When the bureau chief arrives, the crisp swish of his starched white shalwar kameez announcing him, the reporters push their chairs back with their legs, some shuffle their feet back into their sandals or slippers, and then, not quite standing and not quite sitting, they remain in a half-crouch over their desks, each sinking back down the minute the chief passes him.

Azam's beat at the newspaper "keeps shifting." He does whatever stories are assigned to him or whatever he happens to come across. One day he met two friends who said they had a particularly interesting piece of information for him.

"*Yaar*," said one, pointing to the other. "Ask him about Fouzi."

"Fouzi? Who is Fouzi?" Azam asked.

His friend laughed. "Let's go for a meal in the evening. I'll tell you everything. It's quite an interesting chapter." However, when they sat down to dinner that night, the man hemmed and hawed and delayed. He made a big deal about ordering the food and further small talk, teasing the reporter.

Azam finally demanded, "Are you going to tell me or not?"

The friend leaned back, satisfied. "Fouzi," he said, "is Qandeel Baloch."

That's it? That was the big news? Azam had heard the woman's name but didn't know much about her.

"She was my classmate," his friend continued. They had lived close to each other in the village she was from—yes, the village. She was no city girl. They had studied in school together until the ninth grade.

"So everyone in the village knows who this woman is?" Azam asked.

They did indeed, his friend said. There were others like him, people who had gone to school with Qandeel or who knew her family. And, in fact, Azam's friend's wife had been at a school in Multan with Qandeel as well.

Azam went to the *Daily Pakistan* entertainment reporter and told him about Fouzi. The reporter scoffed. So what? he said. Big deal. Most of these women have fake names and identities.

For six months, no matter how often Qandeel featured in the news, Azam sat on the story. There was no point filing it, he insists. As he puts it, the story would not "pinch" in Multan—there wouldn't be much interest. No one in Multan would have cared what some girl from a nearby village was doing in Islamabad, Lahore or Karachi. He concedes that perhaps people might have been interested when Qandeel started making videos for Imran Khan, but he just didn't bother with the story at that point.

It's an explanation that many reporters in Multan are quick to sympathize with.

"Even I knew where she was from," claims J, a reporter for a TV channel. "A guy who lived in Shah Sadar Din called me up and told me, This Qandeel Baloch is a girl from our area. I didn't run with the story. I took it easy. But two days later Azam ran it in the *Daily Pakistan* and then suddenly every paper and channel had it."

J isn't the only one who says he knew Qandeel's true identity. Many reporters in Multan mutter that friends or sources from villages outside Multan or in Dera Ghazi Khan gave them the information, but Azam was the first one to print it. J then got in on the act by revealing that Qandeel had stayed in a women's shelter when she fled Shah Sadar Din.

Azam and his bureau chief, Shaukat Iqbal, rubbish rivals' claims. "If they had broken the news, they wouldn't be saying any of this," sneers Iqbal. "They didn't get the scoop and they definitely would have faced the consequences for that. Ask them just how many angry messages they got. How many colleagues asked them why they didn't get the news?"

When Azam saw the videos of the meeting between Qandeel and Mufti Qavi, he went to the paper's chief reporter. "The *bachi* [girl] is from our area," he told him, pointing to the TV where a clip of Qandeel taking a selfie with the cleric was running. "And by the way, she's not even Baloch."

"How do you know?" the reporter asked.

They went to see the bureau chief together.

"File it," Iqbal ordered.

The story ran on 23 June, tucked away in a small box on the back page of the newspaper's Multan edition. "From Shah Sadar Din's Fouzia Azeem to Qandeel Baloch, a bitter journey to the heights of fame," the headline read. "Her father's name is Muhammad Azeem, from a Ma'arah family . . . " She had been unlucky in love in 2003 or 2004, and that had been her turning point, Azam wrote. He revealed that Qandeel had worked as a bus hostess and after entering the world of modelling had transformed herself from Fouzia to Qandeel Baloch. While he won't reveal how he found out she had worked at Faisal Movers, Azam admits that he was never able to find proof that she had been a hostess—there was no employee record or even a single co-worker who remembered her from that time.

By this point Azam had seen her passport—he won't say how—and learned that Qandeel had travelled to South Africa in 2007. "Her selfies with Mufti Abdul Qavi of Multan have become the hot cake [*sic*] in the media," the story noted. An old photograph of Qandeel, her chin resting on her hands, ran with the piece. The next day the *Daily Pakistan*'s back page featured an image of Qandeel's passport, including her real name, her date of birth and identity card number. "She went back to her father's home three times after she left, but never helped her parents leave the godforsaken village where she first opened her eyes in March 1990 in a mud house," the story noted. "The family cannot tolerate to see her face again." On both days the stories ran under a box containing an interview with "Multan's famous religious scholar, Mufti Qavi." "We met on Qandeel's wishes, she was scared some magic had been done on her," Mufti Qavi said in the interview. "Qandeel Baloch has apologized to me five times, and I have forgiven her."

The stories, which included a high-resolution scan of Qandeel's passport, were immediately run on the paper's English-language website, and quickly went viral. "Controversy queen Qandeel Baloch has been headlining the news for the past couple of days for her scandalous statements on live television and secretive hotel room meetings with religious scholars," the report stated. "Although she now lives a somewhat glamorous life, new details revealed about her past show that she may have once lived an ordinary life of hardship and unrequited love." Clippings of Azam's Urdu story were shared on Facebook and Twitter.

"When Mufti Qavi came into the picture, it became a hot issue," Azam explains. "If I had run the story about her real name back in January, the impact would not have been as much." It was a tantalizing mixture—a religious scholar who loved the limelight, and a woman who had filmed herself alone with him in his hotel room. Mufti Qavi was well known among the media in Multan, and more importantly his family had been running a madrassa in the city for decades. His sisters held classes teaching women from some of Multan's most respected families how to read and interpret the Quran. The information Azam had on Qandeel would finally "pinch."

The *Daily Pakistan* story was picked up by other Urdu newspapers and the English-language dailies. It ran on television. Once everyone knew the name of the village Qandeel was from—it was not hard for local correspondents to call up sources in Dera Ghazi Khan or Shah Sadar Din, a little over two hours from Multan—the media wanted to know all it could about the daughter of Muhammad Azeem.

Ever since the age of ten, Adil Nizami had known exactly what he wanted to do. That year, in July 2001, his eyes had been glued to the TV screen as news broke that the minister of state for foreign affairs had been shot dead in a town in the district of Multan while campaigning in a local election. He was riveted by the coverage.

While at university, Adil dabbled in print journalism, but applied for a job at a small television channel as soon as he graduated. His second job had been with a flashy new network that soon went under for fraud and embezzlement. He finally arrived at 24 News, a current affairs channel, in 2015. At the time 24 had only been around for a year, but it had big ambitions and had recently snapped up one of the country's best-known political talkshow hosts. Adil went for an interview and waited with nine others. He knew his CV wasn't too impressive, but he had something none of the other candidates seemed to have: an interest in current affairs bordering on obsession. "People ask me, 'Have you seen *Devdas*? Have you seen *Taare Zameen Par*?' No, I haven't. I watch the news. That's all I want to watch. My friends call me crazy. But this isn't a passing interest."

"Let's say I am a cleric who wants to be a member of the senate," his interviewer said after briefly glancing at Adil's sparse CV. "How would I go about that?"

Adil rattled off the procedure.

"OK," said the interviewer, surprised. "Not bad. How many four-star generals are there in the army?"

"Sir, there are two four-star generals in the army at a time: one is the joint chief of staff and one is the chief of army staff."

"Tell me this," the interviewer said, leaning across the table. "Who is the Sri Lankan president?"

"Well," Adil replied, "five days ago there was a transition of power. So do you want the last guy's name or the current president's?"

He was offered the job immediately.

On his second day at work a building collapsed in Multan, crushing everyone inside. One man died at the scene while Adil was reporting. He couldn't sleep that night. The next day he arrived at work with puffy eyes. He was quiet, withdrawn. "Sir, this is what we're going to be doing every day," his cameraman said. "If this is how you're going to be, you can't be a reporter. You might as well stay at home." A few months later, Adil found himself in front of a blazing house, reporting live as rescue workers struggled to control the fire. A woman and her five children were laid out on the street, still as dolls. He was relieved that he didn't feel a thing. He quickly learned how to tell stories about things that people hoped would never happen to them.

On the morning of July 16, he received a phone call from a source at 10:12 a.m. He remembers the time because he was running a late for work that day, literally racing up the stairs to the newsroom when his mobile rang. The man on the other line cut through the niceties. "I'm at the police station in Shah Sadar Din," he said. "It's Qandeel. She's been murdered."

Adil flicked through the channels on the television screens in the newsroom: the usual advertisements, the daily bulletins, morning shows. He walked over to his assignment editor. "Heard anything about Qandeel this morning?" he asked. There was nothing. Adil called the source back. "You're wrong, my friend. Must be a mix-up."

Twenty minutes later his phone rang again. It was the same source.

"It's confirmed," he said. "Trust me, it's her. The police are heading out." At that moment all other beats ceased to matter. According to the rules of the newsroom, Adil should have told the crime reporter about the tip. But even though Adil had been with 24 News for barely over a year at this time, the channel had covered Qandeel enough times for him to know that she was one of Pakistan's most controversial celebrities. He was determined to be the one to break this news. Telling no one but his editor about the phone call, he jumped into the station's van with his cameraman and shouted at the driver to take the fastest route to the Muzaffarabad police station, a twenty-five-minute drive away from Multan's city centre, from where his source had called.

The first time Adil had seen her was at work was when one of the video editors had pulled him aside and showed him a video she had posted on her Facebook page. This was in March 2016, right before a cricket match between Pakistan and India, one of the world's biggest sports rivalries. In the video Qandeel was lying on a mound of pillows, wearing a sleeveless Barbie-pink dress with black polka dots.[1] The creamy tops of her breasts peeked out over the neckline. A black tattoo—a leaping deer? a dagger?—snaked across her right breast. She had a message for Shahid Afridi, the captain of the Pakistan cricket team. "Just win this match," she said, staring straight at the camera. "And then see how Qandeel does a strip dance for you. Seriously. I'll say your name as I strip."

Adil couldn't peel his eyes off the screen. He had never heard a woman speak this way. How could she say those things?

The next encounter was far tamer. Not long after the video was posted, someone at the office got her number and Adil was nominated to dial her up on speaker before a group of fellow reporters. He introduced himself and then put the call on speaker. The men hovered in a circle around the phone. She was friendly, Adil found out, especially with the media. Then he was nudged to pass her to someone else. "Qandeel, our assignment editor wants to talk to you," Adil told her. The editor lost his nerve. He couldn't say a word. Qandeel waited patiently on the line, hearing the reporters' stifled giggles. The editor panicked and cut the call. To this day, he is still needled about that incident.

Racing to Qandeel's home on the day he found out she had been killed, Adil marveled at his luck. A giggle escaped his mouth. The van's driver raised his eyebrows. Adil ignored him. Well, he wasn't about to let slip the biggest story in Multan in years—maybe even the biggest story in Pakistan right now—by telling a loudmouth driver with at least six friends on speed dial working for other television channels. Sixty or seventy crime reporters in Multan, and none of them had got the call, Adil mused. This fat little bird flew right into his hands. Just like that. And no one else knew!

The driver glanced over at Adil in the passenger seat. The baby-faced reporter's nose was dotted with beads of sweat, and one leg had had the shakes ever since they'd left the office. "Let's go, let's go, let's go," Adil muttered under his breath as the van crept closer to the checkpoint on Shershah Road in the army cantonment in Multan. His fingers drummed a frantic beat on his laminated press card. Where does this kid need to rush off to so early in the morning on a Saturday? the driver wondered. He knew Adil's beat was the political and religious parties. Had some bloody *maulana* (cleric) died or what? He stuck his head out of the van's window and cursed everything: the beggars slowly weaving their way through the lines of cars when the lights changed from amber to green; the men perched on laden carts urging donkeys that were too tired or starved to do more than strain against their harness as they tried to inch their load forward; the motorbike riders who could wriggle on to the pavement and zoom ahead; the van's broken air conditioning; the goddamn heat; this mystery assignment.

The Muzaffarabad area on the outskirts of the city was mainly known for having one of the largest textile mills in the country, and they had long since driven past the fork in the road that led to it. The police station where Adil's source had called him from was located on a deserted stretch of road with no street signs or markers. It was quiet there, with only a few scattered shops selling mobile phone credit, drinks or snacks. There were no pedestrians. "I don't know what you're talking about," said the policeman behind the desk inside the station. Adil pressed him. "I said I have no idea," he snapped. "No police van has headed out from here."

On his way out, Adil felt someone pinch his elbow. A policeman jerked his head towards a corner. Adil followed him. "Get out of here, drive back towards the cantonment and then take the first lane on the left when you see a sign for a clinic," the policeman whispered. "Go to Karachi Hotel. She lives there." He paused. "Lived."

"Karachi Hotel?" repeated the driver.

"That's what he said." Adil shrugged. Small restaurants and roadside cafés serving tea and snacks were commonly referred to as hotels. "Must be a restaurant."

Adil got a call from his editor. "There's a Shinza Baloch who lives near the police station Adil," he said. "Some singer or actor? Do you think it could be her?"

Please, dear God, don't tell me it's some actress no one has heard of! Adil thought.

They drove through a warren of unpaved narrow lanes that led off the main road. The van had trouble squeezing through. Adil walked to a small kiosk covered in advertisements for mobile phone companies.

"I'm looking for a restaurant," he told the shopkeeper. "Karachi Hotel?"

"You're in Karachi Hotel, bhai," the man replied. "This neighbourhood. This is Karachi Hotel." He looked at Adil's press card dangling around his neck. "A police car just went that way," he said, pointing to a lane.

They drove into the lane. Nothing. Another one. Nothing again. Adil frantically called his sources in the police. One whispered directions to the house, another said that they already knew who had done it. They knew who had killed her. Adil didn't know what was true. He just needed to get to the house fast. The news would spread quickly, and it would not be long before other reporters got wind of it. Then he saw the ambulance. Adil scurried towards it while the cameraman rigged up his equipment. He could hear crying. The ambulance was parked outside a clinic for children. The lane seemed to be a dead end, closed off by a brick wall.

"What happened, son?" Adil asked a little boy standing near the ambulance.

"Uncle-ji dropped dead in Karachi," the child replied. "They brought the body back this morning. He came in an aeroplane, you know."

Uncle-ji?

"Who are you looking for?" asked a woman standing at the gate to a house next to the clinic.

"Do you know where Qandeel Baloch lives?" Adil asked.

"Who?"

"Qandeel."

"No one here by that name. I've lived here for eight years. There's us, the widow of a police officer and a lame old man. He has a wife and son. No daughter."

There was a flash of black and khaki in the corner of Adil's eye. He turned. The lane wasn't a dead end after all. There, to the right, were three small houses nestled in a corner. A pale yellow one-storey house abutted a rose-pink wall. A policeman darted behind the house's cream-coloured front door. The woman glanced at it. "That's the lame man's home. The police just showed up ten minutes ago. God only knows why."

Jackpot! Adil thought.

Adil walked over, cupped his hands around his eyes and peered between the bars of a window next to the front door of the house. He couldn't see a thing. A gate next to the door swung open with the gentlest of nudges. An elderly man and woman sat in a room to his right. Straight ahead, the door to another room opened. Four or five men, some police, stood in a circle around a charpoy, their heads bowed, their necks craned forward. What were they looking at? A pink and white sheet trailed on to the floor. Something peeked out at the end. Was that a foot?

The mustachioed face of a policeman was the last thing Adil saw in that house. "Out!" the officer hissed. "Move back." The gate was slammed behind Adil as he stumbled down a potholed concrete ramp. His phone rang. It was the channel. "We ready to go? I need you to do a live call immediately. We can do the visuals later," his editor barked. Adil stayed on the line and waited. A few seconds before the anchor came on, he heard the producer say urgently, "OK, ready. Wait. Is it her? You're sure it's her?"

At 11:25 a.m. that day Adil Nizami, a twenty-five-year-old rookie reporter from Multan, broke the biggest story of his career. "Famous model Qandeel Baloch has been killed," he blurted out in a live call that interrupted 24 News's regular morning bulletin.[2]

As he stood in the lane outside Qandeel's house, the words that had been on the tip of his tongue for more than an hour now rushed out. "Some are saying that she was shot dead. The police have just reached her house here in Multan. We should find out shortly how she was murdered. The incident took place a little while ago in the area of Muzaffarabad, where model Qandeel Baloch had been living for some time. Her brothers, the murderers, were angry with her because of her behaviour and all the scandals on TV. We also found out that she was planning to travel to India to take part in a reality TV show there. Her family was angry with her. And we have found out this morning that her brothers have either strangled her or shot her, but there's conflicting information about how they killed her."

In the van the driver received a call. He listened for a moment. "Fuck. Are you sure? Adil said so? Yeah, yeah, I'll tell you how to get here." It's going to be a long day, he thought, irritated.

A long day in the middle of nowhere in this heat.

After forty minutes, a line of twelve Digital Satellite News Gathering (DSNG) vans made its way down the lane leading to the house. Adil estimated that more than a hundred people—police, reporters, cameramen, locals—were now buzzing around like flies in a jar on the rough sandy road.

When the ambulance arrived, it took the driver half an hour to cover the last few feet. No one wanted to give up their hard-won spot in front of the small house. It didn't matter. Nothing could save her now, and the police did not seem to be in any rush to get the body out, even as the mercury rose on that sweltering July day. Adil's bright pink knock-off Ralph Lauren shirt was covered in dark patches of sweat. It was nearing 2 p.m. The officers milling around outside the house looked bewildered. Some hadn't even had the time to put their uniforms on before they rushed to the scene. Every time a high-ranking officer arrived, someone inside the house would open the gate just a few inches for them to squeeze through.

The reporters had been breathlessly relaying each drop of information as they received it from inside the house. They were getting restless. Their producers mined Qandeel's social media feeds for quotes and photographs to tide viewers over until they had anything tangible. Adil watched his colleague hoist his camera above the gate of the house, attempting to film what was transpiring inside. It could make for a precious few minutes of footage that the channel would slap its logo on, running it on a loop until Adil could give them something better. A policeman swatted at the camera. An officer had made a video of the body inside the room. The reporters scrambled for it.

Adil didn't want that. I want the real thing, he thought. If I'd only been here ten minutes before . . . If I'd headed out right when I got that first call, I could have been here before the police. I could have got a shot of her.

He knew exactly what he would have done. Shoot footage of the body first. Blur the face of course, but then again that depended on what the bosses at the channel wanted. Maybe a good shot of her face, in case they wanted to run a still. "After that, I'd shift focus," Adil told me. "She's been murdered, she's been identified, she's Qandeel Baloch. OK! Done! Now the parents. How was she murdered? Who murdered her? The story they gave the police—that story could have been mine. I would have been the first to get it."

All eyes were on the ambulance, which had now been wedged up against the gate. "They'll bring her out soon," the reporters murmured among themselves. "Any minute now," they told their producers reassuringly. "The body will come out any minute now." Adil had the best spot, right next to the ambulance's open doors. The other reporters had graciously offered him the space. "You were the first one here," they said, squeezing his shoulders. Adil spotted a photographer he knew from another channel. He called him over. He could hear someone behind the gate shouting for a sheet. It was time. Adil had a plan.

The gate of the house opened. Everyone surged forward. Adil helped the photographer up into the ambulance and told him to crouch at the far end. The ambulance men had forgotten to bring the standard white shroud for the body; they had used the pink bed sheet from Qandeel's charpoy instead. The body was loaded into the back of the vehicle. Inside, the photographer plucked the sheet off so he could quickly take photos of the body. I need to see for myself, Adil thought as he quickly slid open one of the ambulance windows. His hand, holding his mobile phone, snaked inside. He stared at the puffy blue-lipped face for a split second. He began filming.[3]

"Yaar, dead body *ka khyaal karein* [Have some respect for the dead]," City Police Officer (CPO) Azhar Akram, the highest-ranking official on the spot said as he grabbed Adil by the arm and pulled him away from the ambulance. "What do you think you're doing?"

But Adil had got his shot.

The ambulance pulled away. The door to the house opened and two police officials came out with an old man. He could not stand on his own as he had only one leg. The policemen held the elderly man up as the reporters scrambled towards him and pushed their microphones under his chin. With his arm around the shoulders of one of the officers at his side, Qandeel's father, Muhammad Azeem, confirmed the news of his daughter Qandeel Baloch's death. He compared her to Benazir Bhutto, the former prime minister of Pakistan who was assassinated in

2007. His daughter had been as brave as Benazir, Azeem wanted the reporters to know. The loosely tied white cotton turban he was wearing unravelled as he told the media that his son Waseem had killed Qandeel.

Azeem was immediately taken to the police station just a short walk from his home, where he filed a First Information Report (FIR). Azeem formally accused his youngest son of murdering his daughter. "My daughter, Qandeel Baloch, who works in showbiz, came to our house in Multan from Karachi on Eid . . . my son, Waseem, who is twenty-four or twenty-five years old, came to meet us on the 14th of July," he stated for the record. He implicated another of his sons, Aslam, a junior officer in the army, in the crime, saying that he had encouraged Waseem to kill Qandeel. "[Waseem] wanted to stop Qandeel from working in show-biz." "Qandeel Baloch was killed by Waseem in the name of honour," Azeem wrote in the FIR. "This is an injustice. He did this for money. Waseem killed Qandeel Baloch at the urging of my other son, Aslam Shaheen, a subedar [captain] in the army."

Over the coming months, Adil would lose count of the number of times his jerky footage of Qandeel's body in the ambulance would be seen by viewers around the world. Even when his phone crashed and he lost the original video, he could pull it up from thousands of sites where it continued to be shared.

When I interviewed Adil four months later, I asked him what he had been thinking on that day as he filmed Qandeel's body. He thought for a moment. "What was I doing?" he repeated the question to himself. "In that kind of moment—when you don't have control of your senses, can't control what you will do, what you must do and what you shouldn't do—you don't think about this question until later. Then you ask your-self, what could I have done differently?"

Some twenty years ago, or perhaps longer than that, two questions were asked on a TV game show. "Which bank in all of Pakistan has the richest coffers?" "Where do the richest people in the land live?" The answer to both was Shah Sadar Din. At least, that's how people in this village[4] of a little over forty-five thousand tell the story.

"People here might not have education, but they have money streaming in from abroad," explains Javed Siddiqui, a reporter in the city of Dera Ghazi Khan. The people of the district, also named Dera Ghazi Khan, where Shah Sadar Din is located, brag that the area has the most expensive land in the country—yes, more than Karachi, Lahore or Islamabad. Since the 1970s, men from Shah Sadar Din have been travelling to Saudi Arabia for work, Siddiqui says. According to the Bureau of Emigration and Overseas Employment, more than two hundred and thirty thousand residents of Dera Ghazi Khan district are recorded as having left the country in search of employment between 1981 and 2017.[5] Some find jobs in construction while others set up small businesses. It is unusual to find even one home in the district that has not sent a father, son, brother or husband abroad. Qandeel's brother Arif was one of many who set their sights on a life in Saudi Arabia.

According to urban legend, families in the village made fortunes working outside Pakistan. "Labourers were sending home up to a lakh every month," Siddiqui insists. "Some might send five, ten, twenty lakhs. Places here that deal with foreign remittances brag that they have dealt with transfers of twenty million rupees in a month." He says that three servants who worked in his home have left for Saudi Arabia. One of them, a labourer, sends 3,000 Saudi riyals to his family every month. "Yes!" exclaims Siddiqui. "A labourer! He earns more than 80,000 rupees."

It's December 2016. I'm sitting with Siddiqui and a few other local reporters in his small office in Dera Ghazi Khan city, an hour away from Shah Sadar Din. "How much do you think this office is worth?" Siddiqui asks, referring to the 800-square-foot space where he is sitting on a carpeted floor, sipping tea and juice with other journalists. "Thirty million rupees," he brags.

One of the men pipes up with a story he heard recently. A man from

Shah Sadar Din went to a small tea shop—Where? Oh he can't remember where, and that's not the point anyway—and asked for a cup of chai. Ten minutes later he was still waiting. He asked again. An hour went by, and there was still no tea. "Just see what I do to you," he shouted at the server. He bought the tea shop and the land it was built on the very next day and fired the man who hadn't given him a cup of tea.

The others titter and nod knowingly. They have no doubt that this really happened.

Statistics point to an altogether different reality. In 1997 the Asian Development Bank reported that the district of Dera Ghazi Khan is "the least developed division of Pakistan, with more than 50 percent of the population below the poverty line."[6] Even sixteen years later, life was not much better for most of the people of Dera Ghazi Khan—the district was one of eleven in Punjab where a quarter of Pakistan's poor reside.[7]

There's another story about Shah Sadar Din that many of the men I meet in Dera Ghazi Khan are proud of. In March 2009 the Sri Lankan cricket team was visiting Lahore for a match when it came under attack. The bus transporting the players was hit with hand grenades and fired on. Seven people, including six policemen, were killed that day. And, the story goes, two of the attackers were boys from Shah Sadar Din. The following month the *New York Times* reported that Taliban insurgents "are teaming up with local militant groups to make inroads in Punjab" and warned that the "dusty, impoverished fringes of Punjab could be the next areas facing . . . insurgency" in Pakistan. Quoting a senior police official, the story noted that "militants have gained strength considerably in the district of Dera Ghazi Khan."[8]

Religious fervour here is a particularly violent strain. "It has nothing to do with Islam," feels the *Daily Pakistan*'s bureau chief, Shaukat Iqbal. "It's just the society there. People might not even know how to read the *kalma* [declaration of faith], but they'll say they are Muslim." He's scornful of the locals. "Ask them their age and they'll say, 'I've bathed forty times in my life, so I am forty years old.' In this day and age."

"This is a criminal kind of area," Siddiqui says. The locals say land-lords and tribal chiefs hold sway in the villages and towns in the district, and they maintain their influence by making sure no one bands together against them. Petty feuds quickly spiral out of control, often goaded on by the landlords. And when it comes to women, they warn, even a whiff of disrespect can get you killed. In February 2017 it was reported that at least one woman is killed and five others tortured over domestic dis-putes every day in south Punjab.[9] Siddiqui tells me about a woman who had been murdered by her husband just the other day. He only remem-bers this incident because he found it odd that the man didn't shoot the woman, as is the norm here, but strangled her. The others chime in with their tales: a man who killed his mother and two sisters but who can be found in his home village this very minute because he never went to jail; a woman whose legs were cut off because—well, they're not actually sure why; a girl who was found with a boy a few days ago and the boy was immediately packed off to Saudi Arabia, while the girl . . . no one tells me what the girl's father did to her when he found out.

It's not just women who are at risk. Three days after Qandeel was murdered, a man died after five men chopped off his arms, lips and nose. The attackers ran off with the man's severed limbs, leaving him to bleed to death by the side of the road. He had been having an affair with a married woman who lived in Paiga village in Dera Ghazi Khan district.[10] In February 2017 the nose and lips of a twenty-two-year-old man were cut off after he eloped with a girl. Members of the girl's tribe accused the man of kidnapping her. When she was "recovered" and returned to her parents' home, she was declared *kari*—black, a woman who has lost her honour—and sold. In most cases, a woman who is found with a man to whom she is not married is murdered right away. Alternatively, the couple is brought before a *jirga*, or council of elders, and—following the custom in many villages in Dera Ghazi Khan dis-trict—the man has to pay a penalty and the woman is either killed or sold for the same amount as the penalty.

"It might be a big deal for you, but for us these are small things," says one reporter who doesn't want to give his name. "If we started highlighting all these cases, then the entire media industry of Pakistan might as well come and set up shop in the district. It's not that we don't respect women," the reporter wants me to know. For instance, he points out, women are held in such esteem that if there is a clash between members of two tribes and three or four women from one tribe visit the home of the opposing tribe's chief, they can ask for forgiveness or a truce and return to their homes without a scratch or a hand laid on them. "That is how highly we regard our women," he says.

If they want to go to school or college, they are given permission to do so. At the City School in Dera Ghazi Khan—a branch of a well-known expensive private school based in Lahore—many of the female students are the first in their family to be educated. Women who wish to work can get jobs in their village or the district as teachers. "But the way that Qandeel was, we just cannot accept a woman like that," the reporter says. "What she was doing was wrong. And if you're doing something wrong in your own home, but you keep that within those four walls, that's all right. But she was doing things—dancing, singing—for everyone to see. Our religion doesn't allow this, our culture doesn't allow this, our area and our traditions do not allow this."

Since July 2016 the people of Shah Sadar Din have had to explain their culture and traditions to the outsiders who streamed in when news broke of Qandeel's murder. "There have been so many murders here since then," the reporter says. "But Qandeel was a bit famous, a bit well known, so maybe that's why it got highlighted."

The locals find the attention distasteful. If they were initially curious about the media, they now find its presence disrespectful. "Qandeel's relatives say that her father should not continue to meet these journalists," the reporter claims. "People in the village say that they are being given a bad name with all this media coverage." They have started to refuse to give interviews, and Safdar Shah says that some have warned him not to bring any more reporters or camera crews to the village. It has become difficult for outsiders to meet or interview Qandeel's relatives or friends of the family, who don't want word to get out that they have been giving information to the media, particularly as the court case against Qandeel's brother and her cousin Haq Nawaz continues.

The answer to the question of whether people in Shah Sadar Din knew about Qandeel before Malik Azam ran a story revealing her identity changes depending on who you talk to. "We all know each other here," says Hussain, a man who lives a few steps from the mosque around the corner from Qandeel's home in the village. "We knew who she was. We knew that Qandeel Baloch is Fouzia Azeem. It's you who found out later."

He claims that many people in the village liked to watch Qandeel on television when she appeared on talk shows or interviews or sang and danced. Siddiqui says he knows of people who liked Qandeel's Facebook page, even though none of them would admit to it today. "Her brother's friends used to watch her videos," he says. "They wanted her." Hussain explains that as long as it was only people in the village who knew who she was, there was no problem. The moment the rest of the country found out, they felt disgraced.

Few mention Mufti Abdul Qavi. He might visit from time to time and have a family connection to the village, but most of the people here do not seem to revere him. In some conversations the mention of his name elicits titters. "That horny cleric," one man calls him. "Not many people here know Mufti Qavi," Hussain claims. When the selfies and video from Qandeel's encounter with Mufti Qavi went viral, there was chatter in the village about the cleric's roots in Shah Sadar Din. A few days later, when Malik Azam's story revealed that Qandeel was from the same village, hundreds of thousands of people across the country suddenly knew the name Shah Sadar Din, and it wasn't because of the riches in the banks or the expensive land or anything else the villagers are proud of.

But there are also those who say they only found out that Qandeel was one of their own when the *Daily Pakistan* story came out. Five days after Azam's scoop was published, Fayyaz Khan Leghari, the vice chairman of the union council in the neighbouring town of Gadai, sued Qandeel for 50 million rupees in damages for adopting Baloch as her surname. He wanted to threaten her with a greater penalty, but fifty million was the maximum amount he could claim in such a case. He says that the tribe that Qandeel belongs to—the Ma'arah—are not Baloch, and their attempts to claim otherwise are lies.

"I just wanted her to tell the truth and to be honest," says Leghari, a short, mild-mannered Baloch man in his forties. "Baloch people all over the world contacted me—they even offered monetary help if I needed it—because they were so worried about what people would think of them if they believed Qandeel was also Baloch."

A friend sent him the link to a video Qandeel uploaded on to her Facebook page. Leghari watched her kneeling on her bed, wearing a traditional black and pale-yellow Baloch woman's embroidered shirt. She had veiled her face with a dupatta. She called herself Balochi Laila and dedicated the song to her "Indian lovers and fans." She wore an ornate silver headpiece which twinkled and chimed as she shook her hips, raised her arms and thrust out her chest. She played with her veil before finally taking it off.[11]

"That was totally against our Baloch traditions," Leghari says. "Baloch people are honourable and our women cover themselves. They do *purdah* [veil themselves] and she is showing off her naked body and saying she is Baloch. If someone is not Baloch and they—with their behaviour and their actions—defame us and ruin our name, I take offence at that." Giving notice of the case to Qandeel, he warned her that her bid to achieve fame and "cheap publicity" was hurting the sentiments of the Baloch people. They were supposedly extremely dejected by her behaviour.

Ultimately, whether they claim they knew Qandeel's identity all along and or say they were unaware of it, the locals took action. The easiest thing to do was to turn their sights on her family, especially her younger brother. Waseem used to run a small mobile phone shop in the village marketplace, funded by Qandeel. While Hussain claims that Qandeel would sometimes visit the village late at night, arriving and leaving before any of her friends or extended family could find out, others say that she would ask her driver to stop at the edge of town and wait for Waseem so she could hand him wads of cash. When she sent money to her parents, he would allegedly pester them for a handout.

The mobile phone shop, just big enough for three or four men to stand in at a time, is nestled inside the village's main marketplace. It has a clear glass exterior and the latest mobile phones are displayed on glass shelves. Waseem soon sold it off. It was the second business he had run into the ground since Qandeel started giving him money. He liked to drink and lounge at the local dhaba with his friends, sucking on the gurgling pipe of a hookah or smoking hashish-laced cigarettes. He was known as a "loafer type" and a man of short temper. "He kept bad company," Hussain says dismissively. "All their evenings would be spent outside the home."

Waseem's parents say that after the *Daily Pakistan* story revealing Qandeel's real name, their son was taunted. "You have no shame," he would be told by friends and strangers. "You are worth nothing." Hussain remembers someone jeering at Waseem, "Your sister is singing and dancing in her knickers and you're living a luxurious life with the money she earns."

"They would say, 'You have no honour. Your sister dances naked,'" says Hussain. People would go to Waseem and ask if he could download his sister's latest clip on to their phones. Hussain quickly clarifies, "I have never seen them. I've never seen any of her videos."

Soon people from Shah Sadar Din who worked with Qandeel's brother in Saudi Arabia were mocking him, Hussain claims. "They told him that his sister was bringing dishonour to their village. They would have thought it was necessary to do something about this. They would have thought about killing her."

The day Qandeel was murdered, a reporter who did not wish to give me his name was on his way home from a neighbouring district. He stopped to have some tea with friends, five of whom were from Dera

Ghazi Khan; one was a visitor. "The minute I heard what had happened, I said, 'This is great news,'" the reporter confesses. The five men from Dera Ghazi Khan agreed, but the visitor was appalled.

"How can you say this?" he asked. "A woman has been murdered."

"Go ask anyone in our area," the reporter explained. "They will all say the same thing. You can think it's illiterate or savage. But if I travel anywhere in Pakistan and I'm asked where I'm from, if I say Shah Sadar Din, then the immediate answer will be, 'Oh! Isn't Qandeel Baloch from your area?' At least we don't have that to worry about any more."

When I ask if it matters that the murder goes against the laws of Pakistan, the reporter looks slightly puzzled. "The law can be broken, but we can never break the rules of our culture," he explains. "To break the law is nothing at all. These laws can be written and rewritten. But the rules of our culture have been around for centuries. To break them is very, very difficult." At the end of the day Qandeel brought her fate upon herself, he feels. "Islam tells us to hide our sins," he says. "So why did she highlight all of hers?" Then he sighs. "But may her sins be forgiven. After all, she was human too."

The others in the room nod and murmur, "May Allah forgive her."

On the morning of 16 July 2016, Attiya Jaffrey, a police investigator, was at home when her husband called out from his usual spot in front of the television—he was obsessive about watching the news and staying up to date. "Qandeel has been killed," he told her breathlessly.

Just a few weeks ago her husband had told Attiya about this woman and her meeting with a cleric from Multan. Didn't Qandeel live in Karachi? was Attiya's immediate thought. This would mean the murder was outside her jurisdiction. Then her heart sank when she heard the anchor say the body had been found in a house in Multan. What was this woman doing here? she remembers thinking. Then Muzaffarabad was mentioned and she sighed with relief. This neighbourhood was nowhere near her patch. She watched the breaking news play over and over again, saw the media frenzy as reporters jostled for space outside a small house at the end of a lane. "Thank God it's in Muzaffarabad," she said to her husband. "This case is going to get very crazy."

And then her phone rang. It was her superior, City Police Officer Azhar Akram. He wanted her to come to Qandeel's house. He was already there with a few other officers and they needed a female officer to accompany the body to the morgue. He wanted a woman he could trust with the job.

It was no secret that Akram thought highly of Attiya. He would praise her in front of other investigating officers and cite her work as an example of efficiency and professionalism. Even though she was a woman, she was so good at what she did, he would say to some of Attiya's colleagues. Attiya tried not to worry that Akram's request that day could mean he wanted her on the case. She reminded herself that it was routine for additional officers to be called to the scene of a crime if it was a high-profile case or if extra bodies were needed to handle a crowd or family members.

By the time Attiya got to Qandeel's house, the crowd had swelled. It felt like she was in the middle of some festival, not a crime scene. The officers at the entrance opened the gate a crack for her to squeeze through as reporters and cameramen jostled to see past her.

She couldn't believe this small, grubby house was Qandeel's. Cigarette ends, ground underfoot, lay on the floor outside Qandeel's room. Inside, the body was laid out on a charpoy on a red sheet patterned with white snowflakes and crystals, a pillow under the head. The room was a mess: on a table were scattered two mobile phones, a purse, an open packet of hair dye, a bottle of mustard oil, a passport, and a one-way plane ticket. Two suitcases were open on the floor. Clothes and make-up spilled out of them. Attiya could see past a door on the right to a narrow courtyard and a small kitchen, where dirty dishes were stacked at the sink. The room was small—you could walk across it in a few strides, and the charpoy, positioned directly under the fan, took up most of the space.

She looked at the body. The stomach had started to bloat. The green shirt with orange embroidery looked uncomfortably tight. There were small gold earrings in the ears. The face was tinged blue. The swollen lips were a deep plum. There were scratch marks on the face, near the eyes and the nose, the blood dry by the time the body was discovered. A female constable was collecting the cigarette butts from the floor. Tests would reveal traces of Waseem's DNA on the butts. Did he stand outside his sister's room and have a smoke before or after she went limp and stopped flailing and kicking her feet against the man who held her down with all his weight? The constable snapped rubber gloves on to her hands. She took Qandeel's hands in hers and gently swabbed the tips of her fingers and looked under her nails. Had Qandeel clawed blindly at anyone she could reach when her face was covered with the sweat-stained scarf that had been around her brother's shoulders? This is not, Attiya remembers thinking, the work of a single man. The fan spun slowly above the charpoy.

Qandeel's mother was crouched by the charpoy so quietly that Attiya only noticed her when she smoothed her daughter's shirt and covered her chest with a white dupatta with pale flowers on it. She was not crying or wailing. She didn't like it when anyone tried to touch the body. The police needed to check if Qandeel had been raped.

It was stifling in there in the July heat and there were no windows in the room. "Is this really Qandeel Baloch?" CPO Akram asked nobody in particular.

Over the next few days Attiya couldn't stop thinking about the body. She felt furious every time she remembered how a reporter had yanked off that red sheet—the ambulance crew, the fools, had arrived without any white ones so officers had used the sheet to cover the body as it was carried out of the home.

Four days later, CPO Akram dismissed the investigating officer handling the case for negligence. There was too much media interest—not just local but international—in this case, and too many people ready to criticize the Multan police for bungling it. There could be no mistakes. The CPO wanted someone he could rely on to handle it. "Madam, just watch," one of Attiya's wardens commented. "This case will now be hung around your neck." She had never dealt with a suspected honour killing case before.

Attiya had joined the police force as a sub-inspector in 1988, when she was thirty-six. She is from Gujrat, and was posted to Sialkot as a city traffic warden. She stayed there for sixteen years, got married and had three sons. In 2008 she was sent to Multan and has been in the city ever since. On the day we meet, four months after she saw Qandeel's body, she is preparing for another move. She has been promoted, some say because of how well she handled Qandeel's case, and is waiting to find out where she will be posted next. She has had a few days off and looks relaxed, swapping her official black uniform for a bright floral shalwar kameez. She has only come into the office to hand over all the files and records from the Qandeel case to the next investigating officer.

Attiya's family has a history of service in the police. Her father and his father before him were police officers, and many cousins have joined the force since. She has three brothers, and it was expected that they too would join the police. However, it was Attiya who went to her father and said she wanted to carry on the family tradition. "It was unheard of at the time for a girl to do something like that, especially in our family," Attiya explains. Her family is conservative and proudly claim to be Syeds, an honorific title for those who say they are descendants of the Prophet Muhammad's family. "I only managed to do this because I had such a great friendship with and such great love for my father. He took a stand for me, even when everyone else criticized him and said I should just become a teacher." When friends and family members warned him that letting a girl join a profession dominated by men would bring shame and dishonour to his family, Attiya's father would respond, "Respect and honour are in Allah's hands. If it is her fate to be dishonourable and disrespectful, she will bring my family shame even if she becomes a teacher."

Attiya's mother agreed, and when her daughter had completed her studies ignored those who said it was now time to marry her off.

Eventually, she said, her daughter would marry someone her parents chose for her. By the time she did, she was forty-two years old, and she was the first to marry someone outside the family. Even when she was married, and later, when she had children, she couldn't think of quitting the police force. "The thought of just being in the home, cleaning it and sitting there all day and reading magazines—it didn't make sense to me," she says.

Attiya and her best friend took the police exams together and passed them. "I was among the first batch of women in Sialkot to join the police force," she explains. There were only four of them. "There were no senior female officers we could turn to for advice or talk to." It wasn't always easy, but Attiya stuck it out and did not complain because she did not want her parents' critics to say they had been right all along. Attiya and her colleagues had been brought up and educated to be polite, but superior officers would rebuke them if they addressed arrested men and women with the formal "*aap,*" rather than "*tu.*" They'll never fear you and won't tell you anything, they would sneer. When the women patrolled the market together, people would stare at them in their police uniforms and whisper, "Dirty people."

"I remember the first time we got our uniforms and walked out of the station, an old man passed by me and stopped in his tracks," Attiya says. The man shook his head in disgust and pinched his earlobes, a gesture to ward off the evil eye. "Shame, shame," he cried out. "It's a sign of the Day of Judgement."

Inside the station the women had to learn not to be seen talking to male colleagues alone—it was the easiest way to become the subject of a rumour about an affair. "You knew that whoever you were seen standing next to alone, there would be a scandal about the two of you," Attiya says. Male superiors would not call the women into their offices alone, and if they had something to say to them would often use an intermediary to pass on the message. If Attiya or one of the other women complained about a male officer, they knew that the first thing the man would do was attack their character. "It is the greatest weapon they have against us—to say, 'She's not a good woman.' Then they can just sit back and watch the rumour spread throughout the department."

Attiya was given her first murder case in 2015. She couldn't sleep for two days after she saw the body. Even today, after having handled roughly thirty homicide cases, she still feels anxious at crime scenes. "When it's a child, I think of my son," she says. "If it's someone's brother who has been killed, I think of my own."

When she took charge of Qandeel's case, she pored over every piece of information she could find. She would wait for her children to go to sleep and comb through Qandeel's social media pages, her photographs and videos. She watched every interview she could get her hands on. Her children made fun of her obsession and made up a name for it. "Mama has Qandeeliya," they joked.

Attiya swears she could feel Qandeel's presence in her home, drifting through each room. "She was a part of my life," she says. Qandeel wasn't just another homicide case. The police conducted sweeping raids and picked up dozens of people including members of Qandeel's extended family, her sister, brother-in-law and cousins. Many had gone into hiding in nearby towns and villages because they feared being caught up in the case.

Attiya would receive constant phone calls from superiors wanting updates on her progress. "This was being talked about internationally, and we were getting calls every day about the case," she says. The international media coverage tended towards the view that this was a Pakistani woman who had dared to defy the norm and been brutally killed by her own brother. There was pressure to show that the police—and thereby Pakistan—was doing everything possible to bring the killers to justice. "If we [the country] had been trying to make a modern image of ourselves in the world, then that image was being sullied by this case," Attiya explains. "We wanted people to know that we were pursuing the investigation thoroughly."

On 17 July, one day after Qandeel's body was found, her brother

Waseem was arrested. According to many reports, he had made no effort to hide and was spotted riding around on his motorbike in Shah Sadar Din's main market the morning after he fled Multan. CPO Akram promptly held a press conference. He wanted the public to know that the police had been searching for Qandeel's brother. The murder, he explained, "was probably done on the basis of honour."[12] He announced, first in Urdu and then in English, "And now I would like to tell you that we have arrested Waseem . . . He has confessed to the crime." He asked for him to be brought into the room. "I've called for Waseem to come here now," he told the journalists, "so you can have an interview with him."

A striped purple cloth had been thrown over Waseem's head and shoulders. As he walked in, CPO Akram repeated, "This is an honour-based murder." He emphasized that Waseem had been apprehended so quickly because the police had used their "technical and operational teams and all the resources possible" in Dera Ghazi Khan. The forensic samples and autopsy report would also be rushed through a laboratory in Lahore, he said. Qandeel's body had been found on Saturday morning, and CPO Akram promised to have the forensic results by Monday. For the third time, he said that Waseem had choked and strangled Qandeel for reasons of honour. The only question that remained in the investigation, he seemed to imply, was the extent to which any of Waseem's friends had been involved in the murder. Even though Waseem had yet to be fully interrogated about why he had strangled his sister and stolen her money and jewellery, the police had no doubt that this was an honour killing.

The journalists requested that the police remove the hood covering Waseem's face and CPO Akram obliged. Every camera in the room zoomed in on him. A dark, slender man, Waseem wore a pale blue shalwar kameez, the sleeves rolled up, and stared nonchalantly at the room. His curly hair, long enough to cover the tops of his ears, was slightly tousled. He was handcuffed.

"I would like to ask all of you, my friends, to ask him questions in a line, so that everyone's questions can be answered," CPO Akram requested.

A few reporters rushed forward with microphones. The CPO handed Waseem one of them, which he cradled between his cuffed hands.

"Yes, sir, what did you want to say?" Waseem asked one of the reporters in a thin, reedy voice.

"What's your name?" a reporter asked.

"Muhammad Waseem."

"What is your mother's name?"

"I don't know my mother's name."

"Why did you do this to Qandeel?"

The confession was broadcast live by every channel that had a reporter in the room. "The reason is the way she was coming on Facebook," Waseem replied. "We Baloch cannot tolerate this." The reporters pointed out that his sister had been putting photographs and videos on Facebook for six or seven years. Why had Waseem only been angered by them now?

"There were lots of other problems, OK," Waseem whined. "The problem with the cleric. The media came to our house. That hadn't happened before. She made it a problem and so I did what I did."

CPO Akram helped him out. "So apparently what he is trying to say is that ever since she came in the limelight more and more, he felt pressure to do something."

Waseem said he acted alone. No one in his family had known about his plan.

"How did you kill her?" a reporter called out. "Can you describe it?" Waseem nodded towards CPO Akram. "I did it the way sir described it."

When asked to elaborate, he explained, "I gave her a tablet and then I strangled her."

"Are you ashamed?"

"No," Waseem said, sticking out his chin. "I have no shame. I am Baloch."

This was a slap in the face to anyone who said he and his sister weren't Baloch. Hadn't he shown the kind of honour and self-respect that the Baloch were proud of?

Attiya cannot forget how cool and relaxed Waseem remained throughout the investigation. During his polygraph test he told police officials he had given his parents and his sister sleeping tablets in their milk the night before the murder. On 19 July Regional Police Officer Sultan Azam Temouri told the media Waseem had confessed that "the modern lifestyle adopted by Qandeel came under discussion with [Waseem's] other siblings many a time and they were all against it."[13] His brother Arif, who lived in Saudi Arabia, had asked him to do something about their shameful sister. Their cousin Haq Nawaz, a man who had been picked up several times for petty crimes, could help him out, Arif suggested. By 26 July, Haq Nawaz had turned himself in to the police in Dera Ghazi Khan, but Attiya says she could find no proof of the conversation between Waseem and Arif. When Arif called his brother, he would do so online. There were no phone records, she says, and by the time she finally found a phone number for Arif, the phone had been turned off.

On 18 July a news report in the *Express Tribune* quoted Waseem as saying, "I made up my mind to kill [Qandeel] when her controversial video with Mufti Abdul Qavi went viral on social media . . . I had made up my mind that day, and I was waiting for my sister to come home." Attiya says she tried to find some shred of evidence connecting Waseem's actions with Mufti Abdul Qavi and his humiliation after the video of his meeting with Qandeel went viral. "I don't like Mufti Qavi," she says bluntly. "But I could never find any connection between him and the brothers. He came for interrogation every single time we asked. He answered all our questions. He gave us his phone willingly. There were no calls to Waseem. Not a single one. I called all the numbers that had called his phone and then Qandeel's phone." They belonged to reporters who had called Qandeel and then Mufti Qavi to get a quote or an interview about their meeting in that hotel.

But there are some people in Multan who whisper that Attiya is not as efficient as she seems. In the rambling warren that is the city's district and sessions court, lawyers huddle together in a small courtyard to discuss the case. A man who claims to have been closely involved with the investigation and the court case says that Attiya deliberately left information out of her investigation report. "She has done nothing," he says with scorn. "That bitch has done nothing. She has only made things worse." The police are deliberately hiding links—including phone calls between Mufti Qavi and Qandeel's brother Arif—because they wish to remain in the cleric's good books. "Attiya is being dishonest," he claims. "She's clearly joined Mufti Qavi. She's getting his money."

Waseem did not falter during his interrogation, and the police could not bend the rules too much because they knew the media would pounce on any suggestion of torture. They didn't want a single bruise on him and so at most kept Waseem standing in a cell or forced him to raise his arms and did not allow him to lower them for hours at a time. Waseem never complained and didn't seem to care if he was allowed to sleep or not. Attiya tried other tactics. "If you scare them and show them what you have on them, they usually cave," she says. Waseem wasn't like that.

"She made our lives very difficult and I had no other solution," he would say about Qandeel. "She just wouldn't listen. I told my parents so many times to control her, to get her married. But she just would not listen. I had no other way to deal with this."

After fourteen days of court-mandated custody, Attiya had one question left for him: Don't you feel sorry for what you've done? She appealed to his emotions. "You and your sister spent your childhood together," she said. "You must have played together. She was older than you. How did you decide to do this?"

Waseem thought about it briefly. "I do feel sorry," he replied. "But at the time this was all I could think about doing."

As she prepares to leave Qandeel's case behind her, Attiya says she is still not satisfied with the investigation. She believes she did all she could within the limited amount of time specified for the police to submit a report of its findings—extra time was given due to the publicity the case was getting—but she is bitter about the resources and help she was given. "There isn't the satisfaction of leaving every stone unturned," she says. "For instance, I've only just received a reply from the FIA, three months after I requested its help in finding information about Qandeel's social media accounts and her WhatsApp chats. The Saudi embassy never got back to us regarding a request to help locate Arif. The State Bank never got back to us about any accounts Qandeel might have had, and we never heard back about any properties she might have owned or rented."

On the night of 15 July, when Waseem went back to Shah Sadar Din after the murder, he took Qandeel's phone with him. Waseem had owned a mobile phone shop and so knew how to repair phones, but also how to wipe them. By the time he was arrested, he had erased all the data on Qandeel's phone and passed a surge of power through it. None of her photographs, videos or messages were retrievable.

Safdar Shah and Qandeel's parents told Attiya that they had found a laptop and a few diaries in Qandeel's apartment in Karachi, but these items proved equally useless in providing a thread to follow for the investigation, Attiya says. The diaries were filled with quotes, some poetry and the lyrics to songs. There were scribbled notes reminding Qandeel what to say on her social media pages. Attiya gave them all back to Qandeel's parents. As far as the police were concerned, these were just scraps of paper. The parents say they have been unable to use the password-protected laptop. Attiya says she searched the laptop but did not find "anything of use" in it.

On 6 December 2016 a judge indicted Waseem, Haq Nawaz and Abdul Basit—accused of driving the getaway car on the night of the murder.[14] "We have all the forensic evidence we need, DNA reports, a polygraph test and the mobile phone data of the accused," District Prosecutor Jam Salahuddin told me before the hearings in the case commenced. "They murdered her. They cannot be saved."

But Attiya isn't hopeful of the outcome of the trial. "I don't have faith in the justice system," Attiya says. "Some judges can be very cooperative, while others are not. The court follows its own will. I've seen this with a lot of cases—despite all the evidence, nothing happens."

As we wrap up our meeting, Attiya says she wants to clarify something. "This case is important to me," she explains. "It's important because Qandeel was a human and this should not have happened to her. But I don't agree with what she was doing." She is confused by the people who say Qandeel is someone to look up to, and especially by the women who praise her attitude and behaviour. "Qandeel is no role model," Attiya feels. "To make her a role model for young girls is very wrong. Look, Benazir Bhutto is a role model. She integrated with her society. Did you ever see the dupatta fall from her head? She knew how society thinks of women. We need to consider our society, our religion and a modern way of life equally. Of course women have the right to employment, the right to education, the right to good living standards. You can say you want to be totally unfettered, to have freedom, but is becoming Qandeel Baloch freedom?"

Why did Qandeel have to break so many rules so quickly? Attiya wonders.

When I say that I am surprised by her question, especially when I consider all the rules Attiya says she has broken to reach this point in her career, she explains gently, "Society cannot change so quickly. You need to give it time. Maybe in time it will become how you want it to be. No matter how modern we become, as Muslims we cannot expect to have total freedom to do whatever we like. After all, we won't live in this world for ever, will we? We will return to Allah and then we will have to answer for all that we have done in this world. So you have to think about that."

She cringes when she recalls how she had to watch some of Qandeel's videos with her colleagues. "The men couldn't look at me and I couldn't look at them. It was so awkward." She hears women talk about wanting the freedom to behave as they please. "I don't think as women we are missing some kind of freedom," she says. "Do you?"

It's time for her to meet the next investigating officer, the man who will take over the case from her. Some of her colleagues need to sit in on the meeting, but there aren't enough chairs in the room for all of them. Three of them sit on a charpoy that has been pushed into a corner. One puts his feet up; the other leans against the wall and dangles his legs over the side. It is the same charpoy that Attiya first saw Qandeel's body lying on.

"The day she was murdered, I got a phone call from a friend," Malik Azam says. "He said, 'It's you. You did this.'" The *Daily Pakistan* story revealing Qandeel's identity had set in motion a chain of events that would end in her murder, Azam's friend said.

"So when she was putting up all those photos and making videos about Imran Khan, her brother didn't feel dishonoured then?" Azam retorted. "When she posed for the whole world, he didn't feel dishonoured then? But when I run a story he suddenly feels dishonoured?"

He hung up on his friend. They haven't spoken since.

When I meet Qandeel's parents in November 2016 Anwar bibi makes the same accusation. She says that the media is responsible in part for her daughter's murder. If the media had not revealed her real name or made such a big deal of the Qavi meeting, no one from Shah Sadar Din would have cared about Fouzia Azeem. People would not have jeered at her son, and he would not have been driven to kill his sister.

It's an accusation that Malik Azam and his bureau chief have heard many times since July 2016—not just from Qandeel's parents and those who spoke out against her murder, but from colleagues in the industry as well.

Azam's bureau chief, Shaukat Iqbal, is scornful of the accusation. "All we revealed was her real name," Iqbal says. "That's it. The issues that arose after that were her own family's problems. We didn't create those." He and Azam do not believe they did anything wrong by printing pictures of Qandeel's passport. "A passport is nothing personal,"

Iqbal says. "If you go to an embassy or apply for a visa, don't you give them your passport? So what?"

He does not regret the *Daily Pakistan* coverage, although, "I think we underestimated the story," Iqbal says. "Someone else would have run a bigger story, made a bigger deal of it." As for the journalists who criticize the *Daily Pakistan*, he just has one question for them: if the story about her real name was such a danger to her, then why did every other news outlet run it as well? If the *Daily Pakistan* is responsible for what happened to Qandeel, then so is every other newspaper and TV channel that ran a story on Qandeel's real name and where she was from.

Iqbal believes that Anwar bibi blames the media because she does not want to admit that Qandeel's whole family conspired to kill her. They were greedy for her money, he says. They watched Qandeel's interviews and saw the clothes she was wearing, the lifestyle she boasted of, the "side businesses" she claimed to have and the cars she was driven around in. They believed that she was withholding money from them. "This hen was laying golden eggs for them, and they wanted all the eggs at once," Iqbal speculates. "They didn't get that and they slaughtered their hen." After all, Iqbal and Malik Azam say, look at the pictures of Qandeel's parents on the day they called the police to their home in Multan. Look at the clean white shalwar kameez and turban the father is wearing and the embroidered kameez the mother has on. Did they change after they found their daughter's body and called the police? Or did they sleep in these clean, ironed clothes? "The mother is wearing a party dress!" Iqbal exclaims. "Who goes to sleep in such nice clothes?" Their daughter, he says, was nothing special. Of course he feels sad that she was killed, but he does not understand why she is still being talked about. "What was her profession?" he asks. "Simply, she was a call girl. No other word for it. I'm sorry to say this, may Allah forgive me, but that's what she was."

When Waseem returned to Shah Sadar Din after the murder, news of what he had done quickly spread. People in the village say his cousins, uncles and friends congratulated him. They said he had done the right thing. No matter that they had called him shameless. "A man with no honour can discover honour at any moment," they assured each other.

It would be hard to find anyone in Shah Sadar Din today who does not know Qandeel's name. I make my way down uneven sandy trails in a large graveyard, stepping past empty chocolate and biscuit wrappers and dried dog shit as I search for her grave. The previous month, October 2016, Qandeel's father told a reporter, "Following my daughter's wish, I have installed Pakistan's flag on her grave."[15] But I cannot see a flag anywhere in the graveyard. Two villagers standing near a grave ask me who I'm looking for. They point to the far left corner of the graveyard. They have become used to people—mostly the media—coming here searching for Qandeel. Someone has planted a thin reedy sapling a few feet tall next to the grave, which is just another mound of dirt like the many others around it. It is not covered in concrete or marble like some of the others. There is no marker, no sign of her name and no Pakistani flag. Without the villagers, it would have been impossible to find Qandeel in this graveyard.

EPILOGUE

On 22 July 2016, six days after Qandeel Baloch was murdered, a parliamentary committee approved a bill that sought to close a loophole in existing legislation dealing with honour killings which allowed killers to walk free.

By the time Qandeel was murdered, 2016 had already seen an estimated 326 such murders in Pakistan, of which 312 victims were women.[1] According to the Human Rights Commission of Pakistan, the most common motive appeared to be retribution or punishment for "illicit relations" (185 murders) and "marriage choice" (99 murders)—the deceased man or woman's decision to marry someone their family, tribe or former partner did not approve of. Of the 326 murders, it is known that 67 were committed by a husband or ex-partner, 64 by siblings, 41 by parents, 30 by other relatives, 15 by in-laws and 10 by the deceased's son or daughter. Many of the killings took place with the collusion of several family members.

Under the existing legislation, a killer or killers could walk free even after confessing to a murder through the Islamic provisions in the Pakistan Penal Code relating to forgiveness/waiver or compounding, whereby the relatives of the deceased man or woman—in the majority of cases also the relatives of the suspect—could pardon the killer or accept "blood money" as compensation for the crime.

In 2014 Sughra Imam, a senator from the Pakistan People's Party, moved a bill to close this loophole, and the Anti-Honour Killings Laws (Criminal Laws Amendment) Bill 2015 was passed by the Senate. However, the government failed to have the bill passed in the National Assembly.

On 17 July 2016, the day after Qandeel's murder, an editorial in the English-language daily *Dawn* stated that the only "crime" she had committed was to "live life on her own terms," adding, "Women have the right to be themselves even if they offend conventional sensibilities." The state, the editorial continued, "must unequivocally demonstrate that [women] do not deserve to be murdered for [doing so]." The writer criticized the loopholes in existing legislation: "The murderers of women go scot-free they are forgiven and even supported by regressive patriarchies after killing 'disobedient' female family members." While activists and legislators had lobbied for the lapsed amendment to the existing laws since 2015, the government had dragged its feet. "Why the lethargy?" the editorial demanded. "When will parliament be jolted out of its stupor?"

Four days later the newspaper received its reply. In an interview with Reuters the prime minister's daughter Maryam Nawaz Sharif—not a government official—promised that a draft of the amended law would be presented to a parliamentary committee and, once approved, sent for a vote before a joint session of parliament within "a couple of weeks."[2] The draft was cleared the very next day, and three months later, on 6 October 2016, unanimously adopted.

The most significant change under the Criminal Law Amendment (Offences in the Name or Pretext of Honour) Act 2016 is that family members can now only prevent a killer from receiving the death penalty.[3] They cannot "forgive" or pardon the killer and enable them to walk free. Everyone convicted of an honour killing will face a mandatory sentence or life imprisonment.

"We have achieved consensus on anti-honour killing . . . in committee of joint sitting of Parliament," tweeted Maryam Nawaz Sharif. "Great news for Pakistan."[4]

The response to the amendment was overwhelmingly positive, not just in the local media, but internationally. "Pakistani men who kill their female relatives in the name of honour will no longer be able to evade punishment," announced the *Guardian.*[5] The BBC described the new legislation as a "step in the right direction,"[6] while the *New York Times* noted, "Pakistan toughens laws on rape and honour killings of women."[7] A senator from the Pakistan People's Party told CNN, a "vicious circle has now come to an end" with the new law.[8] It was the kind of positive media coverage that Pakistan rarely enjoys internationally.

Prime Minister Nawaz Sharif also received praise and thanks from within the country, most notably from documentary filmmaker Sharmeen Obaid Chinoy. On the day that Qandeel Baloch's body was found, Obaid Chinoy tweeted, "How many women have to die before we pass the Anti Honor Killing Bill?" When the legislation was announced, she said she was grateful to the prime minister.[9] "Thank you to PM Nawaz Sharif for keeping his promise: #antihonorkilling bill," she tweeted.

The "promise" Obaid Chinoy was referring to had been made eight months before, when she won her second Academy Award—for a documentary on honour killings in Pakistan. Called *A Girl in the River: The Price of Forgiveness*, Obaid Chinoy's film tells the story of Saba Qaiser, an eighteen-year-old girl from the district of Hafizabad in Punjab, who was beaten, shot in the face, bundled into a sack and thrown into a canal in 2014. Believing she was dead, her attackers, her father and uncle, fled. However, Saba manged to get out of the sack and trod water till she reached the canal's banks where, grasping at reeds, she pulled herself on to dry land.

When Obaid Chinoy met Saba's father after he was arrested, he explained that he had tried to kill his daughter because she had married a man of her own choice. "Whatever we did, we were obliged to do it," Maqsood says in the documentary. "She took away our honour." He described his daughter's decision as "unlawful" and a choice that had ruined her family's reputation. "If you put one drop of piss in a gallon of milk, the whole thing gets destroyed," he explained. "That is what [Saba] has done."

Proceedings in Saba's case came to an abrupt end when she pardoned her father and uncle. She had come under pressure from her family and in-laws. "Saba can just tell the judge, 'I was angry then, and I want to forgive them,'" her lawyer, Waqas Bhatti, says in the documentary.

"We all live in the same neighbourhood," explained Saba's brother-in-law Shafaqat when asked why she should forgive the men who had tried to kill her. It was for the good of the community and her family. "Some day we may need our neighbours' help. Would they ever cooperate with us if we did not compromise?"

A Girl in the River revealed the extraordinary grip the concept of honour has on men and women in Pakistan—a grip that was only strengthened by the legal right to pardon those who go to any lengths to preserve that honour. In January 2016 the film was nominated for an Academy Award in the Best Documentary—Short Subject category. The lapsed anti-honour killing bill from 2014 leaped back into the headlines, with Obaid Chinoy running a campaign urging the prime minister to "bring this Bill back in parliament." "We need a law that ends impunity for perpetrators of 'honour' crimes right now," stated a petition started by Obaid Chinoy calling on the prime minister to put his weight behind "tighter legislation."[10]

In February Sharif met Obaid Chinoy and invited her to screen *A Girl in the River*. On 22 February the first screening of the film in the country was held at the prime minister's house in Islamabad. The following week Obaid Chinoy made history, becoming the only Pakistani to win two Oscars. "This week the Pakistani prime minister has said that he will change the law on honour killing after watching this film," she announced in her acceptance speech. "That is the power of film."[11]

But until July, when Waseem confessed to killing his sister, the law remained the same. A murder committed in the name of honour in Pakistan was still the perfect crime: when a brother shot his own sister, a father bludgeoned his daughter or a mother burned her daughter alive, there was rarely any penalty. Families protected their own. However, Qandeel's case appeared to be different. A father had accused his sons of conspiring to murder their sister, and he wanted the harshest punishment possible meted out to them.

Qandeel's father had stated in his FIR that his son Aslam had encouraged Waseem to commit the murder. However, Waseem proudly accepted all responsibility. "It's just me," he told the media after his arrest. "I did this all alone." He seemed to want to take all the credit for saving his family's honour. In an interview three months later his mother would say that Waseem thought he would be in jail for "two to three months and then after he will be free," as was common in many such cases. Her son, she said, "was not aware that this would become a high-profile case."[12]

Muhammad Azeem was praised when he told the media that his daughter had been the "best son of all sons"—she had taken care of her parents and supported them when none of their sons had stepped forward to do so.[13] Azeem wept in an interview with BBC Urdu as he thought of how Qandeel must have called out to her parents for help on the night she was killed. "I say shoot my son on sight," Azeem said. "He suffocated my little one." Even in October, when Azeem's right to pardon his son for Qandeel's murder was taken away from him, he reiterated, "There is no pardon from our side." He wanted his son to be punished "at the earliest" and said Waseem "should get life imprisonment or death—I will feel happy."[14]

It's a statement that Azeem would repeat often, and in his last major television interview, in October 2016, he said he would never bow to pressure from his family to forgive Waseem, even though he and Anwar bibi no longer had the financial support that Qandeel had provided.[15] He swore he would never take a rupee from his sons. "God will provide for me," he said. "I don't need these sons . . . I will never take anything from them." When Anwar bibi, sitting next to him in the interview, told him to be quiet, he raised his voice. "I am the petitioner in this case," he asserted. "I will never forgive him."

However, when I met Qandeel's parents in November 2016, Azeem's resolve seemed to be crumbling. After an initial sum of money from a crowdfunding campaign run by a few activists was provided, donations all but dried up. One activist I spoke to confessed that she was reluctant to send Qandeel's parents money through Safdar Shah as there was no way to account for where the money went once he had it.

Azeem told me that his son's friends have visited him in jail and told him that his son cried out in his sleep and sometimes woke up screaming. He dreamed of his sister. Waseem now said that he was intoxicated the night he planned to kill Qandeel. When he tried to strangle her, he could not do it because he felt so weak. When she screamed, he had wanted to run away and so his cousin Haq Nawaz had choked Qandeel. Waseem claimed he had only held Qandeel down. Haq Nawaz surrendered to the police in Dera Ghazi Khan on 25 July.

In December 2016, a month after I met Qandeel's parents in Multan, Waseem and Haq Nawaz were formally charged with the murder of Qandeel Baloch, while Abdul Basit was charged with conspiracy to murder for his role in driving the getaway car. The three men pleaded not guilty.

In January 2017 Muhammad Azeem retracted his statement against his other son Aslam—he apparently no longer believed that Aslam had encouraged Waseem to carry out the murder. A criminal case was then initiated against Azeem and Anwar bibi, accusing them of trying to save one of their sons. If the charges are proved, they face a fine and a possible jail term of seven years. The police officer who brought the charges against Qandeel's parents claimed he saw Aslam give "a sealed envelope to his father and mother and said he had fulfilled their demand, and they should now give a statement in his favour in court." Speaking to the media, Qandeel's parents denied the accusation. "We wrongly nominated Aslam in Qandeel's murder," they said. "We were enraged at that time."[16]

In July 2017, in an interview with Adil Nizami—the reporter who broke the story of Qandeel's murder and who has since progressed to become the host of his own show—Safdar Shah denied that there had been any foul play or bribe from Aslam. Speaking for Qandeel's parents, he said that Aslam had arrived in Multan more than a month after Qandeel's death. "He called me and pleaded with me to get him a meeting with his parents," Shah claimed. "When I took him to the parents, they clung to him and wept . . . Aslam said, 'Baba, why did you put my name as a suspect in the FIR?'" What Shah saw next amazed him. "I have never seen a father beg for forgiveness from a son," he said. "Azeem asked his son for forgiveness and said, 'I made a mistake. I had gone mad.'"[17] Shah also said that Anwar bibi confided in him that on the day the murder was discovered the police had treated her and Azeem badly and demanded the names of people who could have murdered their daughter. In their grief and shock, they could only think of their sons' names.

The district prosecutor, Jam Salahuddin, initially claimed that the murder trial would be wrapped up within three months. But, over two years since hearings first began, another suspect came to the fore: Mufti Abdul Qavi.

On 12 October 2017, a court in Multan issued an arrest warrant for Mufti Qavi after police officials claimed he was not co-operating with them. On 18 October, Mufti Qavi appeared in court for a hearing regarding bail but left before the verdict could be announced. He was arrested by police on the highway leading out of Multan. Mufti Qavi's lawyer insisted that the cleric was simply on his way to a funeral at the time of his arrest. On 30 October Muhammad Azeem testified that Mufti Qavi had offered him money to retract his accusation that the mufti had ordered Qandeel's murder.[18] There were rumours that Mufti Qavi had transferred money to Qandeel's brothers' bank accounts in Dera Ghazi Khan before she was murdered.[19] He has denied everything.

In September 2018 Waseem applied for bail after his parents told the court they had forgiven him for Qandeel's murder. His plea was rejected.

In September 2019, more than three years after she was killed, the case of Qandeel Baloch's murder was finally closed as the court sentenced Waseem to 25 years in prison. Five other suspects, including Mufti Qavi, were acquitted. As he left the courtroom, Mufti Qavi was showered with rose petals by his overjoyed supporters. "The prayers of my supporters have been met," he said. "It is a day of justice, of victory." But many were disappointed in this conclusion to an honour killing case that had received unprecedented attention and media coverage. Their anger was directed towards Mufti Qavi. "It is now proven that a mullah will always escape punishment irrespective of the crime," tweeted journalist Mubashir Zaidi. "This verdict offers an empty, dissatisfying closure," said another journalist, Amber Rahim Shamsi. "The lesson is that the powerful and influential . . . are never held responsible."

An amendment in the legislation regarding honour crimes enabled the court to sentence Waseem to life in prison. However, it will take more than legislative change to end the socially accepted practice of honour killings in Pakistan. Activists say that the law is toothless and mere lip service by the government to the cause of women's rights. After all, as one critic asked, "Why did it take a documentary that won international acclaim to prod the prime minister's conscience on this matter? Aren't the hundreds of corpses each year enough?"[20] Some see the amended legislation as an attempt by the government to portray itself as "pro-women" in order to attract more female voters in the general elections in 2018. While that ploy may fail, such "feminist policies," noted one critic, "help garner the support of educated urban elites and project a good liberal face for the international community."[21]

Meanwhile honour killings continue. The Human Rights Commission of Pakistan estimates that at least 524 such murders occurred between October 2016, when the amendment came into effect, and October 2017. According to one activist, the number might be significantly higher, as perpetrators may now be citing a motive other than honour in order to become eligible for the pardon that is still offered for other categories of murder.[22]

Even in cases where the killer confesses to an honour crime, critics say that the possibility of the death penalty or life imprisonment is not enough to counter the fear of losing the respect of a tribe, community or family, thereby becoming a pariah. In March 2017 it was revealed that Saba, the subject of Sharmeen Obaid Chinoy's Oscar-winning documentary, still feared for her life as her uncle "never forgot the dishonour she had brought on the family."[23] When her uncle reportedly saw a trailer for the documentary, Saba said, he came to her house at night and "started shooting from his pistol."

In some cases the victim's family may be coerced to kill. In September 2017 a teenage couple who tried to elope were electrocuted to death by their families in Karachi after a council of elders in their parents' village, hundreds of miles away, declared that the boy and girl had brought dishonour to the community and had to be killed.[24] The families say they had no choice but to comply if they wished to remain a part of the community.

While the new legislation reinforces the court's ability to punish those found guilty of honour crimes even if they are pardoned by the victim's family, some lawyers say that judges are hesitant to use the full force of the law. In some instances, judges' remarks regarding honour crimes leave much to be desired. The Human Rights Commission of Pakistan noted that 149 of the honour killings recorded between October 2016 and October 2017 took place because of the victim's "marriage choice." In February 2017 a Sindh high court judge, when presented with a couple pleading for police protection from their families after they had married according to their own wishes, scolded them. If "love marriages don't succeed in films, then how will they succeed in real life?" the judge asked. He further noted, "Those who contract love marriage come in the court after some time for divorce."[25]

Well over a year after she made her last video or uploaded her last photograph, people are still talking about what Qandeel did. In a message on Facebook the day before she was killed, Qandeel seemed to reach out to women. "As a women [sic] we must stand up for ourselves," she wrote. "As a women [sic] we must stand up for each other . . . As a women [sic] we must stand up for justice." In the last interview before her death Qandeel spoke for the first time about this kind of feminism. "I don't know how many girls have felt support through my persona," she said. "I'm a girl power. So many girls tell me I'm a girl power, and yes, I am." These words may have been ignored had Qandeel lived. Today they serve as a rallying point for those who defend her choices. In death, she has been adopted and praised by women who enjoy the security she craved and hoped to attain with enough money, enough fame.

A BBC documentary released shortly after her death was watched more than two million times on YouTube. No longer did a reporter have to convince an editor that Qandeel's story was worth covering—the news of her death and interviews with her parents featured as a top story on the BBC's nightly news when she was killed. The year 2017 kicked off with Qandeel's inclusion in the annual vote for "Person of the Year" run by the prestigious Pakistan English-language magazine *Herald*. When the votes were tallied, Qandeel had come second, surpassed only by the former army chief, Raheel Sharif. Sharmeen Obaid Chinoy announced that her next documentary would be on Qandeel, and a short video about her, narrated by Madonna, was released online.[26] On the anniversary of Qandeel's death in July 2017 Pakistani actress Saba Qamar confirmed that she would be playing the role of Qandeel in a TV series about the social media star's life. Qamar reportedly received death threats for taking on the project, and when the *Express Tribune* ran a trailer for the new series on its Facebook page, it was flooded with hateful comments. "Like Qandeel's murder, Saba Qamar should also be murdered in the same way," one male commenter wrote, while another called Qandeel and Qamar "strippers and prostitutes."[27]

Qandeel is no longer "Pakistan's Kim Kardashian"—if anything, the women who walk in her steps, who aspire to the kind of fame she found, like Bushi, the model I met in Islamabad, want to be Pakistan's next Qandeel Baloch.

When Qandeel was buried, her mother covered her hands and feet in henna and kissed them before covering her in a white shroud—a local tradition that shows everyone that the woman being buried was a martyr. She died for some cause and died with honour. "When Qandeel's name is mentioned now, it is not as 'Qandeel the escort' or 'Qandeel the prostitute,'" her friend Jalal says. "It might be 'Qandeel the victim of honour killing,' but isn't that better? I hope that brings her peace." After all, he asked me, for a girl from a small village in Punjab that not many people had heard of, what could be better?

On 24 July 2016 Qandeel's Facebook page was taken down. It went back up a few days later, but many of her posts—the video from Valentine's Day, the trailer for her striptease—had been scrubbed. It doesn't matter. The videos and her photographs have been copied and shared on multiple social media platforms, blogs and websites too many times to count. They cannot be erased.

ACKNOWLEDGMENTS

Thank you. . .

Mustafa, for your unwavering belief in this work from the time that it was just the *sense* of a possible story. For never losing sight of how I hoped to tell that story even when I seemed to forget.

My sisters Mahim, Emma, Zairah and Shehrezad, for your encouragement, for your understanding when I could only think and talk about one woman for months on end.

Niaz Lashari, for working so hard to help me land all the interviews I needed at breakneck speed, for doing more than you signed on to do because you are the best kind of reporter: curious, diligent and comfortable getting into trouble.

Ramzaan, for being a wonderful travel companion and guide across Punjab. I'm very grateful to Dr Farzana Firoz for introducing us.

The team at the *Daily Ibrat*, particularly Mukhtiar Burfat and editor Jai Prakash, for their assistance in Jamshoro and Hyderabad.

Sadaf Sultan Khan and Tooba Masood, for listening to all my stories, for helping me sift through them and for always cheering on this project.

Fatima Bhutto, for being a kind, thoughtful first reader and for your generous spirit.

While I was on the road, I was lucky to find a home to go to at the end of every day. I'm particularly grateful to Dr Bilal and Sarah Ahsan and their daughters for making me a part of their family in Multan. In Lahore I'm thankful to Najma Rahman, Faizan and Fauzia. In Islamabad, my thanks to Sabah and Rahim for being such gracious hosts.

Simar Puneet, for carrying Qandeel with you as I did for all this time, for your friendship and your patience.

Athena Bryan, for your guidance, for steering the work in the right direction. I'm grateful that this book has found a home with Melville House Publishing.

I'm so glad this book made its way to John Ash at Pew Literary. Thank you for keeping it real and telling me true, terrible things.

NOTES

THE BALOCH FAMILY

1 Gishkori, Zahid. "After Qandeel." *News on Sunday*, 2 October 2016.
2 https://www.youtube.com/watch?v=Co6RamOxDa4
3 Gishkori, "After Qandeel."
4 Birmani, Tariq Saeed. "Troubling times for Qandeel Baloch's parents." *Dawn*, 4 October 2016.

"HOW I'M LOOKING?"

1 Hasan, Mehreen. "High and low notes." *News on Sunday*, 15 December 2013.

THE BLUE-EYED CHAIWALA

1 https://www.youtube.com/watch?v=QtiLiNkCUME
2 "Pakistani 'chai wala' turns model after finding fame." BBC, 19 October 2016, https://www.bbc.com/news/world-asia-37704029.
3 Sheikh, Imaan. "This hot Pakistani chaiwala is now a worldwide sensation and has a modelling contract." *Buzzfeed*, 19 October 2016.
4 Web Desk, "10 people Pakistanis were 'most obsessed' with in 2015." *Express Tribune*, 17 December 2015.
5 "Over 44 million social media accounts in Pakistan." GeoTV, 15 February 2017.
6 Malik, Mehreen Zahra. "Female lawmaker in Pakistan accuses Imran Khan of 'inappropriate' texts. Abuse follows." *New York Times*, 5 August 2017.
7 Nauman, Qasim. "See the 'cringe-pop' music video from Pakistan taking the internet by storm." *Wall Street Journal*, 13 April 2016.

8   Ryan Broderick and Imaan Sheikh. "This guy's breakup message to his friend accidentally went viral and it's amazing." *Buzzfeed*, 17 September 2015.
9   Verma, Anurag. "This Pakistani barber sets his customers' heads on fire and no one complains." *Huffpost India*, 19 January 2017.
10 https://www.youtube.com/watch?v=Mi1HKPtFa6E
11 "Shocking: 'Chaiwala' Arshad Khan quits showbiz." *Express Tribune*, 4 January 2017.
12 Staff Desk Report, "10 notable quotes that defined Pakistan's entertainment scene in 2015." *Images*, 28 December 2015.
13 https://www.youtube.com/watch?v=MTiwGvsRm Ww&t=174s
14 Ovais Jafar and Asif Bashir Chaudhary."'Chaiwala' Arshad Khan belongs to Afghanistan, says NADRA." GeoTV, 11 July 2017.

"GUYS, WHO WANT TO WATCH MY NEXT NASTY CLIP?"

1   https://www.youtube.com/watch?v=vN-kxThICRU
2   Agence France-Presse. "Girls tell me I'm their inspiration." *Dawn*, 26 February 2016.
3   Pakistan Press International. "Karachi: Valentine's Day activities disallowed." *Dawn*, 15 February 2002.
4   Agence France-Presse. "PEMRA cautions TV, radio stations over Valentine's Day broadcasts." *Express Tribune*, 13 February 2013.
5   Nazish, Kiran. "Love and politics: Valentine's Day in Pakistan." *Foreign Policy*, 26 February 2016.
6   https://www.youtube.com/watch?v=4c7zbjWdfZ4
7   Ahmed, Imtiaz. "Meet Pakistan's hot new internet sensation: Qandeel Baloch," *Hindustan Times*, 24 March 2016.
8   Trivedi, Hiten J. "Pakistani model to strip naked if Pak defeats India?" *Times of India*, 28 January 2017.
9   https://www.facebook.com/IamMubasherLucman/videos/229187770768989/
10 https://www.youtube.com/watch?v=RcLpHRoGAL4
11 https://www.youtube.com/watch?v=p0z4Flpl6CM. This video is no longer available.

THE HELPLINE

1   Reuters. "Online harassment of Pakistani women turns into real-world violence." *Dawn*, 30 September 2014.
2   "The threats and abuse outspoken Pakistani women receive." BBC, 19 July 2016, https://www.bbc.com/news/world-asia-36824514.
3   http://www.ispak.pk/Downloads/MoITStudyonBroadbandPenetration.

pdf. This URL no longer exists.

4   Internet Usage in Asia, *Internet World Stats*, http://www. internetworldstats.com/stats3. htm#asia, accessed 27 February 2018.

5   "The rise of mobile and social media use in Pakistan." *Dawn*, 10 April 2015.

6   Imran, Myra. "Only 5.8% judges in Pakistan are women: HRCP." *The News International*, 5 March 2016.

7   "Pakistan blocks blogs on cartoons." BBC, 3 March 2006, http://news. bbc.co.uk/2/hi/south_asia/4771846.stm.

8   Zakaria, Rafia. "The web and women's harassment." *Dawn*, 12 October 2016.

9   "Online harassment of Pakistani women." Reuters, https://www.reuters. com/article/us-pakistan-women-internet/online-abuse-of-women-in-pakistan-turns-into-real-world-violence-idUSKCN0HP0Q620140930.

10 Jahanzaib Haque and Omer Bashir. "Banned outfits in Pakistan operate openly on Facebook." *Dawn*, 14 September 2017.

11 Bukhari, Mubasher. "Pakistan sentences man to death for blasphemy on Facebook." Reuters, 11 June 2017.

12 News Desk. "Cyber crime: 'PTI social media activist in FIA custody.'" *Express Tribune*, 17 May 2017.

13 Sune Engel Rasmussen and Waqar Gillani. "Pakistan: man sentenced to death for blasphemy on Facebook." *Guardian*, 11 June 2017.

14 Correspondent, "Man arrested on blasphemy charge." *Dawn*, 19 September 2016.

15 *Gazette of Pakistan*, Islamabad, 22 August 2006.

16 http://dailytimes.com.pk/punjab/07-May-17/lack-of-staff-keeps-fiafrom-clearing-cyber-cases-backlog. This URL no longer exists.

1   Rehma, Maliha. "Who's the boss? Veena for sure." *News on Sunday*, 2 January 2011.

2   https://www.youtube.com/ watch?v=_FJQG0iG8v8

3   https://www.youtube.com/ watch?v=ROlR9YAdjPQ. This URL no longer exists.

4   https://www.youtube.com/ watch?v=WngTpgrLyas

5   http:// www.dailymotion.com/video/x4ho8zc

6   https://www.youtube.com/ watch?v=TQLjHEgrrrI

7   "Mufti Qavi denies association with any suspect." *News International*, 1 August 2016.

"I'M TELLING YOU THAT MY LIFE IS IN DANGER"

1   https://www.youtube.com/watch?v=TuyTR40OBvs

2   News Desk, "Qandeel Baloch's ex-husband comes forward with startling claims." *Express Tribune*, 13 July 2016.

3   https://www.youtube.com/watch?v=uePGv93RvkE

THE MEDIA AND THE MURDER

1   https://www.youtube.com/watch?v=tQtm5n1acoA
2   https://www.youtube.com/watch?v=q-XzzE5iv_ M&t=68s
3   https://www.youtube.com/watch?v=_ MuiOHjNWCs
4   Shah Sadar Din retains the status of a "village" in official records and informally among its residents, even as its population has grown to what we would call a "town." The village remains without much of a town's basic infrastructure and services to cater to that increased population.
5   "Statement showing the number of Pakistanis proceeded abroad for employment registered by bureau of emigration and overseas employment during the years 1981–2017." Bureau of Emigration & Overseas Employment, Government of Pakistan, http://www.beoe.gov.pk/files/statistics/2017/district.pdf, accessed 27 February 2018.
6   "Report and recommendation of the president to the board of directors on a proposed loan to the Islamic Republic of Pakistan for the Dera Ghazi Khan Rural Development Project." Asian Development Bank, August 1997.
7   Usman, Maryam. "Monetary deprivation: Experts term poverty lack of fundamental freedoms." *Express Tribune*, 7 October 2016.
8   Sabrina Tavernise, Richard A. Oppel, Junior, and Eric Schmitt, "United militants threaten Pakistan's populous heart," *New York Times*, 13 April 2009.
9   Correspondent, "Inhuman treatment: South Punjab tops the list in domestic violence cases." *Express Tribune*, 14 February 2017.
10 "Man dies after his limbs chopped off for 'honour' in DG Khan." *Dawn*, 19 July 2016.
11 https://www.youtube.com/watch?v=ZBVTIVq5HEY
12 https://www.youtube.com/watch?v=AcI3h0stYUA
13 Correspondent, "Police may investigate Mufti Qavi in Qandeel murder case." *Dawn*, 19 July 2016.
14 Correspondent, "Three accused in Qandeel case plead not guilty." *Dawn*, 6 December 2016.
15 Gishkori, Zahid. "After Qandeel." *News on Sunday*, 2 October 2016.

EPILOGUE

1   "Honour Crimes Men/Women." Human Rights Commission of Pakistan, http://hrcpmonitor.org/search/?id=5, accessed 27 February 2018.
2   Zahra-Malik, Mehreen. "Pakistan to pass law against honor killings in weeks: PM's daughter." Reuters, 20 July 2016.
3   For more, see Asad Jamal, "How not to legislate." *News International*, 26 October 2016.
4   Bilal, Muhammad. "Pakistan passes anti-honour killings and anti-rape bills." *Dawn*, 6 October 2016.

5   Boone, Jon. "Pakistan makes 'honour killings' punishable by mandatory prison time," *Guardian*, 6 October 2016.

6   "'Honour killings': Pakistan closes loophole allowing killers to go free." BBC, 6 October 2016, https://www.bbc.com/news/world-asia-37578111.

7   Masood, Salman. "Pakistan toughens laws on rape and 'honor killings' of women." *New York Times*, 6 October 2016.

8   Kelly Chen and Sophia Saifi, "Pakistan passes legislation against 'honor killings.'" CNN, 8 October 2016.

9   "Pakistan renews efforts to crack down on honor killings." *PBS News Hour*, 7 October 2016.

10 "End 'honor' killings in Pakistan." Change.org, https://www.change.org/p/help-us-end-honour-killings-in-pakistan, accessed: 27 February 2018.

11 https://www.youtube.com/watch?v=rS2qABXAErw

12 Agence France-Presse. "No pardon for Qandeel's murder, says father." *Express Tribune*, 12 October 2016.

13 Monitoring Desk. "She was our best son, says Qandeel's father." *Dawn*, 22 July 2016.

14 Agence France-Presse. "No pardon for Qandeel's murder, says father." https://www.dawn.com/news/1289678.

15 https://www.youtube.com/watch?v=Co6RamOxDa4

16 Tanveer, Rana. "Qandeel's parents trying to save son, says police." *Express Tribune*, 28 January 2017.

17 https://www.youtube.com/watch?v=oYlHF8kKL3k

18 APP (Associated Press of Pakistan). "Qandeel Baloch was killed at house of Mufti Qavi's friend, police tell court." *Express Tribune*, 30 October 2017.

19 https://www.pakdiscussion.com/news-wise- 12-october-2017/

20 Yusuf, Huma. "The real shame." *Dawn*, 18 July 2016.

21 Yusuf, Huma. "Poll challenge." *Dawn*, 25 December 2017.

22 Agence France-Presse. "'There has been no change': A year on since law passed, men still kill women for 'honour' in Pakistan." *Dawn*, 31 October 2017.

23 Reuters, "Fear of violence stalks honour killing survivor," *Dawn*, 4 March 2017

24 Ebrahim, Zofeen T. "Teenage couple electrocuted in Pakistan in 'honor killing': police." Reuters, 11 September 2017.

25 "SHC says love marriages fail in films, how will they succeed in real life." *Daily Times*, 3 February 2017.

26 Entertainment Desk. "Madonna lauds Sharmeen Obaid Chinoy's documentary on Qandeel Baloch." *Express Tribune*, 12 October 2016.

27 Ariba, R. "Saba Qamar has a Badass Reply to Death Threats for her Role in 'Baaghi.'" *Parhlo*, 29 August 2017, https://www.parhlo.com/here-is-why-saba-qamar-is-receiving-serious-death-threats/, accessed 27 February 2017.

INDEX

Aashiqui 2 (Bollywood film), 47

Abbasi, Iram, 93

Afridi, Shahid, 81, 131–32, 184

Agence France-Presse, xi

Ahmed, Issam, xi

Ajeeb Sa (*Kind of Strange*) (television talk show), 129–33, 145–46, 152–53, 161

Akbar, King, 144–45

Akram, Azhar, 190, 200–202, 205–7

Ali, Javeria, 57–58

Amber (BBC interviewer), 135–36, 139, 163

Anti-Honour Killings Law (Criminal Laws Amendment) Bill (2015), 215–17, 221

Asian Development Bank, 193

Azam, Malik, 177–82, 196–97, 211–12

Azeem, Anwar bibi (mother), xvii–xix, 6–15, 17, 201, 211–12, 218–20

Azeem, Arif, 8, 192, 207–9

Azeem, Aslam, 23, 191, 218–20

Azeem, Fouzia. *See* Baloch, Qandeel (Fouzia Azeem)

Azeem, Muhammad (father), 5–15, 180, 190–91, 212, 213, 218–20

Azeem, Shehnaz, 7, 9, 38–39, 165

Azeem, Shinza, 186

Azeem, Waseem (brother), xviii–xix, 9; and Qandeel's murder, xiii, 11–13, 191, 197–99, 201, 204–13, 217–20

Baloch, Qandeel (Fouzia Azeem): acting career, 51–52, 87; "Ban" video, 169–71; childhood, xvii–xix; fashion modeling career, 24, 26, 38–40, 50, 69–70, 73–74; and fatwas, 84, 88, 133; and feminism, 92, 222; home village of Shah Sadar Din, xiv, xv, 1–15, 25, 87, 171, 180–82, 191–99, 213; "How I'm Looking?" video, 54, 56, 66, 69; Independence Day 2015 performance, 74; marriage and abusive ex-husband, 16–18, 171–73; and martial arts (tae kwon do), 51–52, 89; and Mufti Qavi, 129, 131–33, 137–39, 140–41, 153–61, 163, 167–68, 175, 180, 181–82, 196, 207, 220; name change, 24–25, 75; *Pakistan Idol* appearance, 47–50, 71; passport, 9, 75, 166, 181, 211–12; phone data erased, 209; real identity revealed, 9, 166–67, 171, 179–82, 196–98, 211–12; relationship with her family, xvi, 1–15, 75, 132, 163, 165, 169, 174, 181, 198–99; social media posts and videos, xi–xiii, 52–54, 66, 69–74, 77–89, 92, 134–39, 162–63, 167, 196, 197, 206, 222, 223; son (Mishal), 13–14, 17–20, 171–73; striptease video trailer, xii–xiii, 81–87, 129, 130–31, 136, 184; suspension of

Facebook page, 82–84, 88–89, 162;
televised interview with Sohail, 162–67;
Valentine's Day video, xi–xii, 79–81.
See also Baloch, Qandeel, murder of
Baloch, Qandeel, murder of, xiii–xiv,
11–13, 161, 183–213, 214–23; as
alleged honour killing, xiii–xiv, 93–94,
161, 191, 202, 205–13, 214–23;
funeral, 10; grave, 213; the media and,
177–91, 195–99, 204, 211–13; Mufti
Qavi and, 161, 220; obituaries, xiv, 92;
police investigations, 199–211, 217–20;
social media responses to, xiii, 92–94
Baloch surname and people of southern
Punjab, 10–11, 17, 25, 81, 86,
130, 163, 171, 197, 206–7
Basit, Abdul, 159, 209, 219
BBC, 3, 55, 93, 135–37, 139, 216, 222
Bhatti, Waqas, 217
Bhittai, Shah Abdul Latif, 114, 116
Bhutto, Benazir, 162, 190–91, 210
Bigg Boss (Indian reality-TV show),
135, 145–48, 155, 164
blasphemy, 109, 113, 148
Blogspot, 103
Board of Control for Cricket in India, 134
Bobby, Almas, 149
Bodla, Noman, 106–12
Burfat, Fateh Muhammed, 118–19
Bushi (model), 37–38, 45, 223
BuzzFeed, 55
Bytes for All, 102–3

CNN, 55, 216
cricket teams and players, xii, 78,
81–82, 131, 134, 184, 193
Criminal Law Amendment (Offences
in the Name or Pretext of
Honour) Act (2016), 215
cybercrime, 90–94, 101–26, 168; and
blasphemy, 109, 113; DRF's cyber
harassment helpline, 90–94, 121–26;
Nighat Dad's legal practice and cyber
harassment, 101–6; NR3C and federal
response to complaints, 106–12, 122,
123–24, 126; Prevention of Electronic

Crimes Act (PECA), 112–13, 126; social
media and cyber harassment, 90–94,
101–26, 168; University of Sindh
student's suicide and, 113–21, 126

Dad, Mehar Allah, 96–99, 126
Dad, Nasreen, 96, 98
Dad, Nighat, 90–106, 121–26; education
and conservative family, 94–100; legal
practice and cyber harassment, 101–6
Daily Beast, 92
Daily Pakistan, 177–82, 193,
196–98, 211–12
Darul Aman shelter for women, 18–20
Darul Uloom Ubaidia madrassa
(Multan), 141–45, 182
Dawn (English-language
newspaper), 72, 92, 148, 215
Dera Ghazi Khan (city), 2–3,
17–18, 192–94, 198–99, 219
Dhirkot earthquake (8
October 2005), 29–31
digital rights activism and
cybercrime, 90–94, 101–26
Digital Rights Foundation (DRF), 90–92,
103–6, 110–11; cyber harassment
helpline, 90–94, 121–26; Hamara
Internet (Our Internet) campaign,
103–4, 110; training for female
university students, 119–20
Digital Satellite News Gathering
(DSNG) vans, 188
divorce, 19, 78, 101, 160, 173, 222
Dubsmash app, 70, 135

Eid, 9, 29, 50, 59, 75, 131,
155, 162–64, 169, 191
Express News, 146
Express Tribune, 154–54, 207, 223

Facebook, 33, 34, 38, 44–45, 56–57,
69–74, 77–89; Arshad Khan and,
56–57, 66–67; cyber harassment
of women, 90–94, 104, 108–12,
116, 118, 124–25; Qandeel's fans
and followers, xi, 77, 128–29, 162;

Qandeel's page suspended, 82–84, 88–89, 162; Qandeel's posts and videos, xi–xiii, 52–54, 69–74, 77–89, 169–71, 196, 197, 206, 222, 223; response to Qandeel's murder, 93–94; Sindh University students' page, 118; Virk campaign to shut down Qandeel's page, 82–84. *See also* social media

Fahim, Malik, 59–67

Faisal Movers bus depot, 20–22, 181

fashion models and modeling industry in Islamabad, 26–45; Bushi (as Qandeel Two), 37–38, 45, 223; Khushi Khan and, 26–35, 40–45; Mec and, 24, 34–40, 41–42, 50; Qandeel's career, 24, 26, 38–40, 50, 69–70, 73–74

fatwas, 84, 88, 133, 149

Federal Investigation Agency (FIA), 103, 105, 106–12, 122, 123–24

feminism, 92, 148, 152–53, 221, 222

First Information Report (FIR), 191, 218, 220

A Girl in the River: The Price of Forgiveness (documentary film), 216–17, 221

Golra Sharif district (Islamabad), 57–58

Google, 56, 108

Guardian, 3, 109, 216

Hamara Internet (Our Internet) campaign, 103–4, 110

Hasan, Nazia, 50

Haya Day (Modesty Day), 80

Herald (Pakistan English-language magazine), 222–23

honour killings in Pakistan, xiii–xiv, 214–23; *A Girl in the River* (documentary film), 216–17, 221; legislation regarding, 214–17, 220–22; Mufti Qavi on, 161; Qandeel's murder as alleged, xiii–xiv, 93–94, 214–23; statistics, xiii–xiv, 214, 221; and victims' marriage choices, 222

"How I'm Looking?" video, 54, 56, 66, 69

Human Rights Commission of Pakistan, 214, 221, 222

Human Rights Tulip award, 121

ICC Cricket World Cup, 81, 82

iddat, 101

Iglesias, Enrique, 81

Imam, Sughra, 215

Instagram, 55, 56, 110–11, 127

Internet access in Pakistan, 94–95, 101–2

Iqbal, Shaukat, 180, 193, 211–12

Ismail, Imran, 156

Jaffrey, Attiya, 199–211

Jamaat-e-Islami youth wing, 80

Jay, Muskan, 65, 66

Jinnah, Muhammad Ali, 37

Kaaba, 113

Karachi Hotel (Shah Sadar Din), 4, 186

Kardashian, Kim, xi, 80, 135, 223

Kashmir earthquake (8 October 2005), 29–31

Khan, Arshad (the Chaiwala), 55–68

Khan, Gulshan, 31, 41

Khan, Imran, xii, 78, 82, 138, 152, 155–56, 162, 171

Khan, Khushi, 26–35, 40–45

Khan, Shah Rukh, 134

Khara Such (television show), 84–86, 154

Khaskheli, Anis, 115–17, 120

Khowaja, A. D., 120

Kismat Connection (television show), 60–61

Kohli, Virat, 134–35

Kolkata Knight Riders, 134

Kot Addu (village), 17

Leghari, Fayyaz Khan, 10–11, 196–97

Leone, Sunny, 86, 135

Little Folks school (English-speaking private school), 97

Lucman, Mubasher, 84–86, 154, 155–58, 161

Ma'arah tribe of Shah Sadar Din, 11, 180, 197

Madonna, 223
Malik, Veena, 129, 145–49
Mansoor (Qandeel's friend), 69–74, 80–81, 136, 168–69, 173
Marvi Hostel at the University of Sindh, 113–21
Masih, Nabeel, 113
Matloob, Raja, 129–33, 145
Mec (Qandeel's manager), 23–24, 26, 34–45, 50, 53–54, 69, 75, 81, 84, 169–72, 174–76; Qandeel's audition, 23–24; Qandeel's modeling career, 23–24, 26, 34–40, 50
Meera (Pakistani actress), 162
mIRC (Internet Relay Chat) software, 95
mobile phone ownership in Pakistan, 99–100
Muhammad, Prophet, 5, 109, 147, 153, 202
mureed, 7
Muzaffarabad (neighborhood), 30, 184, 185, 188, 199–200

National Database and Registration Authority (NADRA), 67
National Response Center for Cyber Crime (NR3C), 106–12, 122, 123–24, 126
Nawaz, Haq, 13, 196, 207, 209, 219
New York Times, xiv, 3, 193, 216
Nizami, Adil, 182–91, 219–20

Obaid Chinoy, Sharmeen, 216–17, 221, 223
Orkut (social media site), 102

Pakistan Bureau of Emigration and Overseas Employment, 192
Pakistan Electronic Media Regulatory Authority (PEMRA), 80, 133
Pakistan Federal Ministry of Law, xiii
Pakistan Idol (television show), 46–50, 71
Pakistan International Airlines (PIA), 29, 30
Pakistan National Assembly, 113, 162–63, 215
Pakistan Penal Code, 214–15

Pakistan People's Party, 215, 216
Pakistan State Bank, 209
Pakistan Telecommunication Authority, 102–3, 109, 113
Pakistan Today, 155
Panama Papers, 108
Pandey, Poonam, 82, 86
Parveen, Abida, 174
Pashto language, 59
Patel, Ashmit, 145–46
pay parties, 42
pirs (spiritual leaders), 7
Prevention of Electronic Crimes Act (PECA), 112–13, 126
Punjabi language, 68

Qaiser, Saba, 216–17, 221
Qamar, Saba, 223
Qavi, Hina, 140–41, 160
Qavi, Mufti Abdul, 140–61, 167–68, 175, 196, 207–8; hotel room meeting and photographs with Qandeel (2016), 137–39, 140–41, 153–60, 163, 167, 180, 181–82, 196, 207; image as champion of women's rights, 152–53; madrassa, 141–45, 182; public dispute with Veena Malik, 145–49; and Qandeel's murder investigation, 161, 220; relationships with journalists and reporters, 149–51, 161; talk show appearance with Qandeel, 129, 131–33, 145–46
Quran, 96, 106, 141, 142, 178, 182

Rabbani, Raza, 109
Rahman, Anusha, 113, 126
Rajput, Shafqat, 56
Ramzaan (Ramadan), 24, 29, 59, 131, 137, 159
Rana, Asif, 56
Ratta Matta (town), 96–99
Recep Tayyip Erdoğan Housing Complex, 2
Reema (Pakistani actress), 162
Rehman, Maulana Fazlur, xiii
Rind, Khadim, 115–16, 117
Rind, Naila, 113–21, 126

Roy, Shahzad, 162
Ruet-e-Hilal committee, 131, 157, 167

Salahuddin, Jam, 209, 220
Saudi Arabia, 192, 194, 198, 207
Sawant, Rakhi, 86
Shah, Safdar, 3–15, 171, 176,
    195, 209, 219, 220
Shah, Taher, 56
Shah, Taher Ali, 60–61
Shah Sadar Din (village), xiv, xv, 1–15, 25,
    87, 142, 191–99, 213; Karachi Hotel,
    4, 186; Ma'arah tribe of, 11, 180,
    197; and Qandeel's real identity, 171,
    181–82; wealth and criminality, 191–99
Shahid, Kamran, 146–47
Sharif, Maryam Nawaz, 215
Sharif, Nawaz, 216–17
Sharif, Raheel, 223
Sharma, Anushka, 134
Sheen (Pakistani actress), 152
Siddiqui, Javed, 192–96
Siraiki poetry, 97
Skype, 91, 123, 125
Snapchat, 111
social media: Arshad Khan and, 56–68;
    and cyber harassment, 90–94, 101–26,
    168; Instagram, 55, 56, 110–11, 127;
    Orkut site, 102; Pakistani users and
    viral stars, xi, 56–68; public campaigns
    to suspend Qandeel's Facebook page,
    82–89; Qandeel's fans and followers,
    xi, 77, 128–29, 162; Qandeel's posts
    and videos, xi–xiii, 52–54, 66, 69–74,
    77–89, 92, 134–39, 162–63, 167,
    196, 197, 206, 222, 223; responses
    to Qandeel's murder, xiii, 92–94;
    Twitter, xi–xii, 55, 56, 78, 82, 93–94,
    109, 133–34. See also Facebook
Soomro, Aneela, 120
striptease video trailer for cricket team,
    xii–xiii, 81–87, 129, 130–31, 136, 184
suicide of female University of
    Sindh student, 113–21, 126
Syed Muslims, 5, 6, 202

Taal (Bollywood film), 27

tae kwon do, 51–52, 89
Taliban, 91, 193
Tehreek-e-Insaf (PTI) party, 82, 152, 157
Temouri, Sultan Azam, 207
Time magazine, 92
24 News (channel), 182–88
Twitter, xi–xii, 55, 56, 78, 82,
    93–94, 109, 133–34

UN Women, 103
University of Punjab, 95, 98
University of Sindh in Jamshoro, female
    student's suicide at, 113–21, 126

Valentine's Day video, xi–xii, 79–81
Virk, Farhan, 82–84
Vogue magazine, xiv

WhatsApp, 44, 56, 70, 111, 150, 152, 209
women, Pakistani, xiv; and domestic
    violence, xviii–xix, 16–20, 194–95;
    employment prospects, 30–32, 40–45,
    100, 195; fashion modeling, 26–45;
    feminism, 92, 148, 152–53, 221,
    222; as hostesses, 20–22, 42–43,
    181; and Islamic law, 88, 101, 151,
    153, 160; in the police force, 202–4;
    traditional roles of, xiv–xv; university
    students, 113–21; as victims of
    online cyber harassment, 90–94,
    101–26, 168. See also honour killings
    in Pakistan; women's dress, Pakistani
women's dress, Pakistani: abaya, 98;
    burqa, 2, 80; dupatta, 2, 18, 28,
    32, 35, 115, 154, 164, 167, 197,
    201, 210; hijab, 2–3, 24, 32; niqab,
    96, 98; shalwar kameez, 32, 33,
    35, 37, 50, 164, 167, 202, 212

Yousafzai, Malala, 91
YouTube, xi–xii, 11, 33, 50, 103, 170, 222

Zafar, Ali, 175
Zardari, Asif Ali, 162
zawal, 140–41

A NOTE ON THE AUTHOR

Sanam Maher is a journalist based in Karachi, Pakistan. For more than a decade, she has covered stories on Pakistan's art and culture, business, politics, religious minorities and women. Her work has appeared in the *New York Times, Al Jazeera, The Caravan, Roads and Kingdoms,* and *Buzzfeed. A Woman Like Her* is her first book.

@SanamMKhi